T0271638

WALKING DISASTER

WALKING DISASTER

My Life Through Heaven and Hell

DERYCK WHIBLEY

CONSTABLE

CONSTABLE

First published in the United States of America in 2024 by
Gallery Books, an imprint of Simon & Schuster, LLC

First published in Great Britain in 2024 by Constable

3 5 7 9 10 8 6 4

Interior design by Hope Herr-Cardillo
Photos courtesy of the author unless otherwise noted.
Image of Deryck and Paris on page 11 courtesy of Shamus Hewitt.
Images on page 15 by Ariana Whibley.

A CIP catalogue record for this book
is available from the British Library.

ISBN: 978-1-40871-972-5 (hardback)
ISBN: 978-1-40871-973-2 (trade paperback)

Printed and bound in Great Britain by Clays Ltd, Elcograf S.p.A.

Papers used by Constable are from well-managed forests and other responsible sources.

Constable
An imprint of
Little, Brown Book Group
Carmelite House
50 Victoria Embankment
London EC4Y 0DZ

An Hachette UK Company
www.hachette.co.uk

www.littlebrown.co.uk

The authorised representative
in the EEA is
Hachette Ireland
8 Castlecourt Centre
Dublin 15, D15 XTP3, Ireland
(email: info@hbgi.ie)

This book is dedicated to the Sum 41 fans.
The Skumfuks. The Sum 41 family.

I'm only in a position to write a book because of you. In one way or another we've shared a bond through the words of my songs.

I've always written music honestly about my life, so an honest telling of my life story only seems fitting. I hope you can gain more meaning behind and understanding of those songs from the words in this book.

This is my life. The good, the bad, and the really fucking ugly.

CONTENTS

CONTENTS

WALKING DISASTER

INTRODUCTION

You always start out so innocent. You say to yourself, "Those rock star clichés, they'll never be me." But somehow they find you. The drugs and booze, the sex, the celebrity relationships, the failed marriages—all of it. The fights, the arrests, the near-death experiences, and in my case, surviving an active war zone. All the peaks and valleys of a life in rock 'n' roll await you. As if it's all predestined. And, for me, maybe it was. I was always in trouble growing up. If something went wrong, all fingers pointed at me, even if I had nothing to do with it. It was kind of like *Calvin and Hobbes*. I used to love that cartoon. I even modeled myself after Calvin, spiking my hair and wearing the same striped shirt.

Or maybe I was doomed because by the time I was thirteen years old my idols were Jim Morrison, Kurt Cobain, Guns N' Roses, and the Sex Pistols. I remember watching the Oliver Stone movie *The Doors*—an epic account of Jim Morrison, the band, and their influence on music, culture, and counterculture—and being completely transfixed. The way of life, the chaos, the insanity, the ups and downs, and the wildness of success—it was all so exciting to me. And just as Nirvana came to change the world, I was coming of age in my own right and discovering just who I thought I was.

Picking up a guitar and writing songs for the first time, I knew I wanted to become a rock star one day—and I knew I would do it. There was no question in my mind that music and the rock 'n' roll lifestyle were my path. I mean, what else is a kid who loves music and is always in trouble supposed to do?

I was in bands and on tour before I had a driver's license. I signed a record deal when I was still a teenager. I had multiple hit songs on the radio around the world before I was twenty-four. I toured the world, partied with my heroes, played to sold-out crowds, night after night, had people singing my own words back to me, and I loved every second of it. I wanted it. I was ready for it. And then, I crashed and burned and nearly lost it all, along with my own life. I picked myself up, built it back from nothing, and did it all over again.

OPEN WATER

I was born on March 21, 1980, in Scarborough, Canada, in the east end of Toronto. My mum and I constantly moved to different apartments. By the time I was seventeen, I had moved nineteen times. One time, we moved into a building on a Friday and out on the Monday, because it was so awful. No wonder I was able to tour in vans and sleep in bad motels so easily. My mum, Michelle Whibley, dropped out of high school at the age of seventeen to raise me on her own. She was small, tough, and very pretty. A typical rebel teenager who was barreling down a bad path, hanging out with stoners and burnouts and going to too many high school parties. It was at one of those shitty parties where she met my dad. They had sex in a bathroom and then she was pregnant. It changed her life forever, but him? He stuck around just long enough to see me when I was first born and that was it. I don't know whether it was too much for him or my mum didn't want him involved, but either way he was out of my life for good. Part of me is surprised that I've never heard from him, but I had such a great relationship with my mum and grandparents that I didn't really feel like I was missing out on anything. Plus, even back then I felt that if he didn't want anything to do with me then good riddance.

For the first few years of my life, my mum and I lived with my grandparents John and Mary Whibley, or Nan and Papa. They are very British, very religious, and have always been lovely people. Born in the thirties, they grew up through World War II, my grandfather in London and my grandmother in Kent. I always loved hearing their stories of growing up during the war, even though they thought it was boring to talk about. Their stories fascinated me. During one of the late night air raid bombings over London a German incendiary bomb came through my grandfather's roof and landed in his sister's empty bed, but didn't ignite. How is that boring?! My grandmother and her mother gave tea and sandwiches to the soldiers being rescued by civilian boats from Dunkirk. That's part of history! Life in postwar England was tough, though, and when Nan and Papa were in their early thirties work dried up, so in 1966 they moved to Canada to raise their five children. My grandparents were a big part of my life as a child and I've remained close to them to this day. Even in their nineties they still come to the crazy Sum 41 shows every time we're in town.

I was a one-year-old when my mum met a man named B.D. on a trip to Florida. By the time I was two, they had decided to get married, and boy, did she pick wrong! I'm sure in 1981 he looked kind of cool, with a mustache, cut-off sleeves, and a mullet, but he was anything but cool. He was a mean, abusive, petty drug-dealing homophobe who yelled and hit me for watching TV shows like *Pee-wee's Playhouse* and *The Care Bears*, saying they were going to make me "turn out gay" and no son of his was going to be a "fxggot." I'd then be sent to my room to await more punishment or just be out of his way so he could drink beer, watch *M*A*S*H*, or argue with my mum. Sometimes I would be sent to my room because his "friend" was coming over for a few minutes, which really meant a customer was buying weed in our apartment.

The only shows he'd let me watch were reruns of *I Love Lucy*, *Gilligan's Island*, the old *Batman* with Adam West, and *The Monkees*. I loved *The Monkees*. I had no idea that it was an old show from the sixties and thought they were a current band. I have been obsessed with music for as long as I can remember. I spent so much time in my room listening to my dubbed cassette tapes of the Monkees, the Beatles, and whatever other classic rock tapes my parents gave me. I loved all the early classics. In the eighties, Shell ran a promo where if you spent a certain dollar amount on gas, you would get a free cassette from a collection called *50s & 60s Solid Gold Hits*. My parents always made sure to fill up enough to get me another tape from the collection.

After Mum and B.D. got married, the three of us lived in a pretty rough part of town known as Tuxedo Court. It was a collection of six apartment buildings in an area that had long been considered a "gang area." Years later I was told by some local cops that they didn't even go into that neighborhood if they got a call. They just let that neighborhood sort itself out.

When I lived there, I was too young to realize that the majority of people living there (including us) were extremely low-income. I had no idea that it was a bad neighborhood. Well, other than the fact that the hallway always smelled like piss, and if we left anything on our first-floor balcony even for a few minutes it would be stolen. Life felt normal and I was a really happy kid. I was so young when they got married, that I had no idea B.D. wasn't my biological father. B.D. was adopted and hated that he didn't know his "real" parents. He wanted me to think he was my dad, so they never told me otherwise.

My parents had good taste in music and my mum liked to play it loud. And why not? She was only in her early twenties. I would wake up to the sound of Rod Stewart or Cheap Trick or Patsy Cline coming through the walls of our apartment. Late nights were reserved for B.D.'s music: the Stones, the Beatles, and Pink Floyd. I still remember the sound of the big old twelve-inch speakers in the living room, and hearing incredible songs like "Help!" and "Paint It Black" for the first time.

B.D. drove an orange 1970 Plymouth Road Runner muscle car that looked like the General Lee from *Dukes of Hazzard*. People always stared when we drove around in it. He would take us on trips to different car shows, sometimes submitting his car, but never winning. In the summer of

1986, we went to a car show at Molson Park where I saw my first concert: the Monkees reunion with "Weird Al" Yankovic as the opener. I was in heaven. I sat on my dad's shoulders peering over everyone's head, watching the band from my favorite TV show. Seeing real people performing music left a major impression on me. I knew that someday, I wanted that to be me up there.

That same summer we moved again, this time to a nicer apartment complex in Scarborough. I was told that it even had its own outdoor pool! It was in the back of the building next to the parking lot surrounded by a huge chain-link fence. I ran up to it so fast with excitement only to find that it was absolutely filled to the top with actual garbage. Old furniture, garbage bags, chunks of two-by-fours were in there, and the walls of the pool were stained jet black. All my six-year-old's dreams of being the kid with a pool and living the good life, the movie life, were completely shattered in an instant. While the area was a little better, the anger and abuse from "Dad" only got worse over the next couple of years. Then my mum caught him cheating on her and she kicked him out and filed for divorce. I was about seven when she sat me down and told me that they were splitting up. In my mind, even though I was scared of him, he was still my dad and I didn't want to lose my family. I was upset and cried all day. The only thing that got me to stop crying was my mum promising me he'd be home the next day to say goodbye. He never showed. I didn't see or hear from him again until years later when I ran into him as a teenager, but that's a story for later.

With B.D. gone, my mum and I became a little team. I was eight and she was twenty-five, and our little apartment at 945 Midland Ave had finally become fun and peaceful. No more darkness. We didn't have to worry about his anger and temper anymore. We ate junk food for dinner and watched movies every weekend. We watched everything from light-hearted comedies like *The Goonies*, *Back to the Future*, and *Ferris Bueller* to more mature movies like *Stand By Me*, *Raising Arizona*, and *La Bamba*, the story of Ritchie Valens. I watched *Ferris Bueller* and *La Bamba* over and over again, almost wearing out the copied VHS tapes. They both embodied everything that I felt inside. I knew I loved music and wanted it to be my life when I grew up, and I also thought I could be Ferris Bueller, the charming guy that fucks with all the powers that be, but somehow gets away with it.

At the same time my mum realized there was no relying on anyone else. She had to make her own way in the world and take care of the two of us. The first step was getting her high school diploma. She began taking night school classes and worked in the day as a secretary at the Shell office building in Toronto. Even still, it was tough to make ends meet and we needed a roommate to help pay rent. My uncle Tim lived with us for a bit and then my mum's best friend from high school moved in. It was only a two-bedroom apartment so that meant the hallway closet became my bedroom. I enjoyed it, though, because it felt like my own little fort. It was such a small space that the mattress barely fit and one end curled up the wall. When the hall closet became too cramped for a growing kid, my mum took the closet and gave me the bigger room.

When I think back to those days now, I realize how hard it must have been for her. She was only in her mid-twenties, but already had a kid, had gotten divorced, had recently gone back to high school as an adult, and was working while raising a child. Only once I was in my twenties did I realize the pressure, the embarrassment, the fear of not surviving that she faced. I just couldn't fathom the kind of strength she had. I knew there were times she needed help from my grandparents, and at some points we were on welfare or had to get groceries from the food banks at churches. As tough as it all must have been for her, she never let it show. She was always happy to do anything and everything to make me feel like life was great. There was never spare money, but she always made sure I had a good Christmas. Like in 1988, I nearly fainted when I opened a big box on Christmas morning to see that I had gotten a Nintendo. That was my mum! Somehow always making me feel like the most loved and special kid.

When my mum wanted to go back to school, she told me that with

B.D. gone she needed me to be the man of the house. I was up for the challenge. Money seemed to be a constant hurdle for the Whibleys, and I wanted to start earning my share. I decided to start a business, offering to walk the younger kids to school for $5 a week. A few parents in the apartment building took me up on the offer, and soon I was raking in about $15 a week, which felt like a million to me.

One afternoon, my mum and I came home and noticed the apartment door was open. My mum slowly opened it the rest of the way, and we saw that our apartment had been ransacked. Instead of turning around and running, she picked up a hockey stick and went through the apartment to see the extent of the damage. I was terrified watching her creep down the hall into our bathroom, hockey stick held aloft, ripping open the shower curtain to see if anyone was hiding in there. Our entire apartment had been turned upside down, every drawer emptied, all of our belongings on the floor. We didn't have much, but anything of any value was gone, including all the money I'd saved up. The incident left us both feeling violated and a little unsafe in the building. It also taught me at an early age that just when you think you've got it all, you can lose everything in an instant. It was a valuable lesson, and one that will become a recurring theme throughout the pages of this book.

My mum filled all the roles in my life, so I'd completely forgotten about B.D. by the time I was nine and she finally decided to tell me that he wasn't my real dad. I was sad that I had been lied to, but happy that I had no blood relation to B.D. In fact, I was ecstatic that I didn't have his genes. It also explained why his whole side of the family—the people I thought were my aunts, uncles, cousins, and grandparents—never spoke to us again, just overnight. It all made sense now, but none of it bothered me. In fact, it made me feel strong. I felt both "fuck 'em, I don't need 'em" and "one day I'll show them!" Maybe a therapist would say that's where my drive and determination started. Of course, the only time I've talked to a therapist it's been mostly about the "band problems," but we're not there yet. Being discarded early in life gives you one of two things: incredible abandonment issues or a huge sense of independence knowing that you cannot rely on anyone else to get you where you're trying to go. Looking at myself honestly and objectively, I can confidently state that for me it's the latter. When someone walks out of my life or burns me, I move on almost instantly. I wouldn't be surprised if there's a subconscious drive to prove I can do it without them. I don't spend too much time analyzing it. If I was unhappy, I would try to figure it out, but I've always been comfortable in my own skin. I genuinely enjoy my life. Maybe it's just the way I'm wired or how my brain works but my default is always happy when I wake up in the morning. Of course I go through all the human emotions and I can be horribly upset, angry, or sad, but those feelings don't usually last that long. As an adult I sometimes feel guilty for how happy I am because so many people that I know are not happy. I often find myself playing down my joy to certain friends for fear that I seem like I'm rubbing it in. I know it sounds stupid and I do feel strange doing it, but sometimes I leave out really positive things that are happening in my life or focus on the downside of things with people in hopes that I can be more relatable. I've learned that life can change quickly, so I do my best to live every day like it's my last. Several times, in my case, it nearly was.

I enjoyed school in the early years. My school friends were mostly kids from the apartment complex. We'd play typical apartment games like nicky nicky nine doors, pushing all the buttons in the elevators, and racing up and down the stairwells. I lived on the twelfth floor, so we used my balcony to try to spit on people walking down below, which eventually progressed to throwing eggs or water balloons onto parked cars in the outdoor lot. All of this fun came to an abrupt end when my mum told me we were moving again, this time to live with Nan and Papa up north. They had moved about an hour and a half north to Keene, a town so small that it wasn't actually considered a town. The village of Keene was only 1.2 miles end to end, with one main road, one general store, one school, and a few small businesses in old houses surrounded by trees, a river, and a huge lake. That was it. Moving from the endless city to the endless forest was a culture shock.

What I didn't know at the time was that my mum was being harassed by B.D. and because of his temper she was afraid for her life. She wanted to get away from him and the city. As a ten-year-old kid, I just knew it would be another year with new surroundings, new friends, new school, and new bullies. I was used to getting picked on due to my small size and frequently being the new kid. In my old neighborhood in the city, I had a knife pulled on me when I was just seven. It was only a kitchen steak knife, but when a thirteen-year-old tough kid holds a serrated blade to your neck, it leaves an impression. I figured that if I didn't show people I was tough I'd be beat on mercilessly. So out of fear of getting my ass kicked, on my first day of school, I went up and punched a big kid in the face. He was stunned but fought back. The fight got broken up quickly, and because kids are kids, we actually became good friends later. Keene wasn't "tough" like that, though. They were mellower, kinder kids, mostly into fishing, dirt biking, and four wheeling in the forests.

My best friend was the kid who lived next door to Nan and Papa, who was also in my class at school. His name was Jake McConnell and he was even more into music than I was. At that time I mostly listened to rap music like Run-D.M.C., LL Cool J, and the Beastie Boys, but Jake seemed to know everything about hard rock. He got me into bands like Mötley Crüe, Guns N' Roses, AC/DC, and other eighties glam rock bands. This was back when no one had heard the name Nirvana yet and hair metal ruled the day. Jake and I even did a lip-sync performance of "Unskinny Bop" by Poison in front of our whole school for the talent show and we won!

Living with Nan and Papa was only temporary, and soon Mum and I found a spot of our own. Well, sort of. We moved onto Indian River Lodge, a campground made up of a series of small wooden cabins tucked into a huge forest a few hundred feet from the river. We lived in the maid's quarters of this big old farmhouse that was built in the 1800s and belonged to the family that owned the lodge. Now, instead of playing in the stairwells of the apartment building, I was getting up early in the morning and going fishing before school, catching rock bass, perch, or trout.

The owner, Al, had a few kids, including a six-year-old boy named Shawn who became my little partner. We would catch frogs, play army in the forests, jump off bridges into the river, and sometimes ride out on the lake with his dad in their little wooden single-motor fishing boat. One late summer evening, the weather was perfect, so Al took me and Shawn out on the lake to fish. As we headed farther out to where the big fish lived, we passed a local man in his boat. We waved as we zipped by, but he didn't really acknowledge us, which was typical for him. He never waved, never said hi. When we reached a good spot, we threw out the anchor and started fishing. Within minutes the weather changed drastically—the sky turned dark purple, heavy rain poured down, the wind picked up, and the waves intensified. As the storm roared around us, we wanted to head back to shore, but the anchor was caught in a pile of seaweed. The wind whipped around us and waves crashed onto the boat as Shawn and I huddled under the bow. Al kept pulling and pulling, trying to get the anchor up. He pulled so hard that in all the wind and the rain, he slipped, falling out of the boat and into the water. Shawn was terrified, screaming for his dad. As the big kid, I was trying to comfort him, but I was just as shocked as we watched Al struggle to get back into the boat. For the first time in my life, I was convinced I was about to die. I didn't feel scared, but I was really sad that I wasn't going to see my mum or grandparents anymore. As the rain and wind lashed us, Al managed to drag himself back on board. He finally managed to get the anchor up, but the engine was completely waterlogged and wouldn't start. Al was only about six feet away, and it was so dark that I could barely make him out, but I could see he was desperate. I closed my eyes and gave up hope. Just then, I felt a jolt and the boat started moving. We were being towed to safety by someone. As quickly as it came, the storm disappeared, and when we docked, I finally saw the person who had come to our rescue and saved our lives—it was the man who never smiled or waved at us. He must have realized our little boat was no match for that storm, turned around, and brought us back to safety. We thanked him profusely, but he hardly uttered a word. He just tied his boat up, gave us a nod, and went on his way.

Needless to say, after that I'm not a fan of boats or open water. I'm not afraid, I just don't enjoy it. I never do those rock-show boat cruises either. When our agents and managers send me offers, I always say, "Fuck that shit, I hate water and I hate boats." If they tell me that I can treat it like vacation, I reply, "I hate those, too!" At the time of this writing, I've never actually been on a real vacation in my life. The closest I came was my honeymoon with Avril, and what did we do? We went on a fucking boat for a week! More on that later.

Aside from the boating and the lake, I felt at home in Keene. The village was a great change of pace, but it only lasted for about two years. Just as I was getting used to living there, my mum told me we were moving again, this time to a town called Ajax, the place where I would eventually meet my future bandmates.

CHAPTER 2

CRIME DOESN'T PAY FOR THOSE ABOUT TO ROCK

Twenty-five minutes east of Toronto is a small pass-through city called Ajax. It was once farmland, but eventually became an affordable and safe community for people who worked in the city but wanted suburban life for their kids. There was no downtown. There was no mall. There was no movie theater. There are no restaurants other than suburban outposts of strip-mall chains like Red Lobster and Pizza Hut. The only thing Ajax had to offer was houses and schools. I hated living in Ajax. It felt like a barren wasteland of adult conformity. The film *SLC Punk!* comes to mind. Except Salt Lake City is actually a cool city! I missed seeing the Toronto skyline from my bedroom window like I did in Scarborough. It made me dream of a bigger life. I felt like one day I would take over that city.

One good thing about Ajax was that we had family. My aunts and uncles and five cousins lived down the street from us now, as did our family friends with their son, Mike, who was like a kid brother to me. We all went to school together and hung out on weekends. I actually felt like I had brothers and sisters for once. I loved having close family around, especially since my mum had started going to nursing school full-time, but being the new kid in town again was hard.

I found myself in the same old routine of getting bullied, having no real friends, and getting into fights. I didn't know it at the time, but my school had a bit of a reputation for having some tough kids in it. To me it just felt like the same old thing. When you grow up poor, you don't know any different. Everyone around you is poor and no one has more or less than you do. Everything is even. It was during these years that I got into a series of fights that made me never want to fight again. I had gotten bigger, and so had my bullies. At twelve and thirteen years old, we were able to actually hurt each other. In one fight, a kid came at me and I gave him a hard kick. When he tried to block it, my foot jammed his fingers, breaking one. The fight was over instantly and I felt fucking terrible that I actually hurt someone. The last time I ever punched someone (outside of self-defense) was another pointless schoolyard fight. I can still see the fear in his eyes and hear the sound of my fist connecting with his face. As he fell to the ground, he yelled, "Why are you doing this?" I instantly felt sick. I knew this wasn't me. I decided I would leave fighting to others.

I couldn't have understood it at the time, but the boredom of Ajax was actually a blessing. Boredom breeds creativity, which is probably why it was while I was living there that I started to get interested in writing my own music. At eleven, I formed my first band with my twelve-year-old cousin, Joe. We had a rap group called Powerful Young Hustlers. Of course at that age we had no real life experiences to rap about, so we made up songs about witnessing a fictitious murder or our nonexistent girl problems. My mum would give us each a dollar to perform for her on weekends. It was my first paying gig!

My mum and I still moved around a lot within Ajax, but it was a good thing, because it always felt like each place was a step up from the last. I was very excited when I found we were moving into a townhouse (not an apartment!) and I'd have a real bedroom on the second floor. Of course, it was in the worst part of Ajax, known as Monarch Mews, just below an industrial area, and had a tough reputation, but I didn't know any different. After we moved in, a few houses down from us, a family's garage just burst into flames one afternoon. They were known drug dealers so I guess it was kind of obvious what had happened, and no one paid much attention. Fights were common on my block, too. There was a guy who didn't belong in the neighborhood, who strolled through acting tough and mouthing off to people. It didn't take long before one of my neighbors came along to shut him up. It was fast and ugly. He got roundhouse kicked so hard in the face that it actually tore his nose off. Blood sprayed everywhere, and the people watching, including me, gasped out loud. His nose was barely hanging on as he took off running to get patched up by that free, no-questions-asked Canadian health care system.

We moved to the townhouse when I was halfway through seventh grade. Our next-door neighbor was a drug dealer named Ashley Rodriguez, who was large in both stature and reputation. He was in his mid-twenties and treated me like a little brother, taking me under his wing. We'd watch Rambo movies at his house and he'd tell me to be smart. "Don't fuck up, don't do drugs, stay in school and get your education," he'd say while packing up baggies of weed and coke to sell. Having Ashley on my side gave me protection, making me "a made guy" who no one wanted to fuck with. Well, no one except for the fucking skinheads from the Falby Court area that would walk around Ajax with those novelty-sized baseball bats, like the kind you'd buy at Toronto Blue Jays games, hidden under their sleeves. These guys didn't fear Ashley; in fact, those racists hated him because he and his crew were black and brown. As I said before, Ajax is a boring and generally safe little suburb, but these two pockets of lower-income housing complexes were my world and they certainly had their issues. The skinheads were the one thing I feared most the entire time I lived there. Years later when I was seventeen, I did in fact get jumped by four of these guys in the lobby of the Falby Court apartment complex. It just happened to be bad timing late one night after a Sum 41 show. They started making comments about my spiked hair and the next thing I knew I was on the ground getting pummeled. I managed to land a few punches of my own, which actually made them stop and back off. Unfortunately, Ashley was not around when I needed him then.

In general life was good, if boring, in Ajax. My mum had started her first serious relationship since B.D. Kevin was funny and dorky, but also a kind and generous man. He was recently divorced and had a six-year-old son, so they were taking their relationship slow. He still lived and worked in the city and would come out to Ajax on the weekends. I was happy to see my mum moving on and doing well in life now. I really liked Kevin, but I couldn't help feeling like I was losing the connection with my mum a little, too.

Musically, I wasn't listening to rap anymore and getting into much harder rock music. Nirvana's *Nevermind*, Metallica's Black Album, and Guns N' Roses' *Appetite* and *Illusion* albums were the only thing on my radar. There was something about the way Slash played the Les Paul that got me interested in the guitar and made me want more. I soon discovered Hendrix, Zeppelin, and other guitar heavy bands. One afternoon at my uncle Tim's house, I heard some serious Eddie Van Halen–style guitar shredding coming from a bedroom upstairs. I had to find the source and walked upstairs to find the person unleashing holy hell on his guitar. I stood in the doorway and just stared, mesmerized, until he finally looked up to see some creepy kid he'd never seen before watching him. He uncomfortably said, "Hello and who are you?" I explained that Tim was my uncle and he introduced himself as Phil and explained that Tim was dating his sister. There was an awkward pause until I blurted out the only thing on my mind, "Can you teach me?" He rolled his eyes, but begrudgingly agreed. "What would you like to play?" The first and only song I could think of was "Knockin' on Heaven's Door" by Guns N' Roses. He scoffed and muttered something about it not being Guns N' Roses, which at the time was lost on me. I had no idea it was actually a Bob Dylan song, nor did I care, because Slash was a god and this guy was going to show me how to play a Guns N' fuckin' Roses song! He showed me the three basic chords, and while it was hard, it didn't seem that difficult and I knew I could learn it. The lesson lasted all of ten minutes, but it was a huge moment for me.

That Christmas, Uncle Tim bought me a basic El Degas acoustic guitar for about $100, so I could practice on my own, and that's all I did. I played every day till my fingers bled. It sounds like a cliché, but that's what happens until you build calluses. After learning the chords and changes, I quickly realized I was more interested in writing my own music than playing other people's songs. After playing the El Degas for about a year, I needed to ditch the acoustic and get an electric, so I could play rock 'n' roll. My mum didn't have the money for that, though, and when I told her I wanted a real guitar, all she said was "You better start saving." I had around $80 dollars in my bank account, but I needed at least $150 to $200 for a shitty used electric. I realized that the quickest method to earn money would be gambling. My uncle Phil was a big gambler and taught me how to play poker and shoot pool. He was good at both, and I started getting good, too, which was important because he always liked to play for money, even with us kids. I got good enough that I started beating him, especially when he'd had a few too many beers. After a few months of beating my family at the pool table, I raised enough cash to buy a $150 red Ibanez Roadstar II Series guitar from the "Buy & Sell" section of the newspaper. I was ready to rock!

I wanted to play like Slash, but I knew that even with years and years of practice, I still probably wouldn't come close to playing like him. What I really wanted to do was write music and I wanted to write it now. Kurt Cobain, my other idol, was writing incredible songs with only three chords. Those songs spoke to me more than shredding and soloing, so I started writing my own lyrics. I didn't have a band, though, so I did the only thing that made sense and told my best friends to learn how to play instruments. We only needed to be a three-piece like Nirvana. My buddy Jay Thompson had an older brother that played drums, so I told him to learn from him. Our best friend Robbie Wallace would learn the bass since that was the easiest instrument. They asked their parents for their instruments for Christmas and by New Year's of '94 we were a band! After some quick debating we named ourselves Eternal Death. We played a noisy mess of thrash rock in my unfinished basement, which was set up as the ultimate teenage hang out/jam room plastered with posters of our favorite artists and cutouts from skate and music magazines, and outfitted with hand-me-down furniture and stuff we'd found out on the street. After school we'd put on little mini concerts for our friends. We had a few stand-out songs, called "Killer" and "Billy," that sounded kind of similar to the songs on Nirvana's *Bleach*.

In a short period of time, I'd picked up a guitar, learned to play, and now I had a band. Life was good. The only looming concern was high school. It was rapidly approaching, and I didn't know how I felt about it. Was I scared? Was I excited? When I entered Exeter High School in 1994, I was just another small, insignificant ninth-grader primed for being picked on by jocks and older students, like every ninth-grader that came before me. Luckily, I quickly found some friends to make high school bearable. On the first day of school, I sat next to a girl named Shannon Boehlke in Computer Tech who became one of my best friends for the first few years of high school, and eventually Cone's wife (more on him below). In my second class, Auto Tech, I sat next to a super-friendly chatty guy who happened to be a guitar player, too. We hit it off right away by talking about our bands and musical interests. He was into metal music like Anthrax and Metallica. This, of course, was Dave "Brownsound" Baksh, who at the time had his own heavy metal band called Embodiment. My first day of school gave me one more friend: Jason "Cone" McCaslin. He's always been a creature of habit, and he earned the name a few years later by having "The Great Canadian Cone" every day for lunch. After seeing him eat that same goddamn plain vanilla ice cream cone every day for a year, I finally just started calling him "Cone." It's funny how stupid the back stories are for earning nicknames. Dave named me "Bizzy D" in the tenth grade, because I was always in a rush, moving quickly, bouncing around from his house to record his band, then over to Cone's house to record his band, plus doing my own music as well. One day he just said, "Man, I'm gonna call you Bizzy D from now on." It stuck! Steve Jocz got the name "Stevo32" because he was the anti-jock, who would score on his own team by accident. Since all the jocks in our high school called each other by their numbers, even off the field, we started calling him Stevo32. Dave was always just called "Baksh" in high school. He was the guy who was friends with everyone, and no one had a bad thing to say about him. He was caring, friendly, and also athletic, which made him pretty popular. I was the complete opposite. I was introverted, quiet, and stuck with my same friends from my old school. Although I spoke to Cone and Dave in class, at first we never really saw each other outside of school.

In addition to meeting my future bandmates, that first year of high school was very pivotal for me. I was getting into trouble while hanging around the crew from my old school. Our crew consisted of my Eternal Death bandmates along with a couple other guys we went to school with in seventh and eighth grade. We went from pulling stupid teenage pranks like egging houses and breaking windows in abandoned buildings to breaking into cars and setting fires to the factories behind my housing complex. One afternoon during our March break, we broke into a parked school bus, attacked the seats of the bus with a small hatchet, set off a fire extinguisher, and tried to slash the tires. A man saw us and started chasing after us, so we ran away with the hatchet in hand. We hid in some bushes for a while, reemerging when we felt like the coast was clear. A police cruiser pulled up right behind us. We tried to act cool and keep calm, but he hit the sirens and pulled right in front of us, barking at us, "Get in the car." All five of us piled into the back of the cruiser, and he drove us straight back to the school bus, where another cop was assessing the damage. The officer made us all get out and show him the soles of our shoes. Turns out that my friend and I had left perfect footprints in the powder from the fire extinguisher on the bus.

We were hauled to the police station and charged with breaking and entering, theft, vandalism, and mischief. I had been brought home by the cops in the past, but this was much different than my usual scrapes with the law. I was being charged with four separate crimes and would need a lawyer. We were able to leave the station on our own, but they would be informing our parents soon. I didn't know how the fuck I was going to tell my mum. This was serious enough that it could really affect my life. I was terrified and figured I'd sit on it a few days while thinking of the best way to break it to her. The next day, I was on my way to meet friends when I saw a cop car pull into the complex and right up to my house. My stomach dropped as I watched my mum answer the door. I knew in that moment I was completely fucked. I went back home to face the music. My mum was heartbroken. I knew we had no money, and now she had to hire a lawyer to represent her fifteen-year-old son. For the rest of the year it was back and forth to court. She had to take off days from nursing school. I was so ashamed of myself. The judge couldn't do anything that was going to make me feel any worse than how I felt on those long silent drives to and from the courthouse with her.

In the end, I was lucky and the judge gave me a light punishment of two years' probation, community service, writing an essay, and making a poster about how "Crime Doesn't Pay." On my poster I drew a giant Jim Morrison in handcuffs with the words "Crime Doesn't Pay" written across the top. After a year of lawyers, cops, and courtrooms, I was ready to leave that shit behind me.

The experience helped me realize that I'd been hanging around the wrong people. Soon after I had gotten charged, I decided to cut off everyone I knew from my old school. The next day, I went to high school and just walked by my usual group as they stood outside smoking cigarettes. As I walked by them, they called out to me, "Hey Deryck, what the fuck?" I just ignored them and kept on walking. It quickly turned into name calling and threats. On one hand I knew I was doing the right thing for my future, but at the same time I was giving up all friends, my protection, and my band, which was a terrifying thing to do in the middle of ninth grade.

Having given up my friends, I had nothing else but my guitar and my music. I got used to being a loner. Right before the summer break, I met a guy in my class who I'd somehow never seen before. His name was Gary MacMillan and he played bass. How did it take so long for me to meet this guy? We instantly became close friends. He was into more "indie" music, which was new to me, but we bonded over Smashing Pumpkins and Weezer. This was pre-internet and Gary knew about fanzines, different ways of finding new music from independent record shops, and cool all-ages clubs where we could go see local live bands. He lived in the nicer, more upscale part of Ajax, down by the lake. His house had a pool and a finished basement where we could jam and play music together. The only odd thing about him was, his parents were nudists. They would walk around the house fully naked, and some weekends I wouldn't be allowed over, because it was mandatory "naked family swim day," whatever the fuck that meant. All I know is Gary hated it and was always embarrassed by his mum and dad.

The summer finally arrived, and Gary and I knew we needed to start a band. However, there weren't many people in our school, or even Ajax, that liked rock music. Most people listened to bad R&B or new hip hop, but not the good stuff like N.W.A or Tribe Called Quest. After LL Cool J, Ice-T, and all the eighties rap, hip hop just wasn't fun anymore. It was all slow and looked too flashy. It lost its humor and swagger. Worse than all that the "rock music" that ruled the day were bands like Everclear, Better Than Ezra, Tonic, and Collective Soul. Other than Smashing Pumpkins, Weezer, and Green Day, I was only interested in punk rock. Everything else was meaningless. I had taped a special that aired on MuchMusic (which was Canada's answer to MTV) all about the history of punk. That VHS meant everything to me and I watched it religiously. That's where I discovered Iggy Pop, the Clash, the Ramones, and the Sex Pistols, whose raw energy awoke something inside of me. Kurt Cobain had died that year and those punk bands helped fill that huge void. Punk said everything I felt inside and I wanted in. I had long hair like Cobain, but after finding punk, I cut it all off, spiked it, and dyed it blue using the food coloring that we had in the kitchen cabinet. I didn't have gloves, so my hands were completely blue for weeks. When I went to school the next day, people noticed me—and they didn't like what they saw. I was ridiculed and called a freak; it was provocative and I loved it. I hated all the kids in my class anyway. They were all jocks and losers as far as I was concerned. Dying my hair blue was a line in the sand, a statement that said, "FUCK YOU ALL! I AM NOTHING LIKE YOU!"

That freedom was a pivotal moment for me. Another came later that year when my mum took me to a friend's Christmas Eve party. It was a get-together for adults and I was the only teenager there and bored out of my mind. I noticed a familiar-looking man standing across the room, but I couldn't place him. He glanced my way, but didn't acknowledge me or my mum. He soon ended his conversation, walked right past us, and went out the front door. I only realized who he was when my mum's friend apologized saying, "I'm sorry, we didn't know B.D. was going to be here." I was stunned. This was the first time I'd seen my "dad" since before the divorce. For a second, I felt hurt, but the pain quickly turned into embarrassment, for him. *What a coward*, I thought. *He still can't even speak to me.* Before I could get lost in thought, the owner of the house came up with the perfect distraction. He was getting rid of his entire, massive collection of vinyl records in favor of the CD revolution that had fully taken over by this point. I was free to pick out whatever I wanted. I spent the rest of the night going through hundreds of records without another thought of B.D. I picked out as many records as I could stack into the car. It was the biggest music discovery gold mine I had ever known. Each day, I couldn't wait to get home from school and dive into new records. There was everything—Zappa, Zeppelin, the Doors, the Cars, the Stones, Stevie Wonder, Elton John, Billy Joel. It was endless. Every great record from every essential artist in rock history and I had it all in my hands for the first time.

By the time summer break rolled around, all that music had made my desire to start a new band even greater. Luckily, Gary remembered a rich kid named Chris Shaw who lived down at the lake with his dad, Ken Shaw, a semi-celebrity who had been the *Toronto TV News* anchorman since the eighties. Chris couldn't play drums all that well, but he had a brand-new kit and was a super-nice guy. We called ourselves Kaspir, a name we thought fit in with the *cool* band names of that era like Cracker, Clover, Rusty, and Limblifter. Our music was a cross between Weezer's *Blue Album* and Green Day's *Dookie* and, because we added darker chords, a little Nirvana, too. I would write songs that we would jam to in Chris's basement and then go hang out at the park, where people would smoke weed, drink, or skate. It was there that I met this loud, obnoxious, attention-hogging kid with a dumb voice. This guy had been talking so loud for so long that I later learned he'd gotten nodules on his vocal cords, but just continued talking. The result was a damaged, hoarse, scratchy, dumb-sounding voice. On top of that he smoked cigarettes and a lot of weed. I hated everything that came out of his mouth. I asked Gary, "Who is this guy? I kind of hate him instantly." Gary knew him from elementary school. "His name is Steve Jocz," he said, explaining that he was a year younger than us and would start at our school in September. He added that he was a killer drummer for his age and played in a band called Thrall. I had already heard that this band were supposedly really good musicians with really good equipment. The more times I saw Steve that summer, the more I disliked him. Even if he was some great drummer, I just thought he was a total burnout with a stupid voice who needed to shut the fuck up.

When school started back up, I saw him in the halls, but I didn't speak to him. I had ditched my old crew, but still hung out with Jimmy, this tough guy from my neighborhood. He was a notorious fighter and came to me one day saying, "Hey you know that new kid with the dumb voice? I'm going to kick his ass." That was enough of a reason for Jimmy. He just liked to pick fights. He walked over to Steve in the hall and pushed him to the lockers, making it seem like it was actually Steve's fault. Jimmy's plan was to beat the shit out of Steve after school for bumping into him earlier. While I had always hated Steve, for some reason, I told Jimmy to leave him alone. "Why? Do you know him?" Jimmy said, confused. I pretended like I knew him and that he was a cool guy and he should be left alone. Jimmy said, "Oh shit, I'm sorry, man. I won't let anyone fuck with him." To this day I still don't know what prompted me to save some kid I didn't even like. Maybe it was because Steve was a musician and a skater. Or maybe it was because Steve was just a small, doughy kid that obviously didn't stand a chance against a seasoned street fighter like Jimmy. Or maybe it was because, deep in my soul, I knew Steve and I would become best friends and take over the world together someday. Either way, I put an end to it. Even though Stevo had no idea how close he came to getting pummeled, I decided to go and say hello to him.

Once I got past his voice, he was actually a nice guy and pretty funny, too. We started hanging out more and eventually I got to see him play drums. Everything I had heard about him was true. He was an incredible drummer for his age, his band was really good, and they had great equipment. Way better than we did. In high school the dream was to have big amp stacks like Slash or AC/DC, so I suggested that our bands should practice in the same space so we could combine our gear. It wasn't hard to convince Steve to let us all practice at his house. As with everything with Steve in those days, he just said, in his burned-out stoner voice, "Sure, whatever." The next day Gary and I loaded all of our gear into his basement, stacked it up, and plugged it all in. To test it out and make sure it all worked, we asked Steve to play along to one of our songs. "I know your song, 'Wet Cow,'" he said, enthusiastically. We were surprised he knew the song because he'd only heard us play it once when we were jamming in Chris Shaw's basement before we went out skateboarding. We launched into the song, and with the power of the stacked up amps and Stevo's incredible drumming, we sounded like a band that had been playing together for years. It clicked right away. I could barely contain myself from tearing up as we ran through my song. This was the first moment in my life where I actually sounded like I was in a real band. We finished the song and said thanks, Steve, we'll see you tomorrow. Before we got to the end of his driveway, I turned to Gary and said, "We need him in our band!" Gary agreed, and we came up with a plan where I asked Steve to join, if Gary would kick out Chris Shaw. It was actually simple, because Chris didn't seem to care that much and Steve just said, "Sure, whatever." And just like that the three of us were Kaspir.

THE SUM OF 41

*N*ow that the lineup in Kaspir was solidified, Gary and I poured everything we had into making a name for the band. Gary was great at getting us gigs by cold-calling venues and talking his way into opening slots for bar bands, signing us up for a local battle of the bands, or tapping into the underground scene (playing at basement parties). We were earning our chops, playing in front of strangers for the first time, which I had never done before. We were also putting our own money into it wherever we could. I had saved up a pretty decent amount of cash from all my jobs, including a paper route, working a kiosk selling pins at the local craft shows in Keene, and working for a florist, holding a sign out on the street that said "Roses 9.99" while wearing a full clown costume with makeup, curly wig, and red nose. That last one was humiliating, and I was only getting $5 an hour! Gary had a good job working at a gas station and eventually got me hired there. We just had to sit in the kiosk and take cash and credit cards from people.

Gary and another coworker had a little scheme going, because they had realized that the owner was really checked out. As long as the numbers of what came in and went out matched, the owner never noticed if a little bit of money was missing at the end of the day. Since my life of crime had already forced me into the court system, I didn't want anything to do with this scheme. I wasn't opposed to enjoying the riches of *their* crimes, though! When they first started, they swiped a few twenties here and there, but by the time I was working at the gas station, they were taking hundreds and sometimes thousands a day from that place. Being high school students, they had money to burn but nowhere to spend it. We knew if we started buying amps, guitars, and recording equipment, or started a record label, our parents would have questions. Instead we just lived like kings in ways that our parents wouldn't notice. Gary started taking cabs to school. We took a limo to the mall and had it wait for us while we bought subs from the food court with $100 bills, telling cashiers to "keep the change." We felt like we were in the Mafia with garbage bags full of money hidden in Gary's basement, so we decided to take it to the next level and bought pin-striped suits and trench coats and wore them to school. Kids in class already thought we were weird, so no one even questioned our new style. We gave Steve cartons and cartons of cigarettes that he stashed in his room. While his mom knew he was a smoker, she flipped out when she saw the cartons piled high in his bedroom and he said they were from me. She already didn't like me, always thinking I was up to something, which was true in a sense, but the only thing I was up to was trying to make this band successful. So much for keeping a low profile!

Gary got us a show at the SuperNova Battle of the Bands at a famous Toronto venue called The Opera House. That's where Nirvana, Green Day, Smashing Pumpkins, and other huge bands played, so I was excited. The deal with SuperNova was they would have fifty bands perform on one night, and every band would sell tickets. The band that sold the most tickets got a professional photo shoot or a demo recording of one song. Gary had the genius to use the gas station funds to purchase a shitload of tickets, give them away to people at school, and rent a school bus to take everyone to and from the show. We instantly won the professional photo shoot. Here's the problem, though: Even though we sold more tickets than any other band, they still put us on first at 5 p.m. (the worst slot) and then never returned our phone calls when we tried to set up our photo shoot. Fuckers! Gary knew where one of the promoters lived, so when they never answered our calls, we went by his house and egged it. We carried that grudge all the way into Sum 41 and trash-talked them when people were finally listening, because yes, we were that immature.

Nothing lasts forever, though, and everyone at the gas station eventually got handed a pink slip. It wasn't that surprising really. Someone up top must have realized things were not adding up. The news of my unemployment came while I was playing foosball at our new favorite spot in Ajax called the Chameleon Cafe. Gary, Steve, and I discovered this place while walking down a small back road in the industrial area. It wasn't even open yet, but looked like a place we wanted to hang out in, especially because there were no hangout spots or cafes in town and this place had a cool Bohemian vibe and pool tables, foosball, and a small foot-high stage in the corner. The place was empty except for a woman who was wiping down the bar. She gave us a wary look and said, "Sorry, we're not open." We asked her about the place and she said it was going to be a bar and not an all-ages hangout. She let us sit down and buy a nonalcoholic strawberry kiwi fizzy drink that we'd never heard of. It was the coolest place we'd ever seen, and we asked if we could come hang out until they opened for real. The owners agreed, but warned us we wouldn't be allowed in once it was a bar.

Over the next few weeks we were there every day and told everyone at school about it, so more and more kids started showing up. By the time they were ready to open, there were so many kids hanging around, that they just kept it an all-ages spot. We had successfully turned this place into our own hangout and became the Chameleon Cafe darlings. Naturally, we convinced them to have live bands perform there, so we could play. They were hesitant at first, but as soon as they started allowing bands, it took off. All of a sudden, the Chameleon became a major spot, and bands from all around the country made sure to play there when they were coming through Toronto. To be there at the beginning and watch it grow based on the little ideas of fifteen-year-olds was pretty amazing.

The space had been a mechanic shop and it still had garages with big roll-down doors. Years later they turned those garages into rehearsal rooms for bands, and when we finally had some money after signing our record deal, we rented out one of those spaces to put together songs for *Half Hour of Power* and *All Killer No Filler*. At one point I even thought, if we ever made it, I would buy the Chameleon and turn it into my own compound and park my car in the living room! Of course, once I made enough money to actually do that, I realized the last place I wanted to live was an old mechanic shop in the industrial area of Ajax.

I loved having the Chameleon Cafe as a refuge. My mum and her boyfriend Kevin had been together for a few years, and we had all moved in together. As they formed a family, I started to feel less at home in what was now *their* house. The lighthearted, fun Kevin that I knew had become a hard-ass and angry whenever I was around. He handed me a list of "house rules" that were so ridiculous to me that I can't even remember them. It felt like he was exerting authority for authority's sake. The result was that I either stayed in the basement with my guitar or escaped to Stevo's or the Chameleon Cafe.

Kaspir was playing a few shows around town and we were making a small name for ourselves. Through the band and skateboarding, we started making new friends at the other high school in town, including this cool-looking punk chick I had seen around named Sofia Makrenos. We started hanging out in the basement of her parents' house, and that was where I first heard "modern punk rock" bands like Pennywise, Lagwagon, and Good Riddance. This music was so different than the classic punk rock I loved. It was much faster and had a different kind of energy and paired well with the skate and snowboard videos we watched all the time. One band in particular hit me the same way the Sex Pistols and Nirvana did, but I didn't know their name and didn't want Sofia to think I was lame if I asked. I finally got Stevo to tell me it was a band called NOFX. I asked Sofia if I could borrow her CD so I could dub it. I guess she thought it was cool that we liked the same music, because not only did she dub a few other punk CDs for me, but we also started hooking up. It always seemed like my life went from one cool situation to the next. (In fact it still does to this day.)

I dove headfirst into all this new music. I learned all about NOFX and how its singer, Fat Mike, started his own record label, Fat Wreck Chords, and signed all of these other great bands like Strung Out, No Use for a Name, a Japanese band called Hi-Standard, and the amazing Canadian band Propaghandi. The mid-nineties seemed to have an endless supply of great punk rock bands. Bad Religion, Rancid, the Offspring, and Social Distortion all had big records, and the suburbs of Toronto had an incredible emerging punk scene. This music completely took me over.

Near the end of tenth grade, I saw a guy walk into the school cafeteria who I'd never seen before, which was weird because our school was small. He stood out even more, because he was a skater kid while most of the school was jocks, preps, and other douches. Having been the new kid so many fucking times, I felt bad for him and went up and introduced myself. His name was Jon Marshall and his family had just moved into town. We realized we had everything in common. He played guitar, loved old school hip hop, and was somehow even more obsessed with NOFX and punk rock than I was. From that day on we hung out at Jon's apartment every day, eating Kraft dinner, watching *The Simpsons*, playing video games, and, of course, listening to music and jamming on guitar. Although I was still in Kaspir, Jon and I kept talking about starting another band that was strictly going to be a punk rock band.

As school ended and summer rolled in, we heard that a music festival called the Warped Tour was coming to town. When we saw the lineup, we lost our shit: Pennywise, Face to Face, Unwritten Law, Rocket from the Crypt, and our favorite band of all—the band we thought we would never see in our lifetime—NOFX! There was no way we were going to miss this. July 27, 1996, was a hot and humid day, but we got to the festival early, because we didn't want to miss a single thing. Stevo, Gary, Jon, and I watched motocross and skateboarding events and grabbed a ton of free stickers as we waited for the bands to start playing. We even caught a glimpse of NOFX coming off their tour bus that was parked near the crowd, so anyone could just walk up to their bus. We watched as swarms of punks pestered Fat Mike while he yelled at them, "I just fucking woke up! Leave me alone, fuck!" *He was exactly like we'd thought!*

We were in awe as we watched all of our favorite bands play that day. None of us went near the mosh pit, not out of fear, but because we actually wanted to sit and listen to the music. We thought seeing these bands was a once-in-a-lifetime opportunity, and we weren't going to waste it moshing. As the four of us sat watching NOFX, I turned to the guys with an idea. "We need to end Kaspir," I said. "We need to be a punk rock band. The kind of band that would play the Warped Tour. This is the only music we listen to, why are we not playing it? Kaspir sounds like the early nineties rock music we *used* to listen to, and don't anymore." Everyone agreed. We were starting a new band and Jon would be in it. All we needed was a name. The worst part of starting a new band is always the question: "What the fuck do we call ourselves?"

The four of us brainstormed for days in my basement, even cutting up words from a magazine and pulling them from a hat, but nothing stuck. We liked the idea of having a number in the name, because we thought that could be original, which sounds ridiculous now. Then we thought, *What if the number rhymed with the word?* We almost went with the name 7 Ply Surprise, which is slang for a skateboard to the face, but there was a local punk band named Five Knuckle Chuckle, which meant a punch to the face, and it felt too similar. One word we liked from our magazine cutout experiment was the word "Sum." Since it was like the sum of something, we thought we should add a number to it. What number, though? We looked at the calendar and counted how many days it had been from the start of our summer break to the day the Warped Tour was on and it was forty-one days. That was it! We would be Sum 41, which meant forty-one days into the summer. We had our name and it was original! Or so we thought. We'd been a band for about a year and a half when we started to hear of a band from Southern California with numbers in their name—blink-182. Their song "Dammit" had started getting radio play and people were starting to know their name. Still, we didn't think too much of it, because at the end of the day, who gives a shit about band names anyway?

Throughout the summer, we practiced in Stevo's basement, which also doubled as his family's living room. That meant we had to set everything up and tear it all down by the time his parents came home from work at 5:30 p.m. It was kind of a pain, but we did it until we got signed and moved into the rehearsal spot at the Chameleon. Like all young bands we went through a lot of lineup changes. Sometimes for no reason, like with Gary's departure from the band. Jon, Stevo, and I had become really close friends, but Gary wasn't that into the punk rock stuff. That was enough for us young idiots to decide we needed to kick him out of the band since Jon could play bass. Steve made the call. He dialed Gary's number and we all listened in as Gary answered the phone. Steve excitedly said, "Hey Gary! Guess what! We're kicking you out of the band! So come get your shit in twenty minutes or we're putting it at the end of the driveway for garbage pickup." We didn't even wait five minutes before we grabbed his bass and amp and dumped them on the curb. We then sat on Steve's porch to watch as Gary and his dad pulled up, piled his gear into the car, and drove off. They never looked at us or said a word. Fuck, teenagers are assholes (even Canadian ones).

The weekend before school started back up, Stevo and I had tickets to see the band Treble Charger, who we both loved. Treble Charger had been a band since around '92 and kept writing hits into the early 2000s. They had a lot of cred in the Canadian music scene, because they were big, but never sold out. We had no idea that Treble Charger were really only massive in Canada. Since they were on TV and the radio, we thought they were as huge as Smashing Pumpkins. We got to the venue five hours early in the hopes of seeing the band walk in for soundcheck. We missed them, but we did get a great spot about ten feet from the stage. It was a totally sold out show and the band was amazing. They weren't a punk band, but they had interesting music and a singer with bleached blond spiked hair that reminded me of Johnny Rotten.

Because we had been at the front of the stage, when the show ended, Stevo and I were some of the last in line to exit the venue. We got separated, and Stevo left the building, but I had loitered long enough that the bouncers and security had left, too. Since Kaspir had played the venue once, I knew the dressing room was right off the stage, and I could see no one was guarding it. I didn't hesitate, I just walked straight into the room like I belonged there. All the guys in Treble Charger were sitting around drinking post-show beers and Greig Nori, the spikey-haired singer, looked at me right away and smiled. I went up and told him that it was a great show and that I really loved his band. He smiled and asked, "Did you sneak backstage or something?" I explained that no one was watching the door, so I just thought I'd come tell him I was a fan.

I wanted him to know I was in a band, too. So I told him that we were called Sum 41 and we were playing our first show at a Battle of the Bands in Toronto in a few weeks. "You should come!" I blurted. "That's cool, yeah maybe I will come," he replied. "Put me on the list." I had no idea what the fuck "a list" was, so I asked, "Uh, okay, how do I do that?" He grabbed a pen and paper, wrote his name and phone number on it, and told me to call him a few days before the show to remind him to come by and he would be there. I was fucking stunned. I walked out of the venue in a daze. How the fuck did that just happen? I found Steve outside alone having a smoke. "What happened to you?" he asked. I explained, "Dude, I met the whole band backstage and Greig Nori gave me his fucking phone number! He's coming to our show in a few weeks!" Stevo didn't believe it until I showed him the paper with Greig's phone number. I couldn't fully explain to Steve what or how it all happened. I was still in too much shock from having met one of my idols—and he wanted to come see my band. All I knew was that we had to start fucking practicing for this fucking show.

We had booked another one of those SuperNova Battle of the Bands, but this time we weren't going to play their game of selling tickets or trying to win any bullshit prizes. This was just the easiest way to get a show in a real venue downtown. The week before the gig, I gave Greig a call to remind him to come watch us play. I was so nervous calling him that I kept pressing a few numbers, hanging up, and then starting over. When I did finally manage to dial the full number, Greig didn't even remember me. I reminded him that I was the spikey-haired kid who snuck backstage. He laughed and said he would come with his friend Marc Costanzo, who was in another cool indie rock band called Len. He was about to hang up, but I wanted to keep him on the line. I thought this might be the only time I ever got to talk to a real rock star, so I started asking him random questions about being in a band, how to make it, what kind of guitar he played, anything to keep him sharing the secrets of being a successful musician. He happily obliged me for about thirty minutes before hanging up. I sat there in a daze. Was he really going to come to our show? Were we friends now? I called Steve and Jon right away and told them Greig was coming to the show and was bringing another rock star friend with him! Jon immediately said, "Greig is going to be our key to success." Neither Stevo nor I really understood what he meant by that; we were just stoked that we were talking to one of our heroes and he was so fucking cool!

We knew the show had to be good, so we practiced our set, which was five originals and a cover of NOFX's "Stickin in My Eye." When the day of the show arrived, we were nervous but pretty confident, even though it was our first live performance. When we got to The Opera House to load in our equipment, we were gutted to learn that we had been given the 5 p.m. opening slot, again. Not only would the place be totally empty, but there was no way that a rock star would show up that early to see some new kid band play for twenty minutes. I called Greig, but I had to leave a message on his answering machine, because no one was carrying cell phones yet. We were all bummed and felt the whole night was a bust. As five o'clock rolled around, we took the stage depressed and pissed off to play to a practically empty venue with no Greig in sight. I was mad at myself for getting so excited. I mean, why the fuck would a huge rock star have any interest in coming to see us? I felt so stupid. As we played through our set, we started to feel less bummed, because we were actually onstage playing punk rock music as Sum 41 for the very first time—and we were sounding good. Ten minutes into our short six-song set, I saw two people walk into the nearly empty venue. I couldn't really see them because of the stage lights, but I spotted a spikey-haired silhouette walking straight towards the stage. My heart started racing with adrenaline pumping, thinking could it be? As they walked into the light, the three of us realized, holy shit it's fucking Greig Nori and Marc Costanzo. They made it! We blazed through the rest of the set and grabbed our gear off stage as fast as we could so we could talk to them. Greig said we were amazing, and like most people, he was blown away by how good Steve was on drums, especially for a fifteen-year-old kid. They didn't stay long after that, but we had clearly made an impression on them. The fact that Marc and Greig came to the show and liked us gave us the confidence that we could turn this band into something special. It felt like the best night of our lives.

While Jon was convinced that Greig would open doors for us, I was focused on writing songs, finding a permanent bass player, and making sure the connection with Greig didn't just disappear. I would call him up occasionally to ask him advice and we would end up talking for hours. He told me all the things he'd learned from years in the music business, about booking agents and record labels. He'd already been through so much and had so many great stories and I was more than happy to listen. When '96 turned to '97, Greig and I were chatting once a week and we were regulars at Treble Charger shows. He'd even given Stevo and me our first drink, which were Goldschläger shots handed to us right before they went on stage. We thought it was the coolest fucking thing in the world. *They literally drink gold! That's so fucking rock star!* Even back then my tolerance for alcohol was very high. Stevo would get drunk off of a couple of shots, but I didn't feel a thing. When we started drinking at high school parties, I thought everyone was faking the whole drunk thing, because I barely felt a buzz. This would obviously be a problem for me down the road, but we'll save that for later.

One day Greig asked if we wanted to record a demo. He and Marc Costanzo had some free recording time at the studios at Ryerson University in downtown Toronto and wanted to practice their producing skills. We jumped at the chance. On February 8, 1997, we went in the studio for three days and recorded seven songs:

"Sunday Morning Comics"
"Not My Concern"
"5.0. Grind"
"Neighbors"
"Used and Abused"
"Everything's Okay"
"To All the Herbivores (I Like Meat)"

Walking into a pro studio for the first time felt natural, like we belonged there. We got our gear set up, jammed a little while Marc and Greig got levels, and we got used to playing with headphones on. Then we started doing real takes as they guided us. Steve played his ass off, nailing every drum part with ease. After a day and a half of recording the music, it was time to lay down our vocals and Jon went first. Back then, Jon and I sang an equal number of songs. He quickly knocked out "Sunday Morning Comics" and "Not My Concern." Listening in the control room, he sounded great—punk as fuck with tons of attitude. Then it was my turn to sing. After watching Jon lay it down so quickly, I thought it would be a breeze.

I sang a few lines and the music stopped dead in my ears. I could see Greig, Marc, and the rest of the band talking through the glass, but couldn't hear what they were saying. Greig's voice came over the headphone, "Let's do it again from the top, we had some problems in here." I started again, giving the best version of myself, but once again the music suddenly stopped. This time Greig asked me to come to the control room and listen. When they played it back, I thought it was a joke, like they had put some effect on my voice to make it sound like it was an eight-year-old singing. I was confused, because that was *not* how I sounded. Greig kicked everyone out of the room and told me that hearing your voice on a recording can be really jarring. He said the same thing happened to him when he was starting out. He explained that I needed to over-exaggerate my singing and push harder and sound tougher.

I went back out and did a few more takes, but every time I listened back I sounded like a chipmunk. I was so embarrassed. I knew I looked like a hack in front of Greig and Marc, while Jon and Steve came off so naturally gifted and talented beyond their ages. I felt so *less than* and inferior. Despite my poor performance, we finished the recording and those three long days in the studio were a bonding experience for us. Marc even let down his tough guy exterior, falling for our charms. Everything was a joke to us and we always had fun with everything. We were teenagers and our fun seemed to bring out the "teenager" in people, and they'd find themselves wanting to hang around us for the laughs.

Marc and Greig mixed the songs a few days later, but were only able to finish five of the seven tracks. The other two songs lived on a reel-to-reel tape for years, until I stupidly recorded over them when I was recording new demo ideas for *All Killer*. The good news was that Marc thought the five songs were good enough to release on his indie label, Fun Trip Records.

After that recording session, Greig called me up and invited us to a housewarming party at his drummer's place. The party was exactly a week after my seventeenth birthday. Jon had turned seventeen a month before and Steve was still only fifteen, but Greig asked us to stop by for drinks and head to the party together. Friday night came around and the three of us hopped on the train headed towards Greig's house. Greig had talked about taking ecstasy before, and we were nervous that it might be that kind of party. We only started drinking after Greig introduced us to the liquid gold. None of us had done drugs other than smoke a little weed. What would we do if Greig asked us to take hard drugs like coke or ecstasy? I looked at the guys and said, "If anyone offers us drugs we are NOT doing it right?" Jon agreed and Steve replied with his usual blasé "Whatever you guys do, I'm doing."

When we got to Greig's, the "who's who" of Canadian rock was gathered there to pregame the party. There were members of Treble Charger and Len and Brendan Canning of the band hHead and, later, Broken Social Scene, as well as a few tall, gorgeous models. It was exactly what we expected from rock stars. Drinks were poured, and within a few minutes Greig came over and asked me and Jon, "Do you guys want to do some ecstasy?" We both looked at each other, remembering the pact we had made, and without hesitation looked back at Greig and said in unison, "Yes." Steve was off somewhere else, maybe taking a piss or making the girls laugh, when Greig took us to a back room where it was decided that because it was our first time, we "kids" were only going to do half of what the others got. Jon and I felt that that was a good compromise.

We took our E, had some drinks, and headed over to the real party. We didn't know anything about this drug. How long would it take to kick in? What did it feel like when it did? How long did it last? At first nothing seemed to happen, but as we were walking into the elevator to the drummer's apartment, I started feeling a warm tingling in my head. I looked at Jon and I could tell he was feeling it now, too. Greig smiled and said, "It's kicking in." We got to the party and it felt like the scene in *The Doors* movie when Jim Morrison walked into Andy Warhol's loft. The place was packed with cool artsy-looking people who were all fucked up on one thing or another. There was a DJ, an entire half-pipe skate ramp built into the wall, and a trapeze hanging from the ceiling complete with drunken acrobats. This was absolutely nothing like any "house party" we'd ever been to in Ajax, and probably thanks to being high, we felt like we belonged there, because we came with rock royalty. At a certain point I felt the need to break it to Stevo that we had taken ecstasy without him and that we were super-high. He laughed and said it was cool, because he'd been smoking weed with some guys. He ended up smoking so much fucking weed that he passed out in the middle of the skate ramp and people were either stepping over him to get to the kitchen or were posing for pictures next to him, which even earned him a second nickname: Stevo Pass Out King! Even unconscious, Stevo is an attention getter!

We started playing shows in the local punk rock scene, which meant gigs in basements or at outdoor parties, the occasional set at the Chameleon Cafe, or slots opening for other local bands at shitty dive bars. Stevo's mom or sister would drive us to a gig; we'd pack the car with all our gear, lugging it up and downstairs. We loved every second of it. To us, this was what we were going to do for the rest of our lives. We didn't need MTV or radio play. All we wanted was to find a way to support ourselves by playing punk rock music. That was success.

As we started the eleventh grade, I had been rocking dyed spiked hair for a while, but now Jon had a mohawk and Stevo shaved his head, and we all wore clothes from the Goodwill and Salvation Army. The more "punk" we dressed the more unpopular we became at high school. The jocks at our school routinely threw food at us during lunch, pushed us around in the halls, and called us every unimaginative homophobic slur. We didn't care though. We just had to get through the school day so we could go to Stevo's house and practice. We'd jam for hours after school trying to hone our skills and become the fastest punk rock band around. Every time we heard a band that sounded fast, we would try to play a song faster, pushing Stevo harder and harder with his double kick pedal.

I was constantly working on my guitar sound, too, spending hours standing in front of my amp, fucking with all the controls and searching for the sound I could hear in my head. I would routinely go to bed with my ears ringing. One morning I woke up and the ringing was still there. It was still there the next day and the next. To this day it has never gone away. I had gotten tinnitus at sixteen years old. It drove me crazy for years, but now it's become normal. The only good thing about it was that it made me start protecting my ears so I wouldn't make it worse, and I've managed to keep my hearing intact, which is rare for a touring musician. I wear earplugs constantly, and they live in all my jacket and pants pockets. One of the first things we did when the band made any money was purchase an in-ear monitor system. We were the only young band playing in clubs using an in-ear system, which made us look like total prima donnas to a lot of local soundmen and musicians. But fuck it, I can still hear and I bet they can't!

CHAPTER 4

NO PLAN B

Outside of the Sum 41 dudes and Greig and Marc, I didn't really associate with many people. I was close with Cone and Dave at school, but we didn't hang out much outside of class. My only other friends I talked to were a few girls I would chat with throughout class, lunch, or on the phone after school when I wasn't with the guys. We were just friends, though. I never really had a girlfriend except once in the eleventh grade, when I thought I'd give dating a try. I absolutely hated it. I don't know if I was just too immature or if she was a little too high-maintenance, but we fought constantly about anything and everything. Even if I didn't laugh enough at something she found funny, it would turn into a huge argument. She would scream and yell and hurl insults at me all the time. She grew up in an Italian family who all yelled constantly, too, and she claimed her abusive father was a member of the Mafia and often had her family followed. I never knew if that was true or not. I mean, there is a well-known Mafia presence in Toronto, and her mother looked like she could've been a cast member from *The Sopranos*, but I couldn't be certain. Either way, after six months of arguing, fighting, and worrying if that Cadillac with tinted windows was following us, I had to break it off with her. I did get a song out of the whole experience, called "Crazy Amanda Bunk Face," which ended up on the *All Killer* album.

The whole ordeal scarred me, and I swore I wouldn't get into another serious relationship until I was ready to get married, which is what I did. I wanted to focus on my band and writing music for Sum 41. Besides, most people in high school were only in a relationship to have sex whenever they wanted. That was never an issue for me. From the time I lost my virginity at fourteen and all the way through high school I seemed to be sexually satisfied. Like I said, my close friends outside of the band were all girls. They were the ones I spent my free time with and they were the ones I spent hours on the phone with each night. One thing we talked about? They wanted to have sex, too. We figured why not be friends with benefits? While it rarely works out, for a while it did with one of those girls, my close friend Jessica Whitbread. We met in ninth grade and by the tenth, she wanted to start experimenting with sex and asked if I would be her partner. I was a teenage boy, so of course I was more than willing. It was great, but she lived in a small house with paper-thin walls and her parents' bedroom was right next to hers. There was no doubt that her mom heard everything that was going on. She was very cool and never said a word about it, but there were definitely some awkward looks and smirks in the morning when I left Jessica's house.

School was a joke to me, and by eleventh grade I was only taking bullshit classes like Cooking, Baking, and Interior Design. I saw no future in school, only in music. There was no plan B. Stevo, Jon, and I had become fully accepted in the rock scene of Toronto. Since Jon had his driver's license, at night we would head to Marc or Greig's house, stay up all night drinking or doing mushrooms, going to bars and parties, then sleep for a few hours and show up in class the next morning. I would sneak in and out my window or pretend I was sleeping over at Jon's or Steve's house so my mum was none the wiser—and she never figured it out, so this is probably all news to her. (Sorry, Mum!) Our partying really escalated when Greig introduced us to the rave scene of the mid-nineties. We didn't really know what raves were, but after Greig explained them as underground parties that lasted all night, where everyone danced and took a bunch of ecstasy, we were in. The raves took place every few Saturdays, and for about a year straight we wouldn't miss a single one. The routine became the same. Show up at Greig's or Marc's place on Friday, stay up all night drinking, so we could sleep all day Saturday. Wake up in the evening, start drinking again, take a couple hits of ecstasy, and find out where the rave would be held. It was always somewhere different and unknown, and you usually had to know someone to get in. Of course that was never an issue since Greig had the keys to the city.

We didn't dance at all, but we would take lots of drugs, find somewhere quiet (like the bathrooms), and just sit and talk all night. We'd meet strangers who would become our new best friends for the night, talking and chewing the inside of our mouths apart. We'd be so high that we wouldn't feel any pain, until the drugs fully wore off a few days later and we were left with bloody cheeks and a torn up tongue from chewing on them for hours. After a few months of this, we had done so much ecstasy that the effects weren't hitting us as hard, so someone introduced us to a new drug called crystal, which they said was like coke mixed with ecstasy and would last longer. We didn't know what it was, but with names like crystal and ecstasy, they just sounded like *designer* drugs to us. It wasn't until years later that I realized that those capsules we were taking were actually crystal meth. All we cared about was that it was way cheaper than ecstasy and lasted so much longer.

On crystal we wouldn't come down until Sunday evening at the earliest, which meant we had to find all sorts of secret after-hours parties for us degenerate drug-fueled fiends to hit after the raves. We'd continue going straight through to Monday morning. Sometimes we'd skip the after-parties, and as dawn broke we'd stumble into a park and end up doing tai chi with the older people, or wander into an Ikea and walk around for hours looking at living room sets we might buy one day. You'd think people would be spooked by a crew of cracked out punk rock teenagers crashing their Sunday mornings, but they were always welcoming. I still can't drive by an Ikea without feeling a little sketchy. By Monday morning we felt totally depressed and depleted of all serotonin and electrolytes, malnourished from two days of not eating and delirious from sleep deprivation.

Still, we never skipped a day of school. We always showed up Monday morning completely destroyed for the next four days. I would always tell myself, "This is not okay, I can't keep doing this. I feel so fucking awful. We're hardly playing music or having band practice anymore. It's just partying and recovering. This has to stop." Then Friday would come and I'd feel invincible and ready to do it all over again.

The only thing that was getting me through those long, painful recovery mornings at school was listening to Howard Stern on my portable Walkman radio. The Stern show was new to Canada, and when the Toronto rock station Q101 started broadcasting his morning show, it was like a gift. It was so wild and outrageous. To me, he was like the Johnny Rotten of radio. I saw no difference between what he was doing on live radio and how the Sex Pistols had revolutionized music years earlier. In order to listen, I wore a hoodie with a big front pocket and ran the wire for the earbuds up through my right sleeve to hear Stern, leaving my left ear open to hear what was happening in class. I thought I was so slick until one morning I didn't hear the teacher calling my name multiple times. Finally, she shouted my name loud enough that it broke me from my trance. When she asked me to stay after class, I thought I was busted for the huge radio in my front pocket. Instead, the teacher told me she noticed that I was having trouble in this class. Her plan to help me succeed was to assign me a partner for classwork and then have me take open-book tests in a special class. I paused for a second and thought, *Wait, she thinks I'm dumb and need help with my work.* At first I was offended, but then I realized that I had won the proverbial jackpot. Listening to Stern was not only helping me get through my mornings, but was actually going to help me get the grades I needed to pass, which was my only goal. School got a lot easier.

Unfortunately, things were not as easy with the band. We were playing a few shows around town, but were stuck shuffling in and out new bass players without much progress. The partying definitely made things harder, but on top of that, Jon and I were falling out, too. Our rift grew quickly, and Jon convinced Stevo that they needed to leave Sum 41 and start a new band. They called a meeting at the Tim Hortons near my house to break the news that they were quitting. I was stunned that my best friends had just turned on me. I understood Jon's feelings, but not Stevo, because we never had a single problem. I walked home, fighting tears. I called Stevo later that night and asked him why. He admitted that Jon had turned him against me and he just went along with it, because he didn't know what else to do. I told him to forget Jon, stay in Sum 41, and we would work to make this band bigger and better than ever. Stevo agreed and Sum 41 had its drummer back. It was my first lesson in band dynamics, power, control, and ego.

I could tell Jon had been getting jealous of my friendship with Greig, who had been paying a lot of attention to me and really taken me under his wing. Greig and I spent hours talking late at night, high on ecstasy, bonding over our childhoods, and he was becoming like an older brother or even father figure to me. I wanted to spend all my time hanging out with him, because he seemed cool, generous, and kind. We didn't actually know how old he was and we didn't care. (He was in his mid-thirties. Ancient!) I was young, impressionable, and completely in awe of Greig Nori.

I was glad to have Greig, because things at home were pretty shitty. Kevin and I were now completely at odds with each other, and I felt like an unwelcome guest in my own home. He and my mum had just bought a small but nice brand-new house, and Kevin was always imposing new, and in my opinion, superfluous rules, like I wasn't allowed to use the new cordless phone because it was "for adults only," and he would actually take it with him when he left the house. If I didn't rinse my dishes to his liking I would find a pile of dirty dishes under my covers when I got in bed. If we spoke at all, we were fighting, and it seemed clear he preferred it if I wasn't around. My mum never really saw any of this happen, and because Kevin made her happy, I kept all of our problems to myself. Besides, I knew that in just a few more years I was going to be out on my own or on tour somewhere, so I figured, fuck it, I'll just keep my distance.

I stayed at anyone else's house except my own. Whether it was Stevo,

Jon, Greig, or Marc's house, I was bouncing around from couch to couch. Greig had further moved into his role of father figure, teaching me the things that you would normally learn from your parents, like how to shave, how to put on a tie, and how to drive. Even though I didn't get my license until my twenties, I worked as Greig's pseudo chauffeur/assistant, driving him around in downtown rush hour traffic in his old stick shift 1988 Volkswagen Jetta. We were inseparable at this point and spent most of our free time together. When his band was on tour, he'd lend me his car, but because I didn't actually have a license, I would have to park it down the street from my house so my mum and Kevin wouldn't find out about it. The tricky thing with Greig's car was that he had tons of unpaid parking tickets and couldn't get a new registration sticker without paying them off first. He got away with it for so long because he would have us kids go out at night with a razor blade and cut a brand-new registration sticker from someone else's license plate and put it on his own.

It wasn't all petty theft and unlicensed driving, though. Greig was opening up my world culturally, too. He showed me great movies like *Harold and Maude* and *Run Lola Run*, got me to try new foods, and, most importantly, taught me the foundations of songwriting. Greig would play songs like "Changes" by David Bowie or "This Is a Call" by Foo Fighters and explain how they broke down the verse and the chorus and tell me to follow that structure. He thought I had a lot of potential in my songwriting but needed catchier moments and better choruses. I listened to everything Greig said about everything, so I started applying this idea to my music right away. Marc was a bit like an older brother, too, but in a very different way. Instead of giving me advice or teaching me life skills, he gave me cool random things like a snowboard or a pager, and a cell phone in a time when nobody had one. He had an extra Motorola flip phone because his sister didn't want one. As strange as it sounds now, she didn't want to have to carry around a phone. Now I drove to high school with no license and carried around a cell phone and a pager so I could stay in touch with my rock star friends. *Who was I?*

Greig and Marc seemed to be competing over who could give me the best gifts. To me there was no competition because I didn't care about the material stuff, I was just thrilled to be hanging out with such cool people. The most important gift from Marc was a four-track recorder, an E-mu SP-1200 sampler, a sixteen-track mixing board, and a handful of microphones. He taught me the basics, and I started recording demos for myself and Dave and Cone's high school bands. Marc had always produced his own records in his bedroom, back before it was an easy or common thing to do. One night I was crashing in his studio when he woke me up by working on a new song called "Steal My Sunshine" inspired by the Sunday mornings we spent together after the all-night raves. I sat and watched him build that song up from nothing, putting vocals on it and finishing it really quickly. When it was done, I told him, "Fuck, that song is a hit, man." He thought it was kind of lame, but it became the first single off of his next record and instantly blew up in the summer of '99. It was great to see Marc succeed and see his face on MTV and MuchMusic, but success changed him a little and we lost our tight friendship. Before that song was a hit, he had been a part of our little crew. He'd even played guitar in Sum 41 while we looked for permanent members. But as he got famous, Marc started hanging out with bigger musicians and stars in L.A. and we felt he left us behind. I was hurt by it, and I was pissed at him for a long time, until we eventually made up. It took years for us to speak again, but around 2007 Marc and I ran into each other at a bar in Toronto. We picked up right where we left off. I missed him and our friendship. And we've remained close to this day. Plus, as an adult I could look back and kind of understand why he stopped hanging out with us. Marc was an adult living out his dreams, and while Greig didn't seem to mind, not every adult wants to hang out with teenagers.

Before Marc left for stardom, he did us one last huge favor: He had the president of EMI Publishing Canada come watch us perform. At this point, we'd finally convinced Dave Brownsound to come join Sum 41. We had been bugging him for years to jam with us, but he wasn't a fan of punk rock and wanted to keep playing metal music. Still, he liked me and Stevo and would come jam with us occasionally, showing up with his weird pointy flying V-shaped guitar made by "Jackson," which we thought was so heinously uncool that it was actually cool. After convincing him to play a show with us, though, the chemistry between us on stage was so great none of us could deny that we were actually a perfect fit. We had also found a bass player, a kid from the "wrong side of the tracks" named Rich Roy who we called "Twitch" only because it sounded funny. He had played in Stevo's earlier band Thrall and had filled in with Sum 41 in the past, but we'd kicked him out for adding finger-tapping bass to one of our songs. This time we made him play with a guitar pic instead.

The president of EMI, Michael McCarty, and his partner Barbara Sedun drove out to Ajax to watch us perform in Twitch's run-down old unfinished basement. We were supposed to audition for them with three songs, but "Summer" was our only good song, so we played it twice. We released it twice, too, putting it on both *Half Hour of Power* and *All Killer No Filler*. What can I say? It's a good song! After the performance, we were hoping to have blown them away, but the whole thing lasted barely thirty minutes before they took off. Their lack of interest was confirmed when Marc called them with us listening in on speakerphone. They recognized Steve's drumming skills, but thought I was the weakest link of the band and I did not have a "world class" voice. They said they liked "that Summer song," though. Marc was unrelenting. He swore we were going to be huge someday and EMI needed to sign us. To prove it, he asked EMI to pay for us to go in a studio to record three songs that he would produce. McCarty thought about it for a few days and then decided to take a chance.

We went to Metalworks Studios for a week and came out with: "What I Believe," "Astronaught," and, of course "Summer," produced by Marc. It worked. When EMI heard what we sounded like playing in a real studio with a real producer, they were sold. They wanted to offer me a publishing deal, which is different from a record deal. When a record company signs you, they give you money up front, they own your albums, and keep *most* of your album sale royalties. When a publishing company signs you, they also give you money up front, but they help try to spread the word. They get your songs placed in movies, TV shows, and video games and take a piece of your songwriting royalties later. This was huge for me and the band. Sure, the potential cash advance would be nice, particularly as I was the sole songwriter, but having the backing of the president of EMI could open a lot of doors for us and hopefully lead us to our Holy Grail: a record deal.

When Greig came back from tour, he was not happy about the news. Instead, he seemed angry that Marc had gotten so involved. I was surprised, because Greig had never expressed any interest in working with us professionally. That all changed with the new interest from EMI. Late one night Greig and I were sitting in Marc's kitchen after everyone else had fallen asleep and he told me he wanted to start managing us. He said my songs had shown a huge improvement and that with his help and connections he could get us a record deal and get us on the radio. At seventeen years old, there was nothing more I wanted. He was my hero, my teacher, my mentor, my guru, and now he wanted to be our captain. All I could think was *FINALLY!* Greig had one requirement to be our manager—he wanted total control. We couldn't talk to anyone but him, because the music business is "full of snakes and liars" and he was the only person we could trust. He promised to protect us. We were so young and hungry that we believed him.

So Greig became our manager, and to mark the new role, we started calling him "Capital G." As our new manager, he hired a big U.S. attorney to talk to EMI directly. They got to work on a really great publishing deal. I was still seventeen but soon would be turning eighteen and signing a $75,000 contract with one of the biggest publishing companies in the world. If Sum 41 signed an actual record deal one day, my advances would start to triple and quadruple on every album we released for the next fifteen years!

As somebody who grew up poor, in a family that had always been poor,

I felt so many conflicting emotions. On one hand I was so proud that I got this deal, and sort of wanted to shove it in the face of anyone and everyone who had ever doubted me. I also felt guilty, though, because this was more money than anyone in my family had ever seen. They had all been working so hard for so long and I was just a high school student. I told my mum and Kevin about it, but left out some particulars, like the size of my advance. I made a few reasonable purchases, including a Marshall amp, a used 1987 Gibson Les Paul guitar, and some good recording equipment. I put the rest in the bank, only dipping into it for Sum 41–related purposes.

Greig felt the next step had to be a record deal. After all, signing to EMI was really Marc Costanzo's doing, and Greig had to outdo him with the ultimate prize of a record deal. To secure it, Greig decided we had to re-record our demo. Greig wanted to do it at Twitch's house. It was a little confusing as to why we needed to re-record the exact same songs, but at poorer quality, but Greig's one rule was to trust him, so we did. We rented some professional recording equipment and set up in separate rooms all over Twitch's house, running wires and cables up and down stairs, around hallways into Twitch's basement, and up into his attic.

When the new demo was finished "Capital G" set up some meetings with record labels in New York City, including one with Treble Charger's label, RCA, which we hoped would sign us, too. I was in my last year of high school but wanted nothing more than to come home and announce, "I have a record deal, I quit!" I had always dreamed of living in New York, so this trip was monumental in my mind. My mother, on the other hand, saw it differently. "You're not going to New York City!" she said, after I told her the plan. I couldn't quite blame her. At the time, New York still had a reputation that you could be mugged or killed or maybe both in broad daylight in the middle of Times Square. I begged, but she was adamant that I was not going. The only thing I could do was ask Greig to come talk to my mum for me. He later told me it was one of the most awkward and uncomfortable moments of his life, having to explain to my mum that she should let her teenage son go off to another country because he thought his band had a shot at making it big. My mum never liked or trusted Greig. Probably because he was an older man taking interest in her teenage son's life. She also didn't want to be the one to step in the way of my dreams coming true either, so she was conflicted. He had his work cut out for him. He finally managed to convince her by saying I was a gifted songwriter and this was a real opportunity. "This sort of thing never happens," he told her. "And it may never happen again in his life." Plus, it wouldn't cost her a dime, since I was going to pay for the whole five-day trip with my advance money. After telling Greig he was responsible for my safety, she reluctantly agreed.

I had never been more than two hours outside of Toronto in my life, let alone on a plane, and I was so fucking excited as we descended into JFK, flying by the Twin Towers. We had big dreams, high hopes, and a lot of meetings. Between chatting up labels, trying to convince them to sign our band, we walked around NYC and explored the city of my dreams. We would wander for hours talking about the different areas we could live in and imagining our lives as New Yorkers. Our trip stretched over a weekend, so a friend of Greig's invited us to a party on Saturday night. We bought some ecstasy and took it as soon as we got to the party. Unfortunately, the party was lame and ended early, just as the drugs were kicking in with an edgy, speedy high. Unsure of what we'd taken or where to go, someone told us about an after-hours bar called Save the Robots, in Alphabet City. When we arrived there, the bouncer informed us it was closed but offered to take us to another spot down the street.

We were flying so high that we thought nothing of following a stranger through the streets at 3 a.m. We were walking fast and talking faster, and yep, this had to be straight-up speed. We asked the stranger to stop at the corner store so we could grab some beers. Greig and I went in alone, and I asked if he thought this all seemed like a possibly bad idea. Greig thought about it, and while the guy seemed cool, he decided we should hide our money. We kept $20 each in our wallets and shoved the rest in our socks, just in case. We gave up on going to the bar and just sat on the curb drinking our 40 oz. Olde English and talking about our entire lives with the guy and spilling our inner secrets for about two hours.

The guy asked us if we wanted to smoke a joint, so we followed him around the corner to a fenced-in, unlit basketball court. Then, out of no-where, the guy slammed Greig in the face, hard, knocking his head back. As I tried to help Greig, the guy grabbed us both by our jackets, pulled us onto a bench, and stuck something in Greig's back. He said it was a gun and I didn't look to see if he was bluffing. Greig said, "Dude, what are you doing? I thought we were friends?" He screamed, "SHUT THE FUCK UP! I'VE BEEN LISTENING TO YOU MOTHERFUCKERS FOR TWO GODDAMN HOURS! JUST SHUT . . . THE . . . FUCK . . . UP!" He demanded we give him all our shit, so we handed over our wallets and he was furious that we only had $20 in our pockets, roaring "THAT'S IT?? I WASTED TWO FUCKING HOURS FOR THIS?" He took what he could get and then pointed at a dumpster in the corner of the park. He told us that he had a friend behind the dumpster waiting with a gun and watching us and we had to stay there for two minutes or he would kill us. And then he took off.

We sat there silent for about thirty seconds and then I looked at Greig with a big smile and said, "We just got mugged in New York City!" Greig's face went from panic to laughter. We knew there was no one with a gun behind that dumpster, so we took off running to get the fuck out of wherever we were. We didn't know which way was out of Alphabet City, so we just picked a direction and started running. Unfortunately we picked the wrong direction and went deeper into the neighborhood. We came across a gang, and when they started following us on either side of the street whistling and making calls, we knew we were in real trouble. This was way scarier than the mugging. With my heart pounding and body sweating that cold January night in 1998, I saw some headlights up ahead, which we assumed was a cab. We ran into the middle of the street to stop it, jumped in, and just said "DRIVE!" The cabdriver saw the gang approaching the car and took off. We finally made it back to our spot in

Brooklyn on Sunday just as the sun rose. We couldn't sleep after all of that and stayed up until our meetings on Monday morning.

We got ourselves together and headed to the RCA building to meet with the A&R team and play our three-song demo for Senior Vice President David Bendeth, who had signed Treble Charger. Greig knew everyone and gave them his best sales pitch before hitting play on our cassette tape demo. Within a minute, they stopped the tape, laughing, "Geez, you guys like NOFX much?" They skipped to the next song, and then the last one, not commenting on the music. They were more interested in chatting with Greig about Treble Charger and hearing about our harrowing brush with death in NYC, which got a good laugh. The meeting went so long that we were late for our flight back to Canada. I was so defeated, deflated, and feeling like shit from not sleeping that all I wanted to do was go home. We got in a cab and begged the driver to go as fast as possible, so we wouldn't miss our flight. He tried but quickly realized that the only way to make it would be by train. He sped over to Penn Station and Greig threw open the cab door—and a car smashed right into it. We didn't even have any more American cash, so we just threw the driver a bunch of Canadian bills, said sorry, and took off running for the train. We made our flight, but this time as I sat in my seat watching those Twin Towers again, I felt robbed and defeated.

After we got home from NYC, we picked back up where we'd left off. We had no record deal and no real prospects, so we just went back to partying. Most Friday and Saturday nights we found ourselves hanging out in the overcrowded bathrooms of abandoned warehouses. We'd be talking each other's ears off and popping hits of crystal or ecstasy every few hours trying to stay high. Even though pretty much everyone in the building was on one thing or another, you couldn't just take drugs out in the open. There were security guards and sometimes even police walking through, busting people. Like most savvy drug users, our routine was to dip into bathroom stalls to cut up some lines or drop some pills, and then head back out and join the party.

On one of those long nights, Greig asked me to come to the bathroom to drop some more ecstasy. Even though we were already really high, I obliged. We were jammed in a gross bathroom stall and I was talking non-stop, when he reached over, grabbed my face, and kissed me on the mouth, passionately. Two seconds before I had been talking a mile a minute, and now I was completely speechless. I just stood there having no idea what to say. I didn't even know what to think. My mind started racing as fast as I had been talking. I was very confused. Was that okay? Was I upset? Did I like it? Was he gay? Was he just high and being crazy? So many thoughts were coming at me so quickly that I couldn't comprehend them. I thought Greig was cool, but I had never thought of him like that before. He said, "I'm sorry, but I've been wanting to do that for a long time. I just had to do it. I hope you're not mad at me." I assured him that I wasn't mad, but was definitely surprised. I said, "I didn't know you thought of me like that." He replied, "I've never wanted to kiss another guy before, but for some reason you make me want to. But let's stop talking and get out of this stall before we get busted for drugs."

When I walked out of the stall, Stevo was standing there waiting for us. My first thought was to just blurt out, "Dude, Greig just kissed me on the lips in the bathroom stall!" But I stopped myself. The truth was I didn't know how I felt about it. I was fucking high as shit and couldn't really decipher which feelings were real or drug-induced, so I just stayed quiet about it. I knew one thing for sure, though. While I didn't have feelings like that for him, at freshly eighteen years old I thought it was so cool that this guy I idolized thought I was interesting enough to kiss. I mean, Greig Fucking Nori liked me!

Over the next few weeks, our whole crew continued going out, taking ecstasy, and talking all night, except now Greig and I would get high and wind up talking about us and what we meant to each other and where this whole friendship was going. He told me he'd never had any gay feelings for anyone before and that this was all new to him, too. I brought it out in him because what we had was so special. I reminded Greig that I was into women and not that interested in guys at all, but I couldn't deny that we had a really fucking special connection.

It was really confusing, and being high on coke, ecstasy, or crystal during these conversations didn't help me gain any clarity. To make his case, Greig pointed out that so many of my rock idols were queer. "Look at Bowie and Iggy. Or Bowie and Jagger, Lou Reed and the like," he said. "They're the coolest fucking guys in rock 'n' roll and they all fucked around with each other and with women, too. We can do the same. Most people are bisexual; they're just too afraid to admit it." He was so relentless and convincing that after a while, I started to believe that maybe he was right. Greig had opened my eyes to so many things already, maybe he was right about this, too. I wasn't ready for anything serious like having sex, but Greig and I agreed to take it a little further and try making out a little more. It definitely felt strange and a little uncomfortable, but it also felt exhilarating to be doing something that felt so fucking wild and out of character for me. The drugs helped, too. I also kept reminding myself that this was what people like Iggy and Bowie and Jagger did, and they were the most badass people on the planet, so it must be cool.

As the weeks went on, Greig and I kept hanging out, but I couldn't take things much further than rolling around, making out, and sometimes jerking each other off. I quickly started to realize that I could say yes to things when I was high on ecstasy or really drunk and feel like I was okay with it all and maybe even be kind of into it. But when I was back home in Ajax, alone and even slightly sober, I knew I was extremely uncomfortable with it all. I didn't know how to stop it. It seemed like a cool experiment while I was high, but when I was sober, it felt wrong. Greig kept pushing for things to happen when we were together. I started feeling like I was being pressured to do something against my will. It was a strange feeling because for the most part I trusted Greig completely and still thought he was a great human being, which made it all so confusing.

Writing this now, more than twenty years on, is difficult. I've rarely talked about it before, because for years the only person I had to blame was me. I thought I wasn't a victim, because I did it to myself. Greig never physically held me down and forced me to do anything. I agreed to it and went along with it. When I turned thirty-five, which is how old Greig was when I was sixteen, I started seeing things differently. What made a thirty-five-year-old adult give a teen his phone number backstage at a concert? Why did a famous rock star want to hang out with a kid who looked and acted like he was fourteen years old? Back then, I genuinely thought he wanted to check out my band, but as an adult and in the position I'm in now, that just sounds ludicrous. We had never even played a show! I have to admit that it seems predatory. Looking back, early on in our friendship he always had emphasized how cool the bisexual rockstars were or had shown me movies, such as *Velvet Goldmine* or *Harold and Maude*, that all seemed to lean towards prepping me for what eventually became of our relationship. When the movie *Magnolia* came out, we saw it in theaters. On the way home in the car he asked me what I thought about the ending scene when frogs fall from the sky. When I replied that I thought it was a cinematic masterpiece, he screamed at the top of his lungs, "Are you so fucking stupid you don't see how that applies to us? Is it going to take frogs falling from the fucking sky for you to wake up and see that we're meant to be together?" When this all started, I was too young to know that he was trying to normalize our huge difference in age. It was all just such a mind fuck. I had never heard the term "grooming" until I became an adult. As the #MeToo movement exploded, I started to hear stories that sounded very familiar. Was it abuse? Was it my own fault? Is this why he gave us all drugs and alcohol at such a young age? I don't know. At the very least, I can't deny that he was incredibly manipulative. Thinking about that smile he gave me when I snuck backstage and met him feels much different now.

WORKING LIKE IT'S 1999

With one more year on our sentences at Exeter High School Penitentiary, we all agreed it was time to stop partying as much and start focusing on the music. We practiced every day after school and then I'd go home and work on songs. With money in the bank and my positive intuition, school felt like a huge waste of my time, but I never quit. I knew it would break my mum's heart to have her only child be a high school dropout. I saw her struggle for so many years after quitting school to raise me, and she really wanted me to finish high school. I didn't want to let her down. I just needed to find ways to make the rest of high school tolerable.

Now in my final year, I not only had to keep my sanity, but I also had to get the grades to pass. There was no way I was going to repeat a year. I had heard some kids were getting credits for interning, which I thought was my best way to get out of class all day. The only question was, where the fuck would I work? One night I was lying in bed when it hit me: a fucking recording studio! I told Greig my brilliant idea and he introduced me to his friend Rob Sanzo, who owned a small studio downtown called Signal 2 Noise, where Treble Charger had recorded their first record. Once I got the sign-off from my mum, the guidance counselor, and the principal, I had the green light. I had the rest of the year with no classes and a job as an 'assistant engineer' at a recording studio.

I was excited to go to the studio every day at first, but there weren't a lot of bands coming through and it got really boring, really quick. I stuck around long enough to meet a producer from New York named Daniel Rey, who had worked with the Ramones and the Misfits, but at that time he turned out to be burnt the fuck out. He would sit with his face flat down on the mixing board like he was trying to catch up on the sleep he'd missed for the past three months, and the only things he said to me were "get me more coffee" or "I don't know, kid, talk to someone else" whenever I asked him about how some of the recording equipment worked. After that disappointment, I stopped going in altogether, except of course to get my report card signed: "Deryck did outstanding work again this week!" The owner of the studio was cool about it, too. He understood that I was just a kid trying to ditch school and was happy to be my co-conspirator.

Because I had nothing to do during the day, Greig and I had a lot of time to spend together. He kept trying to take our relationship further and further. After a couple months of experimenting with my sexuality, I'd had enough. I called him and told him that this wasn't me. We had made a mistake and I wanted to just go back to being friends and working partners. He pushed back hard. He told me that I was just feeling self-conscious and that I needed to let go of the stigma of "being gay or bi." He said that my asshole stepdad B.D. and all the homophobic jocks at my school had done a number on me. The last thing I wanted to be was like any of *those* people, and he knew that. Between his arguments and all the drugs I was taking, it was easy to convince myself that he was right. I just needed to get used to it. Was this real love like he said? I was so confused. There was no one I felt comfortable talking to about this either. Certainly not the band. We weren't macho guys by any means, but still, the thought of telling my friends that something like this was going on between me and Greig just felt impossible. I was so embarrassed that I had gotten myself into this mess, but I also felt guilty for being embarrassed, like that somehow made me homophobic. I was still in a place where I needed to believe Greig was great, and the thought of him being a sexual predator was something I chose to bury. I couldn't tell people any of this. I wanted to protect him. My thoughts and arguments were pushed aside and we were right back where we started.

Trying to distance myself from Greig, while still working with him, meant finding new ways to fill the hours when everyone else was at school. I spent my days writing songs while my mum and Kevin were at work and then heading to band practice before they got home. It was during those long, quiet days when I was skipping school and my internship that I started writing the songs that would eventually change my life, songs like "Makes No Difference," "Handle This," and the beginnings of "Fat Lip." The work that I did during this period would ultimately get us signed to a record label and end up on the *Half Hour of Power* and *All Killer No Filler* albums. I had taken the songwriting advice Greig had given me about creating a concise song structure and writing big catchy choruses and was starting to write songs that he considered to be potential hits—but not for Sum 41. This became clear with the song "In Too Deep." I wrote that song in all of ten minutes, while I was waiting for Dave to come pick me up one evening. He was late, as he usually was (and still is), so I picked up a guitar to fuck around and kill some time. I started joking around with a summery little guitar lick that felt to me like Sublime or Sugar Ray, which were all over the radio at the time. I started humming a melody and thought, *Hmm, that's kind of catchy.* When it was clear Dave was not showing up, I grabbed my small tape recorder and started laying it down. It poured out of me faster than any song I had ever written. I thought it was kind of a cool song, not quite punk rock but still really fun, and I could tell there was something special about this one. So could Greig.

Even from listening to my rough cassette demo, he was blown away. "I think you've just written an actual hit song," he said. Most of the song was written when I showed it to him, except for a few lyrics in the second verse. Greig said he wanted to help me finish it and knew what we should do with the song.

He had recently started a side project band with the rapper Snow, who had a huge worldwide hit in 1992 with the song "Informer." Snow had watched his song climb the charts from within the confines of a prison cell. Now a free man, he and Greig had teamed up with another legendary rapper, MC Shan, who came up in the mid-eighties as part of the Juice Crew along with Biz Markie, Big Daddy Kane, Marley Marl, and more. The band was called IKON and they had gotten a record deal with Sony or some other big label for a "Japan only" release. Greig thought that "In Too Deep" was perfect for IKON, and he wanted it and any other songs I could write for them. The only catch was, it had to look like *he* was writing the songs. After all, I was just a high school kid and he was Greig Nori. Still, he would let me work as a "consultant" and let me play guitar as a studio musician. None of that bothered me, because I was where I wanted to be—in the studio, getting to hang out and record with legends.

Despite his reputation and rap sheet, Snow couldn't have been sweeter. He was shy and quiet, but also hilariously funny. Shan had only one speed and it was MAD. He was jaded and angry, and he didn't speak, he yelled. If he got really pissed, he would break and throw things, and was tough to be around. Still, he was rap royalty and super-talented. I was frequently on edge at Snow's studio, either in fear of Shan's temper or Snow's old gang connections. I realized I was right to be nervous when we saw a few police cruisers roll up on the security monitor one day. Shan and Snow looked at each other, jumped up, and started frantically yelling, "You hide the guns, I'll hide the drugs!" Clearly there was more going on at this place than I had previously thought. I didn't know what to do or say, so I did nothing and said nothing, but every time I was at the studio after that, I kept my head down and my eyes open.

When IKON finished their version of "In Too Deep," everyone thought it was a hit. I still have that version of Snow singing the verses, while Greig and I did the chorus, and MC Shan provided a rap bridge in the middle. It's pretty amazing. It's a perfect late nineties sonic time capsule, with irreverent samples and loops in the vein of Beck and Bran Van 3000, mixed with the summer sound of Sugar Ray. For some reason nothing ever came of that album, though. I don't think it ever came out. The band broke up and was never talked about again.

Of course I was still working on Sum 41 songs, too. I had been fucking around with an idea of trying to mix old school rap with punk rock for a while, but wasn't getting anywhere with it, because it was hard to merge the two styles and we were the worst rappers on the fucking planet. We had been working on a new song called "What We're All About" that we were trying to rap on, but it wasn't working. Then Greig had the idea to ask MC Shan if he could teach us to rap, and since I had money in the bank, we could pay him for his time. We all thought it was a great idea, but Shan was less enthusiastic, though he reluctantly agreed. Over the next few months, Dave and I would have rap lessons with MC Shan in Snow's studio. None of us knew what we had gotten ourselves into. Dave and I couldn't get through a few words, before Shan would cut the tape and shout over the headphones, "THAT WAS FUCKING TERRIBLE. DO IT AGAIN!!!" He'd play a few more seconds and then the track would abruptly stop: "YO! STAY ON BEAT!! FUCK! DO IT AGAIN." Talk about a hostile environment! Sometimes he wouldn't even use the talk-back button and just scream at us through the soundproof glass, with veins bulging out of his neck, while Dave and I sat there staring, having no idea what the fuck he was saying. It was absolute torture, but we knew it would pay off eventually. Plus, even if he was always pissed off, I felt privileged to be in the presence of one of the originators of early hip hop. Over time, we started to sound better and even Shan was grudgingly excited about it.

Since IKON had stalled and disbanded before their album came out, I was excited to take back "In Too Deep" for Sum 41. When I mentioned it to Greig, he looked puzzled. He said it wasn't punk enough to be a Sum 41 song and needed to be a Treble Charger song instead. He argued that the song could never work for Sum 41. He was so convincing that I felt embarrassed for even suggesting it, so I gave him the song. And once again he told me not to tell anyone that I wrote the song, because he knew his bandmates would never take it seriously if they thought a kid was behind it. Treble Charger went into the studio and recorded "In Too Deep" as a possible single. I was excited to hear my song become a hit, but when we listened back, it was terrible. The band had no swing, no vibe, no magic whatsoever, and Greig sounded terrible singing it, too. After their failed recording session, Greig decided it was a Sum 41 song after all and gave it back to me.

The year 1998 rolled on and at long last, I graduated from high school. I had earned a 52 percent, which was all I needed. I felt like Tommy Boy in the scene when he gets a D+ and says, *Oh my god . . . I passed*. My mum was pleased that I got my diploma, but she wanted me to either go to college or get a job. Fuck! I couldn't pretend that I wanted either of those options and told her that the only thing I wanted to do was music. Something in that argument made her realize how serious I was about my path in life. She agreed to give me two years to make it work, and if I couldn't break through in the music industry by then, I had to go to school or get a job and pay rent. That was fine with me.

Dave and I were free men, but Stevo still had another year of high school to get through. That didn't stop us from playing more shows. Before our shows, Brownsound and I would borrow his mum's car and drive out at night to plaster the cities with flyers and stickers. We'd leave at midnight, drive for hours to somewhere like Ottawa, cover the whole city with Sum 41 stickers and flyers for the show, and then turn around and drive back. Those road trips were some of the best times of my teenage years, up all night with Dave just talking, planning our future, and listening to music really loud. We were teenage idiots, barreling down the freeway in the dead of winter with all the windows down and the AC on max cold, just to see how long we could last. Sometimes, after hours of driving, with the sun coming up, I'd be falling asleep in the passenger seat thinking, *How the fuck is Dave still up and driving?* Then I'd look over and see that his eyes were closed and he'd fallen asleep at the wheel and I'd have to wake his ass up! We never had money for gas back then, either. For some reason, in the nineties in Canada, paying for gas was on the honor system. You were allowed to fill up your tank and then go inside and pay afterwards. Since we were broke and it seemed like a victimless crime, we would fill up and peel off and onto the freeway. We got away with it for years. We even booked our entire first tour across Canada assuming we would never pay for gas. It saved majorly on costs.

In the summer of 1998, with Stevo on school break and the rest of us out of high school, all we wanted was to get out on the road and do a real fucking tour. So Greig booked us a week-and-a-half-long trip out to Ottawa, Montreal, Quebec City, Fredericton, Moncton, and ending in St. John, New Brunswick. We called it the Beast in the East Tour, and we were ready. To save money, my neighbor, who was the manager of a McDonald's franchise, gave me enough free Big Mac meal coupons that the whole band could get three meals a day for the entire tour, as long as they only wanted to eat Big Macs, of course. We planned on sleeping in Dave's dad's 1984 blue Ford Econoline van, stealing gas, and eating free Big Macs across Canada, which meant this tour could essentially cost us nothing. Before we hit the road, we built a wooden bed frame into the back of the van so we could stow our gear underneath and two people could sleep on the mattress we threw on top of it. The other two guys could sleep on the bench and the floor. Twitch rigged some wires off the car battery and into the van to power a TV and VCR so we could watch movies while we drove. After the shows, we'd park in a residential neighborhood, run an extension cord to the side of someone's house and steal electricity for our space heaters to keep the van warm. We drank, laughed, and tried to get a little sleep before the sun came up. When the sun rose, we'd hit the road, driving like maniacs, blasting music, passing cars on the shoulder, giving people the finger, and hanging out the window like punk rock teenage pirates. People didn't exactly know Sum 41 yet, so we were lucky if there were more than five people in the crowd at most shows. We mostly played to the other bands on the bill and their girlfriends.

There's a lot of space for boredom on the road, so we started filming our own unscripted improv movies and infomercials with some nineties handheld camera. Our movies were usually Mafia-based or spoofs about burnt-out cops. On the last day of the tour, we unloaded our gear and did soundcheck and decided to go grab some Big Macs before the show. As

Twitch pulled out onto the main road, we got T-boned by a giant Dodge
Ram pickup truck. Stevo was the only one not wearing a seatbelt and was
instantly thrown into the front passenger side footwell, suddenly upside
down at Dave's feet in a perfect 69. Miraculously none of us were hurt,
not even Stevo. The police showed up and our van was towed to an auto
shop. We would be stuck in St. John for at least three days while they
fixed it. Since our van was also our home, we had nowhere to sleep. We
sat around on the street weighing our options. Sleep on the street or call
our parents? I argued strongly that there's no calling mommy on tour, but
I was outvoted and Steve and Dave called their parents. They agreed to
pay for half of the costs and got us a room at the Crowne Plaza that we
all shared while we waited for the van to be fixed.

Since we had nothing else to do, we played the show, and it actually
ended up being the best show of the whole tour, with twenty kids there, all
going mental. After the show, reality set in and we realized we'd be stuck
here until our ride was fixed. We made the best of it, drinking booze, eating
pizza, and making more home movies. We were having a great time. Well,
all of us except Twitch. We teased him mercilessly, blaming him for getting
us in the accident, saying, "Twitch, you were driving, so it's technically your
fault and you're going to have to pay the damages yourself." We wouldn't
let the poor guy live it down. When we finally made it home, he called me
up the same night and quit the band. I feel terrible about it all now. We
just didn't see it back then, we were just idiot teenagers.

Once again, we needed a new bass player. We had a stream of random
guys fill in, but no one ever jelled. We had few options and a bunch of
upcoming shows to play, so I asked the guys about having Cone McCaslin
fill in. We were all friends with him from school and Stevo had even known
him since the first grade. The only issue was that he was already in a band.
Plus, he preferred modern radio rock that we fucking hated like Bush and
Toadies, and we didn't know if he could play our kind of music with our
kind of attitude. I also didn't want to look like we were poaching him from
his band, because we were all tight at school. Still, we were desperate, so

I asked Cone if he could fill in for one show. When we all got together to jam in Steve's basement, we asked him to learn "Stickin in My Eye" by NOFX, and he nailed it on the first try. Despite being a Marcy Playground fan, he played our songs way better than all those "punk rock" guys would play. For the first time ever we had a bass player that just felt right. Still, we weren't going to pressure him to quit his other band.

Around my nineteenth birthday, I started to unravel mentally and physically. I hated being at home in Ajax, but I didn't want to stay at Greig's either. I didn't know where to go or what to do. I felt ashamed of myself for giving in to Greig. I had no one to talk to about any of this. I was too embarrassed and ashamed to tell the band. I was isolated and angry and started to feel horribly uncomfortable in my own skin. I started feeling sick about all sex in general. I didn't want to touch Greig, other girls, or even myself. The thought of masturbation made me feel nauseous. For the first and only time in my life, I felt real depression. It terrifies me to think about it now, but I started to feel that the only way out of the situation I had created was to end it all. Luckily, those thoughts didn't last very long. I caught myself and said out loud, "This needs to fucking stop." I wasn't going to let Greig Fucking Nori be the death of me! I knew it wasn't going to be an easy conversation, though.

One night when Greig came out to Ajax to pick me up to go downtown, I told him we had to talk. We drove to a grocery store down the street from my house and pulled into the parking lot. We sat in his car and I told him I couldn't do it anymore. "I've tried but it's just not me," I said. "I thought maybe I could grow to be comfortable with this, but I'm really struggling day to day now. I can't even touch my own dick anymore, it's gotten that bad." When those words came out of my mouth, the gravity of it all hit me and I started bawling my eyes out. "I've even had thoughts of hurting myself lately. I'm scared of myself. I love you, as a person, but not as a lover. We have to end this."

I cried and talked and cried and talked until I had nothing left to say. "Are you finished?" he asked. I wiped off the last few tears and said, "Yeah, that's all I've got." I looked over at Greig and he was fuming. For the first time ever, he started yelling at me. It scared the fucking shit out of me how quickly he changed and how loudly he screamed. He demanded that this continue, because we were not done. He told me this was all my fault to begin with because I should never have said yes to it in the first place. I started this and now he was in it with me so I couldn't just stop. He said I was homophobic like all those awful people in my life. That he knew better than me, and I was too young to understand that what we had was special. What we had was love. I sat there in the passenger seat feeling ashamed, thinking, *Oh my god, what is happening? Is he seriously saying I'm not allowed out of this? Is this all my own fault? Is he right and I'm wrong? Am I really going to lose the best person to ever come into my life? What does this all mean? How do I get out of this car?*

We talked in circles for hours. I don't remember how the conversation finally ended. I do remember that somehow the relationship was going to continue the same as always, but maybe a little slower to address my concerns. I truly believed that it was all my fault. To a certain degree, Greig was right when he said that I had allowed this to start. I had. I just wished that each of the times I had asked for it to stop, he had listened to that, too. I felt like I had signed my life away to someone. I felt trapped in something that was easier to just go along with than to escape from. It had to end at some point. I just didn't know that it would take as long as it did. I was good at separating my personal and professional life, and no one in the band ever knew what was going on because I kept it so secret. At least that's what I had hoped. On the surface, Greig was our trusted leader, and in their minds he could do no wrong. They idolized him the way I used to before all of this. I just kept working with Greig, because he was our manager and I thought he was looking out for the band.

I had to keep working, and after we returned from tour, things were moving pretty quickly. We recorded some of my new songs, like "Handle This," "Rhythms," "Makes No Difference," and "In Too Deep," with me on bass, for a brand-new professional demo tape. Greig was ready to shop our demo to every major record label. Well, every record label in Canada, because as Canadians, we had enough of a patriotic streak that we wanted to succeed in our home country first, instead of going straight to the U.S. for a deal. The Canadian record labels did not feel the same level of loyalty. We were shut down by every single one of them. Universal Music Canada felt the need to tell us we were the worst band they'd heard in a decade! Every label gave us a hard pass, except one small French independent company called Aquarius Records. That was run by a legendary music veteran named Donald K. Tarlton, best known for putting out the Corey Hart hit "Sunglasses at Night." As flattering as their offer was, we had our hearts set on signing to a major. Greig told us the Canadian music industry was notorious for not knowing what the fuck they were doing. We sent the same demo to the U.S. labels, and it turned out they didn't want to sign us either. No one in North America was interested in us. Perhaps surprisingly, I wasn't that discouraged by all the rejection. I just had a sense that we were going to make it. I could visualize it happening.

I had recently put together a little video montage of all our stupid antics. The drive-by squirt-gunning of random people, clips from the dumb Mafia spoof movies we made on tour, some live show footage, various pranks, and the general fucking with unsuspecting people on the streets of Ajax. We didn't have editing programs like iMovie in the late nineties, so I crudely stitched the footage together using two VCRs. I would cue up a cool moment on one machine, hit play on one VCR and record on the other. Then I'd pull up the next cool moment and do the same thing, over and over again, until I had all the visuals on one master VHS tape. Then I put our music over the top of it all. I debuted the Sum 41 prank tape at one of Greig's parties and it was a hit. Everyone thought it was hilarious, except Greig. He made me play it again and then again. After a couple of repeats he turned to me and announced, "You're a fucking genius." He wanted to take this tape of our stupid antics paired with our music, have it professionally edited, and send it out to all the U.S. labels. I was really confused. I mean, the labels had already passed on us, wouldn't they just throw it in the garbage after seeing the name Sum 41? Greig was confident, though. "Labels are so fucking stupid," he said. "They won't even know this is the same band, I guarantee you."

A week later, my video went out as part of a professionally polished EPK, or Electronic Press Kit, to labels in the U.S. A few days later Greig called. Rob Cavallo at Hollywood Records loved the EPK *and* the music. Rob Cavallo, the guy who'd signed and produced Green Day, wanted to fly us all to L.A. for a meeting. This was fucking huge! The next day Interscope Records called, because they wanted to meet, too. It just snowballed from there. All the labels that had passed on us two weeks earlier were now offering us whatever we wanted. What a mind fuck.

Now that we had all this label attention, Cone decided to make it official. "So, I think I'm going to join your band now," he said. I laughed because he had been filling in for six months and it was definitely time. "Welcome aboard!" I said, and that was it. We all knew it was the right fit. Later, we joked that he only joined the band because we were about to get signed, but he was quick to point out that we only started getting label interest after he started playing with us. *Touché!*

In just a few weeks Sum 41 was in the middle of a bidding war. It wasn't a question of *if* we were going to sign a record deal, but *who* we would sign with. First we had to get through the endless meetings, though. Every music exec said the same shit: "Look at what we've done with Limp Bizkit (or Creed or Korn)." One deeply uncool older white executive from Arista Records tried to impress us by reciting all the lyrics to N.W.A's "Straight Outta Compton"—including all the N-words. We only got him to stop by laughing in his face. Going from rejection to the center of attention was such a trip that it was hard to take it seriously. Everything was a joke to us. We'd go to meetings dressed in silly costumes, ask ridiculous questions, and bring the execs gifts like "Women Over 80" porn mags or a "Hot Buns" calendar of nice asses in bikinis, and catch their reaction on video. We just couldn't be serious, especially after sitting through meeting after boring meeting; we just wanted to make each other laugh.

The best part about the whole experience was spending their money. We would see how high we could rack up the dinner bills. We had a $3,000 dinner with a label we had no intention of signing with, because we were four teenage punks and we could get away with it.

Before signing, the label execs all wanted us to perform private show-cases in their offices. That sounded sterile and, worse, boring. Since we had so much leverage, we came up with our own plan. We would play every Wednesday night at the same club in Toronto and the label guys could come watch us play there. We booked a five-week residency at a spot called Ted's Wrecking Yard and put out the word. As soon as people found out that A&R people from every big American label were descending on Toronto to watch a relatively unknown band of teenagers, they wanted to see what the fuss was about. The small two-hundred-seater club was packed the first night with folks from the Canadian music industry and other bands wanting a deal of their own. The few drunk regulars were very confused to see their normally empty bar turned into a rock 'n' roll circus.

We played our *Half Hour of Power* set and did our best to put on an arena rock show in a tiny club. In addition to our frenzied songs and onstage moves, there were spinning sparkler wheels and Roman candle flares on the ends of our guitars, Stevo's burning drumsticks, and two mini trampolines to get extra air out of our jumps. The residency only intensified the demand to sign Sum 41. Even labels that were initially hesitant to get involved in a bidding war jumped in to give us offers.

One of the last labels to be interested in us was a newer one called Island Def Jam, made up of two older labels that had merged. While Def Jam had a long history of success with LL Cool J and the Beastie Boys, that was a long time ago, and the new label didn't have any rock bands. We weren't interested in being the guinea pig at a brand-new label. We wanted to sign with Interscope. It was the biggest label in rock and run by two titans in the industry, Jimmy Iovine and Tom Whalley. Island Def Jam wouldn't take no for an answer, though. They asked us to come to NYC and meet their team before making our final decision. Since we liked free trips and expensive dinners, we agreed. We walked into their big offices planning on being our usual juvenile, immature selves. Something stopped us, though, and without any of us talking about it, we took it seriously. We listened as they laid out a multiyear plan for our future. We didn't make jokes or try to be funny at all. For the first time, we were interested in what they had to say. Halfway through the meeting, Lyor Cohen, the president of the company, came to speak with us. Cohen had built Def Jam with Rick Rubin and Russell Simmons, and had a reputation for being tough, intimidatingly smart, and incredibly successful. He helped break acts like the Beastie Boys and Run-D.M.C. and saw us as the same kind of group. He could see our path to success. We left the office all thinking the same thing: we had found our home.

It wasn't quite that easy, though. To this day that was one of the toughest decisions I've ever made in my life. We had every huge label willing to give us whatever we wanted. We had Jimmy Iovine and Lyor Cohen vying for our band. I was completely stumped, so I sat down with Michael McCarty, the president of EMI, and asked for help. "You've been around," I said. "You must know who I should pick, right?" He told me the truth: No one knows. It really was a crapshoot and I just had to go with my gut. A few weeks later we headed to the top of the CN Tower in Toronto and signed our record deal, becoming the first rock band on Island Def Jam.

Because of our unique position we were able to ask the label for a few special deal points, the main one being that we excluded Canada from the record deal. That's because we wanted to give Canadian rights to Aquarius Records, the small label who were the only ones to show any interest in our original demo. I can be fiercely loyal.

We started 1999 as nobodies, fresh out of high school and with a two-year ultimatum from my mother. By December, we had signed a record deal worth over $3.5 million. It was the biggest deal ever signed by a Canadian band.

STORMIN' THROUGH THE PARTY

Island Def Jam was wasting no time. In the first week of January 2000, just two weeks after we signed the deal, we were on the hunt for a producer. The top contender was Jerry Finn, who had recently produced blink-182's *Enema of the State* and had also worked on Green Day's *Dookie* and *Insomniac* albums. We knew he was a great producer, but we wanted to forge our own path and we didn't want to draw comparisons to blink or Green Day by working with the same producers. Then there was Greig Nori. He was lobbying hard to be the producer, and since he was our manager and had helped us get the record deal, we liked the idea. The folks at Island Def Jam, or IDJ, were persistent about getting Jerry to do the record, though. They also wanted us to work with a booking agent named Stormy Sheppard, so Jerry, Stormy, and our A&R reps, Rob and Lewis, all flew up to freezing cold Canada in January to watch us perform. We were going to do the exact same showcase that we'd played a million times, but this time at the famous Horseshoe Tavern on Queen Street. At showtime, Jerry, Stormy, Greig, the record company folks, and for some reason Twitch, our old fucking bass player, were the only ones in attendance. I guess Twitch had heard we had gotten signed and wanted to see what he'd missed out on.

Since we felt like veterans of this showcase game, we walked on stage confident that we would blow them away. The lights went out and we launched into "Machine Gun," but as I was halfway through singing the

first line, *"And I'm up and I don't know why but I guess . . . ,"* Cone accidentally stepped on Dave's guitar cable, pulling it out. The whole place
went silent. I panicked, scrambling to get my guitar plugged back in. I
threw out some half-assed joke about how Cone could fuck up because
Twitch was there to step in on bass. We resumed playing, but things
went from bad to worse. Our fireworks didn't go off, Stevo's drumsticks
didn't light up in flames, our guitars couldn't stay in tune, and our jokes
weren't funny. On top of all that, the sound was just fucking terrible and
no one could make out what the fuck we were even playing. When we
got off stage, neither Greig nor the record company could pretend it was
any good. When our label rep Lewis asked "What the fuck was that?"
we had no answer. We were horribly embarrassed and worried that Jerry
would refuse to work with us.

The record company felt the only way to save this night was to take
everyone out partying like it was, well, a week ago, 1999. Back then,
Toronto was famous for having wild strip clubs, so we ended up at a place
called For Your Eyes Only. Island Def Jam pulled out all the stops: private
back room, three dancers for every one of us, bottles of vodka and Jack
and champagne, and through our own connections, lots of blow. It didn't
feel like 2000, it felt like the 1980s. We had been to strip clubs before,
but never on the record company's dime. We were still wide-eyed teens
(the drinking age in Canada is nineteen) in a brand-new band that they
had just signed to the label, and they were throwing down thousands of
dollars like we'd already sold ten million records. This was Mötley Crüe
shit! While "Hot Blooded" by Foreigner blared through the speakers and
boobs were smashed in our faces, Jerry and I laughed about how bad our
show was. As much as I wanted a more unknown producer, I couldn't
deny that Jerry and I got along extremely well and spoke the same musical
language, which is so important when making a record. I shouted over
the music that I thought we could make a great record together and he
shouted back, "I agree, let's do it! Now, enough about business, let's have
some fun!"

The plan was that Sum 41 would record the EP that became *Half Hour of Power* in February and March with Greig and me working as producers. Then, a month later, we would record the full-length record with Jerry. Feeling confident about the timeline and glad to have Jerry on board, I needed to start writing, because I didn't have enough songs for two back-to-back albums. As the sole songwriter in the band, there was a lot of pressure on me, even before we got signed. Now that we had a contract and real timeline, that pressure increased tenfold. There was also the problem that I didn't actually enjoy the process of writing music. I didn't feel like I was great at it, either. I could strike gold, but it wasn't every day or even every week, and it caused me a lot of mental turmoil. I loved having the songs once they were written, but hated the torture of getting them to the finish line. I also didn't understand myself as a writer yet.

These days, if I'm stuck on something or am not feeling creative, I just put it down and come back to it later. Back then, I thought I needed to write all day, every day, no matter what. While that works for some people, I don't operate that way. I can write a lot and create a lot of stuff I like, but then I feel creatively depleted and it takes time to build it back up. I didn't really have the luxury of working on my timeline, though. Island Def Jam wanted us to release our five- or six-song EP as soon as possible. Then they wanted us on the road crisscrossing America for a year. Once we had built up a solid fan base, they would put out the full-length album. That may seem backwards now, but back then you wouldn't be taken seriously by fans or the industry if you hadn't paid your dues. To their credit, Island Def Jam knew this and was willing to spend the time and money helping Sum 41 build a lasting, credible career by paying for our albums, videos, and all of our touring expenses indefinitely while we built a following. Luckily, touring nonstop was all we'd ever dreamed of. But first, I had to write some goddamn songs.

Greig and I looked at all the songs I had written, or even half written, and decided which ones should go on the EP and which would be held for the full-length. The label felt that "Makes No Difference" could be a hit on the EP, while "In Too Deep," finally and firmly a Sum 41 song, would be the single from the full-length. We returned to Metalworks Studios in March of 2000 and were able to knock out the EP *Half Hour of Power* in two weeks. It was quick, because it was basically the set we'd been performing for the label showcases, plus a little metal song called "Ride the Chariot to the Devil," which I whipped up while sitting on the couch in the control room of Studio A. The song "What We're All About" had been kicking around since we practiced rapping with MC Shan, so we stuck it at the end of "Dave's Possessed Hair." Stevo, Dave, and I quickly wrote the lyrics while sitting on a curb in a parking lot we had pulled into while on a food run. At first we were trying to write a "dis" song about all of our old bass players, but we couldn't get anywhere with it. Steve then had the great idea to make a rap song about rock music like a throwback to Run-D.M.C.'s "King of Rock," and the words quickly poured out of us. We even hit up MC Shan to come in and rap on it for us. Always a legend, he laid down the vocals in one take.

Once we finished recording the EP, I had four weeks to finish writing the songs for the full-length album. I felt a lot of pressure, but I had a problem: I couldn't write at home. I was still living with my mum and Kevin, and I couldn't create an album in their house with paper-thin walls, where making any kind of noise at night was unacceptable. Also, they went to bed at fucking 8 p.m., which is when I was just starting to feel creative. It was a fucking nightmare. I ended up sitting out in the car in the driveway writing with an acoustic guitar and a tape recorder. One time the cops showed up, knocked on the car, and asked me for my license and registration. I rolled down the window and asked, "Am I seriously getting pulled over in my own fucking driveway right now?" I showed them my guitar and recorder and they left me alone.

By the time Jerry flew up to Toronto to start preproduction for the full-length album, I only had six songs to work on. I picked him up at the airport and took him out for ribs and beers at Jack Astor's on Front Street, in the hopes of delaying the inevitable. I was terrified to tell him that I didn't have enough songs for the record yet. When I finally worked up the courage to admit the problem, he shrugged. Apparently every artist he'd ever worked with ended up writing songs in the studio. It was reassuring, but I wasn't sure that it would work for me. Back then—and even now—I need to be locked away somewhere completely private to write anything more complicated than the metal riffs of "Ride the Chariot." I have to try out weird ideas by myself, before I can even think about sharing with anyone. I had my doubts that I would be able to write in a crowded studio, but Jerry was a pro, so I figured he knew what he was talking about.

We had never done preproduction before where we would figure out all the right tempos and keys for the tracks and play the songs over and over again until we knew them in our sleep. We found a cool rehearsal spot in a finished basement next to Mama's Pizza (our favorite spot for 'za!) and got to work. It was here that we turned the song "Handle This" from a Third Eye Blind–ish tune into the heavier pop punk ballad that you hear on *All Killer*. We even gave "In Too Deep" a new intro, ditching the little picking guitar lick at the beginning and replacing it with the main guitar riff that normally comes after the first chorus.

One of the best things about working with Jerry was his collection of musical equipment. He had every great guitar and amplifier you could imagine, as well as microphones and all sorts of other studio gear. It all showed up in huge road cases, and we got to go through it all picking what we wanted to use. When you listen to that album, my guitar is on the left side and Dave is on the right. I played the few guitar solos on "In Too Deep" and "All She's Got," but Dave and I both did some leads when playing live. I know it sounds strange now, but Dave Brownsound didn't play all the lead guitar back then. He was always a great guitar player, but he hadn't become the incredible solo god yet.

Once we were back in Metalworks Studios recording the album, it devolved into productive chaos. After all, we were still teenagers, but now we were teenagers who'd been given too much money and were hell-bent on having fun. We also had teenage egos, thinking our record deal meant that everything we did was the shit. Jerry was quick to point out that actually, no, we were terrible musicians and had somehow *miraculously* got a record deal. He had no problem making us do take after take, like MC Shan had, but Jerry had an incredible ability to make you laugh while he was tearing you apart. He would say things like "Let's try that again, but leave out all the parts where you sucked!" Or "Perfect! Do that again, but nothing like how you just played it." Back then, everything was recorded to tape, with no computers for editing. It was just, play it until it's good. This proved to be really difficult for me as a singer. My voice was so underdeveloped back then, and I did everything you're not supposed to do as a singer: I sang from my throat, I didn't drink any water, I ate the wrong foods, and we never slept because we were still partying all night. My voice was so damaged and hoarse that just listening to that album now makes my throat hurt.

As the recording process stretched on, we started to show up to the studio later and later, doing a little less work each day, and getting mushrooms or ecstasy delivered there. We weren't a good influence on Jerry (and he wasn't a good influence on us either!), and he went along with us when we would leave the studio early to go to get (more) fucked up at strip clubs or at his apartment. One night after the studio, we were high on mushrooms and I started to have a really bad trip—and a strip club is the last place you want to be on a bad mushroom high. All my joy and laughter turned into anxiety and panic as I started to hallucinate, thinking the lint on my clothes was bugs. The band and Jerry were laughing hysterically as I frantically tried to brush the bugs off me. Out of nowhere a dancer in a fluorescent yellow bikini, with big blond eighties hair, grabbed my hand and said, "Come with me." I thought she was going to lead me to safety, but turns out my asshole friends had paid for a lap dance thinking it would be funny because I was so fucked up. As she led me into a back room, the woman morphed into a fluorescent yellow monster with fangs, a lizard tongue, eyes bulging out of her head, and blood pouring from her nose. I sat watching her naked boobs melt down her body for about thirty seconds before I lost it, running out of the club, past the band guys laughing, and out the front doors onto the street. As soon as I hit the fresh air, I felt better, and I just waited outside until they came out.

We had seven weeks to finish a twelve-song record, but when the label reps flew up to hear the finished album, we only had five and a half songs done—and nothing else to show for it. They were understandably really fucking pissed. "Who the fuck do you think you are?" screamed the head of A&R, Jeff Fenster. "This is your first fucking record, you haven't even sold a single goddamn album yet! You guys still have something to prove, not something to lose! Do you know how much money you've wasted already?!" They all took turns dressing us down, one by one. Even Greig got angry with us, which was rare. His beef was mostly with Jerry, who he felt had been handed this record on a silver platter and couldn't be bothered to keep it on track. The label was pissed that the album wasn't done, but they were also unhappy that we had significantly changed some of the songs from the demos, particularly "In Too Deep." They thought we had ruined the first single, and while I didn't necessarily agree, I caved. I wish I had stood my ground and had more confidence in myself as a writer, but I was only nineteen and they did this for a living.

We were in trouble, and the label decided the only way to save the album was to send us to our rooms, figuratively. We were forced to take a break, go write more songs, and then finish the record in L.A., where none of us were of legal drinking age. No more friends stopping by, no more drug dealers showing up to the studio, and no more staying up all night at strip clubs.

Determined to finish writing songs for the album, I rented a rehearsal room, and there, in the dirty roach-infested garages of the Chameleon Cafe, I was finally able to focus. I ended up writing the rest of the record pretty quickly. There was only one song I couldn't quite finish, which was trying to meld punk rock with old school hip hop. I had been piecing the song together, section by section, for over a year. I had the intro riff down, because I thought it was going to be a ballad, but I couldn't figure out how to finish it. I then started working on a different song, writing a fast chorus that I thought was almost as good as Elvis Costello's "No Action" off of *This Year's Model*, which I was listening to on repeat. Then came a verse riff that I thought maybe I could rap over. It had taken me a year of staring at the pieces to realize that they were actually one song. I sped up that original intro riff and made it heavier with a half-time drum feel, giving a punk edge to the Limp Bizkit, Korn, and Linkin Park songs that were big on MTV at the time. It worked. I recorded a rough demo, rapping some gibberish lyrics, except two key lines that came to me when I stood at the mic: "Storming through the party like my name was El Niño / When I'm hanging out drinking in the back of an El Camino." I was usually a procrastinator when it came to writing lyrics, but that day, those two lines came out instantly and set the theme for the rest of the song. The El Niño line came from one of the band's favorite Chris Farley skits on *SNL*. We had never seen an El Camino in person before, but after seeing them in movies and TV, we thought it was the most ridiculous car we'd ever seen. We joked that if we ever got money one day, we'd all buy El Caminos, but sadly, even though I've done more promotion for the El Camino than Chevrolet ever did, I still do not actually own one.

I was afraid to play the demo of the song I had been calling "Punk Hop" to anyone, but there was something about it that I couldn't shake, so one day I showed it to Jerry, alone. The second the song ended, he turned to me and said, "That is the best thing you've ever written. It is a fucking smash and it needs to be the first single." I was relieved because I felt the response could've gone either way, but it still needed a lot of work and we were running short on time.

We showed up in L.A. with the best intentions. We knew we needed to get some real work done, but it didn't take long for us all to fall back into bad habits. Our friends Heidi and Mike had just moved from Toronto to L.A. and were well connected and big partiers. Between them and Jerry's friends, being underage in L.A. didn't seem to matter, and we managed to have some fun. This time, though, Greig and Lewis Largent, our A&R guy, were there to babysit us and keep us on track. We had seven songs done by the time we had to leave for tour.

The EP, *Half Hour of Power*, was due out in July, but the label had already released the single "Makes No Difference." It had started to get some airplay and, much to everyone's surprise, was on the *Billboard* chart. We shot a video for the song right before we left for L.A. It was based on a true story about an infamous house party we'd had at Stevo's back in high school. His parents had gone away for the weekend, and Dave and I made it our mission to throw the biggest party Ajax had ever seen. We printed up flyers and handed them out around town, telling everyone to bring as many people as possible. If you watch the "Makes No Difference" video, you can see a full recount of what happened, minus DMX riding a four-wheeler through the living room, of course.

While the song was doing well, IDJ didn't want to push the single too hard, because back then, overnight success could actually hurt your credibility as a new band. As much as we would've loved to be instantly successful, we also knew that bands that blew up really quickly didn't al-ways have longevity in the industry. We wanted to have a real career and a solid, enduring fan base. So instead of pushing the single, we got in a van and hit the road, because we were playing the Warped Tour. Since we were a brand-new band, we were playing on the Tiki Tent Stage at 1 p.m. Not the best time slot, but we didn't care. Four years earlier, we had started Sum 41 after going to the Warped Tour and now we were playing it! Plus, we were meeting bands like Green Day, MxPx, Jurassic 5, and our heroes, NOFX. Their lead singer, Fat Mike, even came by to see us play after he heard we had trampolines on stage. We'd often see the Green Day guys walking around backstage, and one day Cone and I got up the courage to give our EPK VHS tape to Mike Dirnt. He was so cool, and even though we were a no-name teenage band, he treated us like equals.

After wrapping the Warped Tour, we set out on back-to-back tours.

The first was with Face to Face, who were headlining a four-band bill with us as the opener, along with New Found Glory and Saves the Day. Other than becoming good friends with New Found Glory, the tour was unfriendly and disappointing and made us worry that touring the U.S. might not be as fun as we'd thought. Then we hit the road with the Mighty Mighty Bosstones and it was like a whole new world. Flogging Molly was direct support, and from day one we were welcomed by both bands and their crews as if we were long-lost family members. We would all hang out after the shows, getting wasted backstage or at bars. We played dice on the Bosstones' bus with Dicky Barrett, the lead singer, and he would unapologetically walk away with whatever little money we all had, laughing, "Them's the breaks, kids!" Watching those bands play every night was a master class in putting on a show and how to treat other people on tour. To this day, it's one of our favorite tours that we've ever done.

Dicky Barrett is an incredible front man, and it's odd to think that some people only know him as Jimmy Kimmel's longtime announcer. He knew how to work a crowd and was such a character, on and off stage. On the tour, we realized that he and I had a similar look, so he started calling me his son and I would call him Pops. He took the bit further one night. I was sitting backstage while the Bosstones were performing, and I thought I heard Dicky say my name on the PA. Stevo came running back and said, "Dicky's calling you up on stage right now. Get up there!" I was shocked and kind of concerned, but when I walked on stage the crowd started cheering. "There he is, there's my son. Get up here, Deryck!" Dicky was saying into the mic. "Ladies and gentlemen, give it up for my son Deryck from Sum 41. We've been estranged for years. His mother's a whore and we haven't seen each other until this tour." I waved and thanked my pops for having me out. He then shooed me off the stage, saying, "Now, go run along and play, kid!" He kept that gag up for the rest of the tour, on and off stage. He even scolded me like he was my actual father after he heard that Cone and I were breaking beer bottles backstage and getting rowdy with Nathan from Flogging Molly. Talk about committing to the bit! To this day, we still play it up, reuniting like father and son, whenever we run into each other.

Those endless tours meant just getting in a van and going wherever the schedule took you. There were no breaks, no time off, no going home, just city after city. We would drive all night, blasting music, or comedy records by David Cross, or Neil Hamburger's *America's Funnyman*, eat every meal at Denny's (better than Big Macs!), and sleep in motels that were so shitty one even had dried blood on the walls. We would drive straight to the gig, arriving close to showtime, and have to lug all our gear out. Since we were still putting on our "arena rock show in a club," we had to set up our trampolines, fireworks, and whatever ridiculous gag we were doing in addition to hauling around our amps, guitars, and drums. We were learning a lot on tour, like how to play to a different audience in a different city each night and develop a consistent show. It was on these tours that I started putting Xs on my equipment. I had two blown speakers in my Marshall cabinet, so I marked them with big white Xs of gaff tape so sound engineers wouldn't bother putting microphones in front of them. I liked the way it looked, so when we got rid of having cabinets on stage, I started putting them on my guitars instead. We also found a solution to one of our biggest problems on stage, which was that our guitars were constantly coming out of tune. I strum my guitar really hard and every night I would come off stage with bloody knuckles and a completely out-of-tune guitar. Then a veteran guitar tech suggested we tune our guitars a half step down and use heavier gauge strings. We tried it the next day and sure enough our guitars stayed in tune and we even sounded a little heavier. We've been playing live like that since 2000 and never looked back.

The good thing about touring is that it kept me away from Greig, too, and I wanted to stay far away from him.

After those tours were finished, we went back home so I could finish writing the remainder of the album. I had been working on lyrics and trying to write songs during the tours, but it was hard to find a quiet space.

I would retreat to the back of the van or a dressing room or work in the hotel bathroom while Dave, Stevo, or Cone slept or watched a movie. We were scheduled to be in L.A. for the first two weeks of December, to put the final touches on the still untitled full-length album, and we had some work to do. In Toronto, we got together at Signal 2 Noise studios, where I had done my internship, and recorded demos of "Heart Attack," "Never Wake Up," a newly reworked "Handle This" and "Punk Hop," which was now called "Fat Lip." Everything went smoothly except for writing the rap lyrics for "Fat Lip." I had written the song by myself up to that point, but I always wrote rap lyrics with Dave and Stevo. We tossed around ideas, but nothing worked. Greig had stepped in as pseudo-producer in Jerry's absence and kept pushing us to write funnier and more clever lines. It all clicked one day when he said that this song needed to be our mission statement, telling people who we were. That made sense, and all of a sudden the lines just started flowing. When Stevo came up with the line "I trashed my own house party, because nobody came," I knew we were nailing it. That one line was funny, self-deprecating, and said we didn't give a fuck and liked to party! It was Sum 41 in one sentence.

The next day I walked into the studio and everyone was laughing about some silly metal song that Dave and Stevo had just written. Dave had been fucking around with a little metal guitar riff, which Stevo overheard while walking to the bathroom. When he came back from taking a shit, he said, "I just wrote all the lyrics to that song while sitting on the toilet. It's called 'Pain for Pleasure.'" It was the first time anyone other than me had written a song for the band, and I loved it. I told him, "This has to be the last song on the record!"

A few weeks later we were back in L.A., listening to the final versions of everything we had recorded to date. That's when Joe McGrath, our engineer, said, "Jesus, this album is like all killer, no filler." We all looked at each other, and someone, I don't remember who, blurted, "That's the name of the fucking record right there!" Everything was sounding amazing, except for "Fat Lip." Something wasn't working vocally, but I couldn't figure out what was wrong. I played it back over and over, but no one could hear what I was talking about. I started to get the feeling that everyone thought I was being an annoying perfectionist, where *nothing* would ever be right. But then it hit me: I didn't have the right delivery when I rapped the opening lines. I knew Stevo's voice would be better, so he went in and recorded it and it sounded *almost* perfect. We listened again and realized there was a short pause between some of the lines that was interrupting the flow. We then made minor changes to the lyrics that in my opinion took it from being a cool song to a hit. I knew it, too, because before those changes I wasn't feeling goose bumps. I didn't get excited at playback. No one was jumping up and down saying, "This song is a smash!" And now they were. Everyone agreed "Fat Lip" needed to be the first single. Well, almost everyone. Stevo and Cone didn't think it even needed to be on the album. While they both came to love "Fat Lip" later, Cone admits that he just didn't see it at the time.

We finished out the rest of December with our very first headlining shows in the U.S., playing Chicago and Detroit because their radio stations had given "Makes No Difference" significant airplay. As we wrapped up touring, we were on a high from everything we'd done and everything we'd gone through over the past year. We were asking ourselves, "How could this get any better?" Just wait, it does.

INTRODUCTION TO DESTRUCTION

*Y*OU KNOW YOU HAVE TO PAY FOR THAT SHIT, RIGHT?!" screamed Greig Nori on the other end of the phone. This was starting to become a common occurrence as we toured across North America trashing hotels, dressing rooms, and even our own rental vans. We were barely making any money at these shows, and whatever little earnings we did make, they were all going towards paying off damages. It wasn't the smartest use of money, but it sure was fun.

Besides, we had a green light from our label. Before we hit the road, IDJ had told us, "Go out there and destroy the world. Break everything, and as long as you get it on tape, we'll pay for it." While we just looked at our goofy videos as us being us, and thought it was funny to get on film to show our friends back home, he saw the value in what we were doing. There were no other bands filming themselves in the same way. Before every band was on YouTube and TikTok desperately making goofy content, we had already been there, done that, using those videos as marketing. Cohen saw the future, and needless to say, we took his words to heart, storming the country and wreaking havoc in every city with a "get out of jail free" card tucked in our chain wallets. We emptied hotel rooms into pools—mattresses, desks, chairs, everything. We swiped keys to other people's rooms and let fire extinguishers off in them. We slashed tires in hotel parking lots, broke lamps, mirrors, and TVs, and pulled fire alarms in the middle of the night just to watch the fire department show up. In a just-off-the-off-ramp hotel in Syracuse, we lined up with members of the bands Saliva and American Hi-Fi and hurled bottles of Jack through the giant bay windows of the hotel, shattering glass all over the lobby. The more havoc we caused, the more we were encouraged. Everyone around us (labels, agents, the press) applauded our behavior and laughed at our videos of the carnage. The only problem was, the bill never seemed to go to the label. It came straight to us. None of it mattered to us. We were broke anyway, so what if we had to pay for all the destruction? We couldn't be *more* broke. Broke was broke.

Here's some music industry math for you: Even though we had signed a huge deal, we weren't getting the money anytime soon. Most of it was held back to be given to us as we put out future records. For the first one, we were given a $600,000 advance from the $3.5 million. We had to pay 30 percent of that to our management (Greig) and lawyer for their commissions. That's $180,000 down. Then we had to pay for recording costs, which was $250,000, plus Jerry Finn's fee of $100,000. That left about $70,000 for all of us to split over the next two years of touring. Greig worked it out, and if we were on the road for the next two years straight, we could pay ourselves $750 a month. We bought great portable CD players and headphones and could now afford to buy all the albums we wanted to take on tour with us. The truth was, we were broke and only getting broker, because the bills were coming out of our pockets.

But back to the chaos: We loved stopping in Walmart, which we didn't have in Canada, because you could buy really cool high-powered pellet and BB guns. In Texas (of course), Stevo bought a huge Dirty Harry–looking gun and I bought one that looked like a Glock 9mm. We returned to the hotel and shot out all the windows, mirrors, and glass cups, not thinking about the fact that we had to sleep in that room, which was now covered in broken glass. In Dumas, Texas, we rolled into a Holiday Inn late one night and the front desk guy recognized us. We told him to come party in our room and somehow convinced him to trash the hotel with us. This dumbass from Dumas joined right in, smashing tables and lamps and everything. The manager watched the whole thing on the security cameras the next day and fired him on the spot. At least he got a good story!

Even our own home, aka the van, wasn't off-limits. We were driving through the night after a show, and after way too many drinks, when someone got the brilliant idea of tearing off the lining from the ceiling. For some reason, it became almost a tradition, and every van we rented was sent back torn apart and trashed. Greig pointed out that no one wanted to rent us vans anymore, and if we didn't knock it off, we wouldn't be able to tour. We stopped destroying the vans, but everything else was still fair game.

Even though Island Def Jam never paid the bill, we still filmed everything and used it as new footage for our album marketing materials. Someone was always holding the camera, because even though we never discussed it, we all instinctively knew the importance of capturing everything on tape. We did it because we thought it was funny and we wanted to share it with the world. It started with VHS tapes, which we would hand out for free at our shows. Then we moved to DVDs, throwing them off the stage into the crowd. When we released albums, we included video content on CD-ROMs or an extra disc. When we were still unknown teenagers, before we were on MTV or radio, we were making a name for ourselves by handing out copies of our VHS tapes to bands like Green Day, Mighty Mighty Bosstones, and NOFX. Whether they liked the music or not, we knew the videos, like our live shows, would leave an impression.

It was the early days of 2001 and we were making ourselves known all over the U.S., for better or worse (definitely worse when it came to hotels and rental van companies). As we looked to the year ahead, our schedule included touring, another album release, touring, video shoots, the whole summer on the Warped Tour, and more touring, with big bands like the Offspring. We were also touring with blink-182, who were some of our earliest supporters, particularly Mark and Travis, who always talked us up. Travis even came to one of our early shows in Pomona to check us out, which blew our minds. Then there was more touring, but overseas for the first time. The first outing of the year was opening for Social Distortion on their reunion tour, because we shared the same booking agent, Andy Somers. Andy wanted to test us under pressure, and there was nothing tougher than a sold-out crowd of older, rockabilly punks when we were the only opening band, aka the only thing standing between the fans and their beloved Social D. We knew this was not going to be easy, but decided to just be us and lean into all the onstage theatrics. If they spat on us and booed us off stage, at least we'd get it on tape! Every show went the same, with the crowd going from boredom and confusion to smiles and applause as they recognized the entertainment we provided, even if they didn't like the music.

The last show with Social D was in Las Vegas, and we had to be in Halifax, Nova Scotia, three days later to open for Treble Charger across the East Coast of Canada. Cone, Dave, and our tour manager Simon Head took turns driving, staying up for days on trucker speed, stopping only to gas up, piss, and get a little food. Stevo and I didn't drive back then, but Stevo stepped up to take the legal crack for "moral support." He rode shotgun and made sure whoever was driving stayed awake. All I remember from that trip is waking up early one morning at an off-the-highway strip club with a sign that read "All Nude & All You Can Eat Breakfast." Obviously, we had to go in. Who wouldn't want to order eggs and bacon and watch strippers dance at 10 a.m. in the middle of nowhere America? If you haven't already guessed, it was incredibly depressing. Decent food, though!

When we finally pulled up to the Marquee Club in Halifax, it felt like a huge victory. Greig and his bandmates were all standing outside in three-foot snowbanks ('cause it's fucking Canada in January, eh) when we rolled up, and they cheered as we jumped out of the van. This tour was going to be very different from the Social Distortion tour, because we were touring with friends and we weren't an unknown band anymore. "Makes No Difference" had gotten significant airplay on both radio and

TV in Canada, and there was a lot of buzz around us. In fact, there was more buzz around us than Treble Charger, and it was their headlining tour. While Greig was our manager, he was used to being a star, and this was starting to cause friction.

I could feel Greig becoming jealous of our band's success, even though he had helped us find it and, as our manager, benefitted from it. He never showed it with the rest of the band, but with me, in private, he seemed angrier in general now. He didn't seem excited about "Makes No Difference" doing well in Canada. He didn't care to hear our funny stories from the road. He always brushed aside the good news and instead would grill me about meeting girls or get mad that we were all having wild times on the road without him. It was all such a mind fuck, and there was so much tension that there was no way it wouldn't snap. It finally did in the middle of that tour. We played a great set at the Savoy Theatre in Nova Scotia. It was so great that when Treble Charger went off before their encore, instead of chanting their name, the crowd started shouting for Sum 41 to come back. While it was nice that the crowd liked our set, I felt devastated for Greig and the rest of his band and kind of wished the chanting would stop. Treble Charger went back out and played another song anyway, but the vibe after the show was terrible and they were visibly humiliated. Most of Treble Charger left immediately, but Greig stuck around watching as I chatted with a few girls backstage and invited them back to the hotel for the inevitable party.

After driving back to the hotel, I planned to join the band at the hotel bar, but I stopped by Greig's room first. He was seething mad. I thought he was pissed because he and his band had been humiliated on stage. I was wrong. He started yelling at me about talking to those girls and inviting them back to our hotel. As he screamed at me and I processed what he was saying, I fucking lost it. It's one of the few times in my life where I felt like I lost total control of myself. Every emotion, every thought I had been thinking for the past two years, about him and his treatment of me, all boiled up. In an instant, I was done. I started bawling and screaming.

"I CAN'T BE WHO YOU WANT ME TO FUCKING BE! I'M NOT GAY! WHY CAN'T YOU GET IT THROUGH YOUR FUCKING HEAD? I CAN'T FUCKING DO THIS ANYMORE. I HATE THIS! IT'S NOT WHO I AM!! CAN'T YOU UNDERSTAND?!"

I was so worked up that all I could see was bright white light. I started punching the walls and smashing the lamps and kicking everything, as I ran out into the hall. Greig sounded panicked as he yelled after me, "Deryck! Okay, I'm sorry! Stop!" He'd never seen this much emotion in me before. I'd never *felt* this much emotion before. As I tore down the hotel hallway, I grabbed a lighting fixture and ripped it down, shattering it on the ground. I ran to the elevator, picked up a giant potted plant, and smashed it against the wall. I slammed the elevator button thirty, forty times. I had so much adrenaline pumping through me that I was shaking and my knees were buckling. The elevator took too long, so I ran for the stairs, still bawling and hyperventilating. As I was running down flight after flight, I felt some sticky goo on my hand and when I looked I realized my entire hand and arm were covered in blood. I must have cut myself on the lighting fixture and it actually hurt quite a bit, and I had left a trail of blood down the hallway and stairs as I ran searching for an exit. I finally made it to the bottom floor, and I stumbled into the lobby crying as I ran past a horrified front desk clerk and out the front door into the freezing cold night with just a T-shirt on, still dripping blood. I just kept running with no idea where I was going. I wasn't making much progress, though. It was dark and the snow was up to my knees and I could barely see. I kept falling in the snow, picking myself up, and desperately trying to escape to somewhere, anywhere.

I saw flashing lights coming down the road and knew they were for me. I ran behind the hotel in fear of the police, in fear of Greig, in fear of facing my band. As I started to calm down, I realized that the trail of blood in the snow would lead them all right to me. I gave up and walked back to the lobby. The whole band, Greig, the police, the hotel manager and security were all waiting for me. The hotel and police wanted to charge me with vandalism. Greig instantly took charge. He put me in the van with the heat cranking. As he smoothed things over with the cops and hotel, I sat in the passenger seat looking at my hand. I had sliced my left palm, all the way from my thumb to my pinkie finger, and it was deep. I could see my tendons. I knew this was bad. Greig eventually got into the van. "What the fuck was that?" he asked. I told him I needed to go to the hospital, and when he saw the extent of the wound, he freaked out. He didn't take me to the hospital, though. He wanted to talk.

I tried to tell him that it was over, that I couldn't do it anymore. Being on the road so much had limited our sexual interactions, but when a tour was ending and I knew I'd be home for a week or two, the darkness would set in. I found myself giving in to Greig's pressure, just repeating the same cycle of going through the sexual motions over and over, whether I was sober or fucked up. I tried to tell him that I loved him as a friend but nothing more. He refused to hear me, giving me a list of reasons I had to stay with him: I was throwing everything away. I was wasting our friendship and our professional partnership. He had saved me from Ajax. I owed him. Everything great in my life was because of him. He went on and on listing all the reasons he always listed. Plus, if I refused, he wouldn't be our manager anymore. He wouldn't help me with the band. He wouldn't do anything for me. He also blamed me, saying I had allowed it to start. I couldn't turn around and stop it now. I felt trapped. There was no way out. And worst of all, I thought he was right. Everything good in my life would disappear without him. It would all be over. He *did* save me, everything great in my life *was* because of him. I couldn't do anything on my own. Everything that had happened was my fault. I had allowed it all to happen. I cried as we sat in the van for hours going back and forth.

Finally Greig came up with a compromise of sorts. He said he understood it was uncomfortable for me, but there had to be some sort of "special connection" between us. However, it didn't have to be all the time, just sometimes. I was so beaten down and seriously worried about my hand, that I just said okay. Greig gave me a big hug and laughed and said, "Let's go get you to the hospital, buddy!"

I got to the ER as the sun was coming up. The doctor looked at my hand and said it was too late for stitches. "You should've come here hours ago," he said. We told him I was a musician and begged him to reconsider. After a second opinion they put fourteen stitches across my hand. I couldn't play guitar for a month. The guys just assumed that I had cut myself while trashing the hotel again. I never told them the real reason. I couldn't wait to get back to America and away from Greig.

We headed back to L.A. to shoot the video for "Fat Lip." We had picked the director Marc Klasfeld because we liked what he had done on the rapper Nelly's first video, "Country Grammar." We met up with him when we were in Vegas, and he told us he came from a documentary background. That inspired us to make a video that was almost a documentary—no real treatment or concept, just invite a bunch of fans to come hang out. We set up in two different locations—a skate park and a liquor store parking lot—and filmed the kids doing whatever they wanted to do. We shot for two days in Pomona, California, because we knew we had a small but dedicated fan base there already. It was surreal that we had fans anywhere outside of Toronto, let alone in California! That small but hardcore fan base that had formed in Pomona was so special, because it felt so random. But it also boosted our confidence, 'cause if some kids in Pomona were into us, then kids in other cities might like us, too! The video shoot with those fans was fun and spontaneous. Except for the synchronized jumps we did, everything that happened in that video, from the girl getting her head shaved to us rapping in the convenience store, was all thought of on the spot.

After the shoot was done, we put on a real show for everyone at the Glass House in Pomona. When we hit the stage, we were so tired from the past two days of getting up at 6 a.m. and shooting for twelve hours straight, jumping nonstop, and doing take after take, that we could barely walk. We covered our legs in so much fucking Bengay that the stage and front row reeked of it. At the after-party, all I could hear people saying was "Why is it so fucking minty fresh in here?"

A few weeks later "Fat Lip" went to radio. It had a bit of a slow beginning, but things picked up once the video started being played on MTV. Soon we were getting recognized walking down the street. We were opening for blink-182 in Philly, and went to grab something to eat on South Street after soundcheck. Almost immediately someone stopped us and said, "Holy shit! You're Sum 41!" We didn't even make it down the block before it happened again, with more and more people coming up and asking for autographs. It quickly got a little overwhelming, and we ditched the idea of getting food and went back to the venue. It blew our minds, because the video had only been out for a few days and here we were getting mobbed on the street.

After we started doing well on radio and MTV, IDJ finally got us a tour bus. They cared about optics just enough that they couldn't have their band driving around in a shitty van anymore. This was still the heyday of the music business, when there was money to burn, and sometimes they liked to live large and show it off. Julie Greenwald, the president of Island, asked if we wanted our bus wrapped with pictures of our faces like Redman or Ja Rule, but we politely declined. In hindsight, what a missed opportunity to do something ridiculous!

We were so excited to move out of the van and into what was basically a rolling bar with no last call and an actual driver. At each show, I would announce on stage, "We're having a party on the tour bus after the show. If anyone wants to come, it's parked in the back!" After the show, there would be a line of a few hundred people trying to get on the bus. Our tour manager played bouncer, checking IDs at the door. We almost burned the whole thing down on the first night. We were trying to make food, but passed out while it was in the toaster oven. We woke up as smoke filled the whole bus and as we were airing the place out we found some random dude who must have come to our party the night before.

Our endless touring continued with a stint with the Offspring. We had met Dexter Holland back when we were teenagers (you know, a year ago) and recording with Jerry Finn in L.A. Dexter was having a little 4th of July party at his house and Jerry brought us along. *Half Hour of Power* was coming out in a few weeks and we had boxes of CDs sitting in our van. We decided to plant CDs all over Dexter's house, so he would never forget the name Sum 41 (and to have a laugh). At first we put CDs in all the obvious places, like on his coffee table and the kitchen counter, but after a few drinks, we started getting more creative. We put them in the freezer and cupboards, behind pictures on his wall, inside cereal boxes, two discs in his toaster, a pile of them in his microwave. Years later, once we'd become friends, Dexter told us that he was finding those things for years. He even saw one when he moved fifteen years later!

With "Fat Lip" slowly climbing up the charts and all the work we had done building a name through touring, we were finally able to do a headlining tour of our own. It was small theaters across the U.S., and we brought two bands that we'd grown up listening to and loved, Unwritten Law and a Canadian punk band called Gob. We were so proud of what we'd accomplished. A year and a half ago, we had never played a single show in the U.S. and now we were selling out venues across the whole country. The nonstop work was actually paying off.

All Killer No Filler came out in May and sold more records in its first week than any of us had expected. It didn't stop there. With "Fat Lip" steadily in rotation on radio and MTV, the sales just kept increasing. It went gold in four weeks and then platinum about a month later. It wasn't just the U.S. either, we were selling records all over the world. We were an "overnight success" that only took five years.

To keep the momentum going, we just kept playing shows. We had a reputation for playing more than three hundred shows a year. We never took days off. It was just back-to-back tours, interviews, in-store meet-and-greets, autograph signings, and radio station visits, and we were loving every minute of it. We finally got invited to spend the whole summer on the Warped Tour. As usual, so many of our favorite bands were on the bill, like the Vandals, Rancid, and Pennywise. While NOFX was not performing, the singer Fat Mike was on the tour with his other band Me First and the Gimme Gimmes. The only shitty thing was that we had booked this tour long before "Fat Lip" came out, so we were playing a small side stage and only getting paid a couple hundred bucks a day, when we could now earn much more. It was a bummer, but what were we gonna do? A contract is a contract and we weren't going to drop off the tour. Warped is exactly where we wanted to be. It was Punk Rock Summer Camp!

On the first day of tour, we were a little nervous that our punk rock heroes would shun us or kick our asses for being sellouts. No one else was on MTV or the radio, and we were all over both. Some of our own fans were even calling us sellouts online, and we even heard them sometimes outside our bus when we were signing autographs after our shows, all for having a video on Carson Daly's *TRL* that was played next to *NSYNC and Britney. I never saw that as selling out, because we didn't get any money for being on *TRL*. Plus, as I saw it, we were planting our flag in enemy territory. We were winning on our own terms with our own music.

To our surprise, everyone was very friendly towards us. All of my anxiety disappeared on the first day when I met Todd Morse from the band H20. He told me, "If you're worried about being the band who's on TV and selling a lot of records, don't be. That's what we're all trying to do as well. Everyone here wants to be successful, too!" Later, Fat Mike came to our bus and hung out for a bit, probably trying to suss us out. We had a couple drinks and some laughs, and he reported back to the other bands we were cool, and not to fuck with us. Within a few days we were making friends with the Vandals, Pennywise, and Tim Armstrong from Rancid as well as Kevin Lyman, who owned the Warped Tour. It became the best summer of our lives.

There seems to be one moment in the life of every successful band or artist when everything changes. And it usually comes when you're not expecting it. For us, that moment came near the end of the Warped

Tour when we were asked to open *The MTV 20th Anniversary Special* in New York City. We knew it was a cool opportunity and wanted to do something really interesting like the mashup collaborations we'd seen at MTV Awards in the past. Our A&R guy, Lewis Largent, had worked at MTV for years. We had some big ideas and he had the connections to make things happen. We wanted some people to play a medley with us and started tossing around names like the Beastie Boys and Slash, but they declined. Lewis told us that Mötley Crüe's Tommy Lee was going to be at the show, and since they were friends he could ask him to play with us. We also asked Rob Halford from Judas Priest to join us on stage. This was going to be the most epic performance of our lives.

Once the shock that we'd be playing with our heroes wore off, the reality set in. We had to figure out what to play and how to play it. I worked out a rough little sketch of how the medley could work. Since we were still on the Warped Tour, we didn't have anywhere to practice except the bus. The only real rehearsal we would have was the night before the show, the same time we were meeting Tommy and Halford. We had to make it work.

We left the Warped Tour and headed to NYC so we could get ready. We had rehearsal space at SIR Studios in Midtown. We showed up early, Halford showed up right on time, and due to flight delays Tommy was really fucking late. We'd all been reading the Mötley Crüe book, *The Dirt*, since it had recently come out, and we had no idea if Tommy was going to be cool or a total rock star asshole. We waited and waited, but he wasn't showing up. Hours went by and I started to write the whole thing off. It was too good to be true. Why would *the* Tommy Lee want to play with us? We were nobodies. I was bummed and planning to pack it in, and went to the bathroom to take a piss. All of a sudden my mood changed. I could actually feel a different physical feeling in my body, like a release of serotonin or dopamine. I smiled and said to myself, "There's something in the air, and it's not this piss. He's here!" I then told myself to shut the fuck up, because what the hell was I even talking about?

I went back to the studio to prove to myself that I couldn't possibly have felt someone's energy enter the building. When I walked into the rehearsal room, though, there was Tommy Fucking Lee. He was super-nice, chatty, excited, funny, everything you wanted in a rock star. He shook my hand, leaned in, and said, "Duuude! You wanna do a Jäger Bomb with me?" I had no idea what the fuck a Jäger Bomb was, but I said "Fuck yeah, of course I do!" He took me behind his drum kit, where his drum tech Viggy (RIP) dropped a shot of Jäger into a pint of beer and handed it to me. How the fuck had I ended up here? I had just been reading *The Dirt* in my bunk yesterday and now I was chugging Jäger Bombs with Tommy Lee and about to jam a medley with Rob Halford of Judas Priest. This was fucking crazy!

Once we got through the MTV red carpet bullshit and the press line, there wasn't much time until we hit the stage. We were all nervous as hell. Not because it was MTV, but because we didn't want to fuck up the music in front of all the famous musicians and celebrities in the crowd. While "Fat Lip" was doing really well, we were still a new band that most people didn't really know or care about. We had a lot to prove. Right before we went on stage, Lewis, our A&R guy, grabbed me and Stevo and just said, "Dudes, come with me. You will thank me later." I thought he was taking us to meet some musical icon, but instead he drags me in front of two similar-looking blond girls. He says, "Sum 41, meet the Hilton Sisters." We looked at each other and thought the exact same thing, "Who?" I had never heard of the Hilton Sisters or Paris Hilton in my life, and it seemed clear they had never heard of our band either. It was so awkward and embarrassing, but to break the tension, I just said, "Uh, hey, how's it going?" Paris looked at me completely uninterested and said, "So, what cool band are you?" I laughed and walked away and told Lewis to never do anything like that to me again. I walked over to Tommy and the band and got ready to go on stage, more nervous than I'd ever been for anything in my entire life.

The one thing about Sum 41, especially in those crucial early days, is that whenever the pressure was on, we always delivered. Well, except for that one horrible showcase for Jerry Finn. That doesn't mean we didn't make mistakes, but the end result was always a major win. Not this time, I thought. We hit the stage and the sound in our monitors was terrible, we could barely make out what we were playing, the audience seemed stone-faced, and I was counting all the mistakes I was making. Luckily, when Tommy came out on the drums, it felt amazing, and Halford took it to a whole new level. While the whole performance went by in a flash, and I felt like we were blowing it, I couldn't help but feel like it was just so fucking awesome that it was even happening. Walking off stage, I thought we'd failed and had totally collapsed under all the pressure. I knew people were going to be disappointed, and as we walked backstage I said to Tommy, "I'm so sorry I fucked up some parts, I was having too much fun up there and with all the adrenaline and everything—" He cut me off. "Dude, it was fucking killer! What are you talking about?" He gave me a big hug, and when we entered the green room we were bombarded with applause.

People lined up to give us hugs and get us drinks; Greig Nori and the label folks were beaming. We were introduced to the top executives at MTV, who promised us "a great future together." Then we were ushered out into the audience. I was supposed to meet the press from outlets like *SPIN* and *Rolling Stone*, but the first person we ran into was Slash. He immediately thanked us for asking him to be part of the performance. I couldn't believe he cared enough to thank us and take a photo! I barely got two words out before I was pulled further into the crowd, shaking hands and meeting new and famous people. It was a surreal experience. It felt like when the President walks into Congress for the State of the Union address and everyone is cheering and shaking his hand as he walks through the crowd, except this was for us, and the people coming to us were Puff Daddy, Method Man, Carmen Electra, TLC, and more. I met Jamie-Lynn Sigler, who invited me out to grab food after the show. I wanted to, of course, because who didn't have a crush on Meadow Soprano? I couldn't, though, because we had to get on our bus and drive back to the Warped

Tour that night. That was the story of our lives in those days—always working, even when Meadow Soprano invited us to dinner. Right before we left New York City, Lewis Largent pulled me in for a hug and said, "Just so you know, your life is never going to be the same ever again." I didn't really know what he meant, but I soon found out.

CHAPTER 8

NO BRAINS

*A*fter the MTV performance, the "Fat Lip" video went into heavy rotation around the world. The power of television back then was enormous, and MTV seemed like the biggest network on the planet. There were millions upon millions of viewers watching our video around the globe. We thought our workload was heavy while we zipped around North America, but once we went worldwide, it was almost impossible. On our first tour of the UK we were slated to play *Top of the Pops* in London in the late afternoon, but had a show in Manchester that evening. The problem was that Manchester was seven hours away, if we sat on the bus in traffic. To make it work, they stuck us on the back of four high-speed motorbikes that zigzagged through the London rush hour traffic to Heathrow Airport. From there we jumped in a helicopter, flew for an hour, chugged a bunch of Stella Artois, and then landed in a park outside of the venue, fifteen minutes before showtime. We ran on stage straight from the helicopter and had one of the best shows we'd ever performed. The label released "In Too Deep" a few months later and everything got bigger and better. We were invited to perform on late night talk shows, morning shows, radio shows, and even *SNL*, with Seann William Scott hosting, in case you forgot it was the early 2000s. We got guest spots on *King of the Hill*, too. The album just kept selling and selling.

As we got closer to the end of the year, the folks at the legendary L.A. radio station KROQ asked us to record a Christmas song for a compilation disc. We decided to write a heavy metal Christmas song, because we'd never heard one before and thought it would be funny if we asked Tenacious D to collaborate on it. We had been fans of "The D" since we saw their little HBO shorts from the late nineties, way before Jack Black was a superstar. They were game, so we booked two days at Sunset Sound Studios in Hollywood to write and record the song. We showed up to the studio on September 10 to get ready for Jack and Kyle. We hit it off pretty quickly, chatting and joking around, before getting down to songwriting. I was stunned by how much funny shit Jack Black would come up with. He would write lines that would have us dying laughing and then he'd think for a second, and say, "Nah, this is terrible," and then start rewriting. After a long day, we had a good outline for the song, planning to finish it the next day. Unfortunately, we all woke up to the horror of September 11. There was no way we were going into the studio to write a funny metal Christmas song. Months later, when the world felt a little more normal, we finished the song in separate studios. It's called "Things I Want," and we thought it brought a little joy to the world.

As the year turned to 2002, we continued working at a breakneck pace, and the *All Killer* cycle was quickly coming to an end. Greig Nori and the label had their sights on us making a new record, and this time, Greig didn't want Jerry Finn to produce it. He'd always felt that he got screwed out of producing the last one and wanted his chance to shine. He argued that the majority of what was normally the producer's work had been done well before it ever got to Jerry, and he wasn't totally wrong. Greig did help select my best songs, urged me to write a better chorus here or there, and pointed out parts that needed to be longer or shorter. He even helped write some lyrics, if I had procrastinated too long and we were sitting in the studio. Thanks to our success, Greig knew we had the leverage to make demands of the label, so he convinced us to go to bat for him. I had mixed feelings about Greig at this point, obviously, but I still believed we had a special creative partnership and that maybe things could go back to the way they used to be. I thought maybe some of his anger was because he wasn't as involved in making the records as he'd like. So I didn't mind Greig producing the album, but I did mind the timeline set out by him and the record company. For some reason, they thought four weeks was enough time for me to write an entire new album. Four weeks! It took me a couple of years to write *All Killer*. The agents, management, and the label weren't listening. They had committed us to be on festivals and TV, and headline tours were booked, so our entire year was mapped out and there was no other time to record. I was able to squeeze an extra two weeks of writing from them, but that was it. Despite my protests, we were scheduled to go in the studio to record the new album just a few short weeks from the last day of the *All Killer* tour. I didn't have any songs written.

The *All Killer* tour ended on May 8, 2002, and I flew home to Ajax the next day to start writing the new album. Despite all our success, I was still living in my mum and Kevin's basement, but I knew there was no way in hell I could make another record living under their roof. I also didn't want to write in my car in the driveway or go back to the roach-infested Chameleon rehearsal rooms. I needed an apartment of my own, but we were still completely broke. Here's a little more music industry math: While our album had gone multi-platinum worldwide, we weren't seeing much more than a dime. That's because we had to reimburse the label for the studio time, the music videos, and the tour support they'd provided us. It would be years before we'd see any of that money trickle down to us. We had a little bit of walking around money thanks to touring nonstop, but there was no way I could afford my own place. So I rented an apartment in Toronto on the record company's dime (which was really my dime, since I would have to pay them back). Then I holed up and did nothing but write songs, all day and night. I didn't drink, party, or even speak to anyone. I never left the apartment except to get food. I barely slept, just repeating the same schedule over and over trying to get twelve songs together. I was fucking miserable. That misery filled me with self-doubt. When "Fat Lip" exploded, all I could think about was *Oh god, what if I'm a one-hit wonder?* We had two more big songs, so I thought I was safe, but then I saw a VH1 countdown of the "Best One Hit Wonder ALBUMS of All Time" and started to panic again. *Oh no! What if I'm on that list one day?*

Greig used to be able to lift me up and make me feel confident, but things between us were incredibly strained and instead of making me feel good about myself, he did the complete opposite. What I understand now is that Greig had become incredibly jealous of our success. Plus, he was losing power over me. After finally confiding in someone—our mutual friend Heidi—over the course of several months I had completely ended any and all sexual relationship with Greig. Having someone to talk to was huge, and Heidi was an incredible help to me with that situation. While she and I were close, she was old friends with Greig, too. He had told her about our relationship in some misguided attempt to get her to convince me that it was okay to be bisexual. Of course, being bisexual wasn't the problem. I told Heidi what was really going on and she told me that it was abuse. She told Greig the same thing. I think having a friend call him out helped put a stop to everything; unfortunately it also made his attitude towards me a lot worse. Sure, he was getting rich off of us, but on top of the money, he wanted power. He took every opportunity to put me down. He would dish out insulting backhanded compliments and say things that were just mean. Telling us things like our merchandise profits were low because people were too embarrassed to be seen wearing Sum 41 shirts, or saying "It's great you're selling a ton of records, but only little kids and losers are buying the albums." All of this, compounded with my lack of self-confidence in my writing, made me feel horribly insecure and embarrassed of our own success. It was hard to see back then, though, because I still believed Greig wanted what was best for me and for the band. Even when he was putting me down, I saw it as constructive criticism and brutal honesty. Besides, the rest of the band still loved him. He was always so different when the rest of the guys were around. I think they sensed something was going on since Greig and I spent so much time together, but I was too mortified by the whole thing to ever confide in them. So to those guys he was just same old cool and fun Greig who wanted us to succeed.

One thing I knew for sure, though: His constant cutting remarks reinforced my insecurities, making it harder than ever to write. Adding to my songwriting difficulties was that his attitude towards the "pop punk" that had propelled us to this point was changing, too. He argued that the music on *All Killer No Filler* was kids' music. On one hand I was offended, but on the other hand the music I was writing was evolving, becoming darker and heavier anyway. I didn't have any full songs yet, but I had been stockpiling the riffs I had written in the back of the bus, backstage, or in hotel rooms. All of them had a darker tone than the tracks on *All Killer*. Some of that was inspired by the metal bands that we loved, like Metallica and Iron Maiden, as well as the punk sounds of Bad Religion and the minor-chord progressions on Social Distortion's *White Light White Heat White Trash*. I played some of my new music for Greig and he was enthusiastic, encouraging me to write "heavier, darker, and even more metal shit." He told me, "Forget this pop punk shit, because only young girls and little kids like that stuff." I didn't necessarily agree that only little kids liked punk, but I couldn't deny that my writing was naturally getting heavier. It also seemed like nobody was doing guitar solos anymore—not even Metallica. I felt that maybe we could carve out our own lane within this genre, bridging heavy metal and punk rock in a way I hadn't heard before. It would definitely be a major U-turn to go from "In Too Deep" to metal in one year, but I liked the challenge. It was something new and actually got me excited about writing a new album, now with the goal of reinventing Sum 41.

My lyrics were also changing. How could they not? I've always written about my life, and our lives had changed so much in such a short amount of time. One of the biggest things to shake my entire world had happened near the end of the *All Killer* tour. My high school friend with benefits, Jessica, had come to one of our shows and we had picked up where we left off. We were fooling around in the back of the bus, when we realized she had just gotten her period, so we stopped before having sex. She called me a month or two later with some devastating news: Her cheating ex-boyfriend had tested positive for HIV. She needed to go get checked—and so did I since I technically had been exposed to her blood. We were both shaken, but I didn't think we had any reason to be alarmed yet.

Two weeks later, I happened to be off the road and was able to accompany her to the doctor's office to get her results. She was positive for HIV. We were stunned. The virus still felt like a death sentence back then. There was no cure and few treatments. She had, at best, we thought, ten years to live. I held her in my arms as she cried. It was fucking heartbreaking and agonizing to feel so helpless. I realized that I really needed to get tested now, too. Those were the two longest, scariest, sleepless two weeks of my life waiting for the results. I was at a Denny's somewhere in the U.S. when I got a call from an unknown number. It was the doctor telling me I was negative for HIV. "Thank god, fuck yes!" I shouted in the middle of the restaurant, startling the families eating at their tables. It was strange to feel so elated and happy, but also feel devastated for Jessica. Thankfully, science has come a long way to help people living with HIV, and Jessica is alive and amazing and working as an activist helping other people living with HIV and AIDS. It was during that two-week period of knowing about her HIV diagnosis and awaiting my results that I wrote "The Hell Song" in its entirety, music and lyrics:

Everybody's got their problems
Everybody says the same things to you
It's just a matter how you solve them
And knowing how to change the things you've been through

I feel I've come to realize
How fast life can be compromised
Step back to see what's going on
I can't believe this happened to you

It's just a problem that we're faced with am I
Not the only one who hates to stand by
Complications ended first in this line
With all these pictures running through my mind

Knowing endless consequences
I feel so useless in this
Get back, step back, and as for me,
I can't believe.

Part of me, won't agree, 'cause I don't know if it's for sure
Suddenly, suddenly I don't feel so insecure.

I liked the song and took it to Greig because I hoped it would work on the new album. When I told him the backstory, though, he flipped his shit. He was instantly irate and just started yelling. I was so confused, but figured it was because I had been having a sexual relationship with Jessica and he was so jealous. As he ranted, though, I realized it was because he had been sleeping with her, too. Now he was concerned about his own HIV status. This confused me even more. Was he not gay? Did he just want to fuck everyone? Even my high school friends? As much as this revelation confused me, it didn't shock me. I was starting to realize there was a lot going on with Greig that I didn't really know about. Either way, as time went on, he was losing all my trust and admiration. If you're worried, don't be: He was tested and was negative, too.

With "The Hell Song" completed, I had one song down, and so many more to go. I was writing so intensively that I lost all perspective. I had no idea if anything was good or bad anymore. Sometimes Greig would come by, fill the room with his bad attitude, bark at me to change a line, move a chorus, rewrite a lyric, and then quickly leave. Other times he would analyze my lyrics and claim songs like "No Brains" were about him. Maybe they were, or maybe I wasn't the only one with low self-esteem. I never intentionally wrote any lyrics about Greig or our situation, but looking back on the words now, he might have been right:

> *I hate you today, I can't find a way, Don't drag me down now.*
> *Goodbye, I've had enough frustration, I won't get stuck*
> *Goodbye, this dead end situation, is just not worth my time.*

Luckily for me, Greig had found a new young band to divert him. They were called No Warning, and he was already pitting us against each other, claiming the singer, Ben Cook, was a tougher, more credible version of me, and that Sum 41 would be opening for No Warning someday. He still wanted me to write songs for them, though, and when he wanted something from me he became the old Greig again. He would be so kind and generous and complimentary, and I'd be so desperate to be out of the darkness that I'd fall for it. I ended up working on songs for No Warning and even Treble Charger when I was supposed to be writing my own record. As an adult, it's hard to look back at that time, because I just want to shake my younger self and say, "WAKE THE FUCK UP!" The only way I can explain it is that he'd been shaping me since I was sixteen. I believed that everything good in my life came from Greig, and he encouraged that belief, telling me that if he were out of the picture, we'd all be fucked and our careers would be over. He was so good at manipulating us, especially me. I look back and feel like I was brainwashed. I grew up without a dad, and even if you've never flipped through a pop psychology book can probably figure out why I was clinging to Greig's friendship. Still, I've never felt like I needed a father figure. What I always longed for were brothers, and that's what Greig and my bandmates were to me. Even with all the pain I was feeling around him, I wanted to get back to the way it was before it all went to shit. I wanted to keep this whole family together. Like I said, I'm fiercely loyal, but sometimes it's to a fault.

At the end of the six weeks, I was supposed to have twelve songs written, but had pulled together only eleven, well, eleven plus the tracks I had written for Greig to give to Treble Charger, as well as some riffs and choruses for No Warning. I was completely fucking exhausted, emotionally and creatively. I had nothing left. Luckily, everyone liked the songs, and agreed that "Hell Song" would be the first single, followed by "Over My Head" and "Thanks for Nothing." I felt so relieved and positive. The only thing darkening my life was Greig. He wouldn't stop taunting me and bragging about his new band, saying they would be bigger, heavier, and better than we could ever be. His negativity was unrelenting. I just wanted to shut him the fuck up, so one night before pre-production started I picked up my guitar and wrote the heaviest, toughest, most badass thing I'd ever written. I had so much hate and anger on my mind, that the lyrics that came out of me were dark:

> *So am I, still waiting, for this world to stop hating.*
> *Can't find a good reason, can't find hope to believe in.*
> *Drop dead, a bullet to my head.*
> *Your words are like a gun in hand.*

"In Too Deep" had come to me in minutes, and so had "Still Waiting." I originally called this song "Drop Dead," and the minute I put down a demo of it, I knew it was something special. I brought it to our rehearsal the next day, and when it was done playing, Cone said, "That's the best song you've ever written." What more did anyone need to say?

We wanted to record the album in NYC, because other than the Strokes, hardly any big rock bands were making records in New York, opting for L.A. instead. We also thought this harder, darker record would benefit from being recorded in a tougher, grittier city. It didn't hurt that I wanted to move to New York and this felt like my way to get there and not come back.

Dave, Cone, and I kept a very similar recording setup, as we had on the previous record, using one sound for the entire album. The main difference now was that Dave had become a much better guitar player. He had used all the downtime on tour to practice scales and solos, playing along with his favorite bands. Although I was still writing some of the guitar solos during my demo stage, Dave would be performing them all. I wrote the framework of the solos on "Hell Song" and "Hooch," just to show Dave the style I was thinking, and then he took it from there, always coming up with the most incredibly iconic shit.

The label had agreed to let Greig produce this record, and a week into recording, I started to worry he was in over his head. I didn't think I knew a lot about recording or producing, but I had studied every fucking move Jerry Finn made when we were making the last album and I could tell Greig knew far less than I did. He was always second-guessing himself and would get angry if we ever doubted him or said, "That's not how we did it on *All Killer*." And while it was still early in the process, sonically the album wasn't sounding as good as even the demos I was making in my apartment. One thing that wasn't Greig's fault was the humidity. It was so hot and humid in New York that summer that our guitars were going out of tune every couple of minutes and we kept having to stop and retune. It was a fucking nightmare. New York was killing us in other ways, too. For some reason the electricity was shitty and caused a weird buzzing noise, or the power would drop in the middle of takes, which was ironic because the studio was literally named Power Station.

Not all of us were suffering: Stevo did his drum parts in a week and fucked off to the Bahamas. While he sat on the beach sipping mai tais, I was locked in a studio cursing at the power grid or sitting in my hotel room trying to finish "Still Waiting." At the time George W. Bush was using the tragedy of 9/11 to go to war in Iraq. As I walked from SoHo to the Midtown studio, I realized I wanted to write "Still Waiting" as a protest song against Bush and that bullshit war. I also realized while walking the New York streets that Toronto had everything New York had, but was much cleaner and nicer, with less anger and hostility. I definitely didn't need to move after all.

Four weeks later, the instrumental tracks were done and we were headed back to Metalworks Studios in Canada to finish up vocals. When I showed up to the studio, Greig was in a total panic screaming, "Everything is out of tune! The whole thing is fucked!" I didn't understand, what was out of tune? Greig said, "The whole fucking thing, the whole record is out of tune!" I thought, there's no way, we would have noticed it in New York. He played me "Still Waiting" and then "Hell Song," and I listened intensely, but I honestly couldn't hear it. Greig was adamant, though, and so was his engineer. I figured I must be wrong, since they could all hear it. To fix the phantom problem, Greig wanted to re-record the entire record. We had originally recorded most of the songs in half step down tuning, which made the songs sound heavier. But Greig was second-guessing everything at this point and made us re-record all the possible "hit songs" back to standard tuning for fear they wouldn't work as well on radio for some reason. There was no way we could do that. We didn't have time, because we had to leave for yet another tour in two weeks. Greig had a plan: "We'll rent two rooms here, you sing in one room and Dave and Cone will record in the other, and when you're done vocals, you can come over and put your guitar parts on it, too." He laid it out like this plan made any kind of sense. I pointed out that we had recorded the album on rented and borrowed gear, but Greig said our own stuff was decent enough and it would sound great. So we re-recorded the album.

For the next two weeks we feverishly scrambled to lay down all the tracks for our incredibly important, make-or-break follow-up album. We ended up spending less time, working on worse equipment, and recording it at lower quality, but at least it was done and, according to Greig, in tune. Years later I was able to get the master tapes and listen back to what we had originally recorded. As much as I was hoping to hear horribly out-of-tune guitars so that I would know we had averted disaster with our frantic re-recording, it wasn't there. The original album was great and big and filled with perfectly in-tune guitars. Greig had lost all perspective and, that day, his insecurities won.

To no one's surprise, the album wasn't finished on time. We had to leave for England to play the Reading and Leeds Festival and continue the recording on the road. The silver lining was that we got to rent the famous Olympic Studios in London where the Stones, the Who, Zeppelin, Jimi Hendrix, and Bowie all had made seminal records. While staying at the Trafalgar Hilton in London, we ran into the Strokes in the lobby. We'd hung out with them a few times at festivals and had found common ground in our interest in drugs and alcohol. We all got along surprisingly well. After spotting them in the lobby, we headed to the hotel bar together. We all had things to do the next day with us due in the recording studio and the Strokes headlining at the festival, even though the singer Julian had a broken leg. We didn't let our responsibilities slow us down. Come 9:30 a.m., Julian and I were still sitting at the twenty-four-hour lobby bar, drinking Jack and vodka and solving all the world's problems. I pitched him an idea that we had been kicking around for "Still Waiting," which would be the first video off the new album. At the time, it was really popular for bands to have "the" in the name. The Vines, the Libertines, the Hives, and, yes, the Strokes. The idea for the video was a spoof on the music industry and how nobody cares about bands with numbers in their names anymore, but they only wanted bands with "the" in the name. To make the point, we would use the set design from the Strokes' "Last Nite" video and then we would trash it. Julian loved the idea, saying, "Please do that! That would be so fucking amazing." We shot the video with Canadian comedian Will Sasso playing a record company president who wanted us to change our name to the Sums to get with the times. He improvised that entire scene, and the hardest part of shooting was not laughing every time he did a new take, because he kept adding new bits. When the video came out, most of the press at the time either got it wrong or intentionally tried to make it look like we were making fun of the Strokes, which couldn't have been further from the truth.

By September 2002, the record was finally finished, in time to make the release date pegged to American Thanksgiving. We barely made it, though, because on top of all the other issues we had, we still didn't have a title for the album. We'd already created all the artwork for the packaging and had done a zombie photo shoot to promote the album, but we just couldn't think of a title. We were all on the tour bus, when Rob Stevenson from the label called us frantically relaying the news: "If you guys do not pick a title today, this record can't come out this year." The current front-runner for the title was *No Brains*, but none of us liked it *that* much. We were looking at the pictures of the zombie Stevo we had picked for the cover as we tried to come up with better album titles. I said, "It looks like Stevo is asking a question in this photo. What would he be asking?" Then it just hit me: "*Does This Look Infected?*" We all laughed and that was it.

I finally felt like I could relax. I had been under such intense pressure since the year started, trying to write and record a new album that was as good as or better than *All Killer*. On top of all that, I had just spent months in close quarters with Greig, who was seemingly engaged in a master class of mind fuckery. He was either making me feel like a horrible person for destroying our "special bond" and making him angry all the time, or he was building me up as a great writer who just wrote an amazing album that was going to be huge. If I had been smarter back then, I would have realized that he was only nice when he wanted something—and he really wanted something on this album.

Here's even more music industry math: When a song comes out, whoever is listed in the publishing credits gets paid, which is usually the songwriter, along with producers and other folks involved in the song's creation. Getting those credits right is very important if you want to make a living in music. When I started out in the industry, I was a teenager. I didn't know what publishing was or that the people listed in the publishing credits were the ones who got paid. On *All Killer No Filler*, Greig made it clear that since we'd already told so many people that he wrote "In Too Deep," he should be listed as the songwriter or it would look strange. He also said Sum 41 would be taken more seriously by radio stations and the music industry if they saw his name as a cowriter on more songs. So he took 40 or 50 percent of the credit on a lot of songs on *All Killer No Filler*, supposedly for our own good. That meant he got anywhere from 20 to 50 percent of the money for almost every track.

When it came time to submit the publishing credits for *Does This Look Infected?*, Greig suggested the same kind of publishing splits. I was a little wiser now and pushed back, pointing out that I had written these songs on my own. He instantly became angry and laid on the guilt, which he knew always worked on me. "Oh, now that you're successful you have an ego and you're forgetting about the people who made you?" he said. Feeling small, I tried to defend myself, pointing out that I did all the writing. All he did was come in and say he liked a chorus or I should shorten an intro, and maybe some help on lyrics here and there, but that was it. I had spent weeks holed up in that rented apartment writing alone. That only made him angrier. He gave me the same old line about how I wouldn't be here without him, how he had taught me everything, that songwriting was him telling me to extend a section or write a better chorus. I reminded him that it was part of the job as a producer to do that, which was why he was getting producer royalties on every song, plus a producer fee. I didn't mind giving him credit when he contributed to songwriting, but not on every song. It went back and forth and back and forth, with him making me feel greedy and unkind. In the end, I caved. Was there ever any other possible outcome? Sure didn't feel like it. Greig ended up getting publishing credit on large parts of songs he had nothing to do with. Maybe the song "No Brains" was actually about me.

Around this time, Coors approached us about using the song "What We're All About" in one of their commercials. The song was a new version of the track we had included on *Half Hour of Power*, which had been reworked for the *Spider-Man* soundtrack. We had been hesitant to redo the track in the first place, but the label had been relentless, because this was going to be the lead single for the biggest movie of the year.

We still said no. Then the label pulled out the big guns. Greig called and said, "Look, Rick Rubin says he wants to produce this song for you. Sony wants to put a couple million dollars into marketing this track and Island Def Jam is willing to put ten thousand dollars into each of your bank accounts tomorrow and you will never have to pay it back, if you say yes." Since we were essentially still broke, the cash sounded great. The real motivator, though, was Rick Rubin. If the legendary producer thought the song was good, how could we say no?

While Rick was great, we still hated the song when it was finished—and the video was even worse. We shot it over two super-jet-lagged days in Toronto, having flown in from our European tour and headed straight to the shoot. The video had us suspended upside down in harnesses trying to perform naturally. Not only was it extremely difficult, but we looked ridiculous doing it. The whole thing was a flop, and I was so embarrassed and pissed that I had allowed myself to be seduced by the idea of working with Rick Rubin and a little bit of money. I vowed I would never again do anything just for the money. So when the Coors Company called and asked us to use the song in their new campaign, I immediately said no. They kept coming back, offering more and more money, and I just kept saying no. Greig called and told us that the final offer was a million dollars to use thirty seconds of the song. It would have been life-changing money for us, but I told them it wasn't going to happen. I told Greig, "I am never making a decision based on money ever again in my life." And I still live by that vow to this day.

COCAINE, STRIPPERS, ECSTASY, ORGIES, AND PARIS

One of the best pieces of advice we've ever received was from Ice-T. We met him at a party in NYC, pretty early in our career, and he decided to share some words of wisdom. "Yo, I fucking love you guys, so I'm gonna give you a piece of advice," he said. "Remember this: The only thing harder than being the Mac, is staying the Mac." We've never forgotten those important words and kept them close as our reputations and careers grew and we wanted them to stay that way.

Even before our new record came out, 2003 was looking to be a very big year for the band. Our single "Still Waiting" was released in the fall of 2002, and by the time the New Year rolled around, it had surpassed "Fat Lip" in radio spins. Soon it became our most played song on American radio. It was a staple on MTV, and fans bought so many copies that the album was hitting gold or platinum in countries all around the world. All that off just the first single! Things only got wilder after "Hell Song" was released. While it was exciting, it was exhausting, too. We were releasing a new album just a year after *All Killer*, which itself had come out only a year after *Half Hour of Power*. We were on the hamster wheel and it was spinning at full speed.

Our band had started out playing basement parties in Ajax and now we played arenas. We were on the covers of magazines. Every major press outlet wanted interviews with us; every radio station wanted us to play their festival. There were more late night talk shows, more early morning radio shows, more everything! We had journalists asking to travel with us hoping to go behind the scenes with the band and see our rapid-fire rise firsthand. We did it all and never questioned it, because when your dreams are coming true, all the work is fun. This is what it took for us to be the Mac, and more importantly, to stay the Mac.

Not everything at that time was fun, though. With all the new attention, there were a lot of eyes on us, and not all of them liked what they saw. There was a lot of critique of my appearance. People would mock my height and my looks, and it felt like almost every article about the band made sure to comment on it. I was ridiculed online for being short and ugly with a big nose (which still happens to this day!). I even got nominated for the dubious honor of the Ugliest People in Rock award from *Kerrang!* magazine. Obviously, it hurt, but I also kind of liked the fact that I had beaten the system. I was successful despite being too short, too unattractive, and bearing the horrible un–rock 'n' roll name of Deryck Whibley. I started to take a dark pride in it, getting in on the joke and telling people that it was all true and that was why I went into music and not male modeling. The constant critique took a toll, though. To prove I was where I was supposed to be, I tried to keep my head down and work harder than everyone else—and we had a lot of hard work ahead of us.

When we were on the road, every day was a grind. Each evening we were handed schedules for the following day that looked like this:

Wake up at 6am
Pickup at 7am
Morning Radio station interview 730-830am
-Travel
Morning TV 9-10am
-Travel

Print Press / Photo shoots til 1pm
Lunch - 30 min
-Travel
Afternoon Radio Station visits
-Travel
Soundcheck - with meet and greet
Interviews at Venue
Dinner
Showtime
After show Meet and Greet with Radio Station and contest winners
Travel to next city - 12:00am

It was so grueling and there was so little time for fun, let alone hotel trashing, that at one point, Stevo and I vowed that if we were going to work this hard, we should party just as hard. After all, everyone told us that we were "famous rock stars" now, but it sure didn't feel that way. The relentless schedule made it hard to live out any of the rock star fantasies we had ever heard of—unless rock stars secretly fantasized about waking up at 6 a.m., spending hours smiling at strangers, and shoving Subway sandwiches into their mouths between interviews. If we were going to be living our dreams, we needed to have a little more fun.

The first step was to take some control of our schedule. There wasn't much we could change, but we could move the after-show bus call. By switching the time we had to be on the bus from midnight to 4 a.m., we could stay in the city after our work was done and try to squeeze in a little action. The only problem was, it was becoming increasingly difficult for me to go out in public. The more famous I got, the more difficult it was for me to blend into a crowd or grab a drink in a bar. While the other guys got left alone or even had people offer to buy them drinks, I was getting fucked with wherever we went. People would shout, "Sux 41 is here!" They would intentionally bump into me, throw ice or drinks at me, or just try to stare me down from across the room. It was clear the only reason these idiot men were trying to fuck with me was because wherever we went girls would pay attention to us and not them. After two back-to-back incidents where I walked into a bar and got punched in the back of the head while I was ordering a drink, I stopped going out to bars altogether.

So where do you go when you can't go to a bar, but want to have some wild booze-soaked fun? A strip club, of course. We were always welcomed with open, uh . . . arms at strip clubs. It became a routine. We would finish a show, hop on the tour bus, drive over to the closest gentlemen's establishment, and head inside to get to know all the dancers. When the bar closed, we'd invite the girls onto the bus, turning it into our own private dance club to burn away the last few hours of night. Strip clubs apparently talk to each other, because soon wherever we were touring, clubs started reaching out. We put their girls on our guest lists and they would bring us back to their clubs. We weren't the only rockers who liked strip clubs, of course. Vinnie Paul, the late drummer for Pantera, had opened his own adult-entertainment spot, the Clubhouse, in Dallas. We made sure to stop by every time we were touring through. It was a mutual fandom that evolved into friendship—we had gold and platinum record plaques made out to Vinnie Paul and the Clubhouse and they hung them up on the walls at the bar.

There were some risks to hanging out with dancers, though. Late one night, in our early days of touring, we were in our hotel with a few dancers and some guys from a local radio station, when a stripper OD'd in front of us. We had no idea what she had taken, but we knew something was very wrong when she started convulsing and foaming at the mouth. We were still only nineteen and twenty and had no idea what to do. We knew we had to call someone and get her some help, but we didn't want to get in trouble, either. We decided to wheel the convulsing girl down the hall to the elevator in the hotel desk chair. We got her to the lobby and left her in the care of the front desk clerk. Paramedics came and took her away.

Another night we were in Florida and two girls were giving Cone and Stevo lap dances. The quarters were tight, though, and the girls kept gyrating into each other. One of the dancers suddenly took a swing, hitting the other girl square in the face and knocking her wig clean off. Grieving her lost hair hat, the girl grabbed a martini glass, smashed it on the table, and stabbed the other dancer in the neck. Blood sprayed all over the guys and they took off running back to the bus. We saw the ambulances and police racing in as we tore out of there.

Sum 41 earned its reputation as hard-drinking, hard-charging pranksters honestly. It wasn't uncommon for us to stay up all night, crash at noon, and wake up twenty minutes before showtime. This is when I invented my own not-so-traditional version of Jack and Coke. I'd have lines of cocaine dropped into shots of Jack Daniel's that I could drink on stage to wake me up. On some tours, our tour manager paid us our per diem in cocaine instead of cash, citing "you're just gonna give it back to me to buy coke anyway." We knew we were known for wild antics, and we didn't mind living up to it. In classic Sum 41 fashion we took it way too far during a two-week promo tour of Australia and Japan—and a lot of it was witnessed by a writer who was writing a cover story on the band for *SPIN* magazine. We were touring with our friends Unwritten Law, and that meant a lot of drinking and a lot of drugs. It's well known (at least among touring bands and other degenerates) that drugs in Australia are usually shit. Stevo and I wanted some ecstasy, but because we had been burned in the past, we told our promoter to buy fifty hits, just in case it was weak. It ended up being some of the most intense ecstasy we'd ever had—and we were taking two at a time. Cone and Dave never went as crazy as Stevo and I did, but they joined us for this party and were hitting it just as hard. This ecstasy was quicker than normal and faded fast, so every time it wore off, we'd take more. Besides, we had fifty pills to get through. As the night blazed on, our tour manager, Jeff Marshall, came knocking on the hotel room door. The room was completely trashed and raging with close to thirty people rolling hard.

"What the fuck are you guys still doing up?" Jeff yelled. Turned out it was 8 a.m. and we were due at the Japanese consulate in thirty minutes. We had to be interviewed for our Japanese work visas and we were high as fuck. Luckily I had a solution: "Let's just move the interview to tomorrow!" I yelled from across the room. Jeff screamed back "Our fucking flight to Tokyo is tonight, you idiot!" Jeff proceeded to go Full Tour Manager. He kicked everyone out of the room and dragged us down to the lobby. As we were marched down the hall like naughty schoolchildren, Stevo looked at me and smiled slyly. He flashed me his hand revealing a couple more pills. We looked at each other, nodded, and gulped them down. They kicked in right as we arrived at the consulate to ask Japanese immigration officers to let us into their country. Miraculously they approved our visas and took our photos for the passports. (I wish I still had that photo.)

As we arrived back at the hotel, Jeff informed us he had flushed the rest of our pills down the toilet. Stevo lost his mind and threw Jeff against the wall. "You did what?! You had no fucking right to get rid of MY fucking drugs!!" Stevo screamed. Stevo almost never got angry like this, so it really freaked us all out. I pulled him off Jeff and told him that we needed to cool it for the day. Things had gotten a little out of hand. Nearly missing our interviews at the consulate wasn't even the worst of it. The hotel was furious with us because during the course of the all-night party, every-thing from the room had, uh, accidentally ended up falling off my balcony and into the swimming pool. Chairs, lamps, TVs, the bed, including its frame. The hotel was freaked out and the police had been called. Even that wasn't the worst of it. A member of our touring party apparently attacked a maid, threatening to kill her for coming into the room and throwing a glass coffee table at her. It didn't hit her, but managed to shatter all over the floor and gave her a real scare. It was definitely time to leave Australia.

When we arrived in Japan, we knew we needed to mellow out a bit. Luckily, touring through Japan meant long workdays with tight schedules and very little time for partying. Every time we were in Japan we knew we would be worked to the bone and then on the last night we'd let ourselves go wild. On earlier tours, we had learned that mushrooms were legal in Japan, so the ritual became that we spent the last night tripping balls while walking through the streets of Tokyo.

Unfortunately in 2002 the country had changed its mind about magic mushrooms and made them illegal. So what was a hardworking band supposed to do? Luckily, the local photographer traveling with us had a line on a new legal drug that was kind of similar to mushrooms but came in a powder form that you mixed in a drink. It was called Mystic Blue Powder.

It was our last night in Japan, and like most stories on tour, it all started in a bar. We were having a few drinks and Stevo decided he was going to go find this Mystic Blue Powder. He took off with our translator and returned later with a bunch of premixed vials. We had no idea what it was or what it would do, but we each took one and returned to drinking, waiting for it to kick in. At this point, Dave somehow got separated from us and we didn't know where he'd gone. Stevo and Cone and I waited about an hour, and when none of us felt anything, we all took one more vial. We considered ourselves talented drug users and weren't afraid of pushing things closer to the edge. We had a few more drinks and slowly started to feel a little something. That was encouraging, but it was still very minor. We gave it another hour or so and then Stevo and I downed a third vial. I knew the Blue Mystic had taken its grip when all of a sudden it felt like we were on a boat rather than solid ground. The bar had a Scooby-Doo poster on the wall, and as the characters on it became hideous monsters, leaping out of the picture towards us, we knew we were in for a high unlike any we'd had before. This was not a trip of spiritual enlightenment or expanding our minds; it was pure fear and loathing in fucking Tokyo. And, where was Dave? Did he take this potion, too? He was always the smarter one and must have gone to bed. The bar was no place for us in this state, and besides, it was 5 a.m. and we were being kicked out anyway. Back at the hotel we rode the elevator for another hour, just going up and down looking out the floor-to-ceiling windows, laughing hysterically, and spitting on each other (drugs, man). We tried to enter the lobby, but we were blinded by the bright lights and white marble floors and became convinced it was heaven and God would punish us if we proceeded. We dove back into the elevator and hit the button for our floor as fast as we could. When the doors opened, our floor was dark and ugly and it felt like we were entering hell. Holding on to one another, we slowly walked the hall as the patterns in the carpet began forming into snakes that were trying to bite us.

As the drug kept on hitting, I kept thinking, how could I possibly get any higher? But I could, and I did. Every thirty minutes it went to a new level of intensity. And with every new level, more hallucinations and terror took over. We sat in the hallway too frightened to enter our own rooms. Stevo was the first to brave the unknown and disappeared into his room. He reemerged twenty minutes later holding a pineapple he believed to be a girl he'd met at the bar named Mai. He proclaimed they were in love and would be getting married one day. As high as we were, I was thankful I still had some semblance of sanity, because Stevo had clearly lost his. After a few minutes, Stevo took off with Mai back to his, I mean, *their* room. Cone and I sat on the carpet praying this high wouldn't get any worse. Minutes later Stevo opened the door looking terrified. Something bad had happened. "I killed her," he said, solemnly. "What are you talking about?" I replied. With panic in his voice he said, "Mai. I killed my girlfriend. I don't know what to do. I need help!" Cone and I both laughed and said, "Chill out, you're just tripping balls, like us."

Stevo then presented us with a pineapple, ripped open, with a steak knife stuck in it. "I killed her," he wailed. "I don't know how to cover this up. I'm going to jail." Now I started getting concerned, thinking this is the type of high that you hear about where people jump off buildings or stab a human (not a pineapple) to death. We told Stevo to go to his room, so we could deal with it later. He was starting to remind me of Benicio del Toro's character in the movie *Fear and Loathing in Las Vegas*.

Cone and I decided to ride this out together in his room. We jumped in his bed, got under the covers, and put on Oasis for some reason. We were swapping funny stories when out of nowhere, Cone panicked, blurting, "I can't do this anymore. I need to be alone. You have to go!" I said, "What are you talking about? I can't fucking be alone right now." He was adamant and pushed me out of the door into the hallway of hell. I ran to my room as fast as I could, freaking out in a way that I know now was my first full-blown panic attack. I started chugging vodka, which helped take the edge off a little, but not for long. It dawned on me that we had an entire day of press booked and it started in a couple of hours. I called Jeff Marshall and begged, "Cancel everything, we're too fucking high!" His reply was "Tough shit. You're doing it."

We rolled into the lobby to meet the press, still high. We hadn't seen Dave since the night before, but he showed up in the lobby looking like he'd been through hell. Which he had. He only took half a vile and had the worst night of his life. He had ended up naked and hiding in his bathroom worried his luggage was trying to eat him. Then, thinking he could wash the drugs away, he jumped in the shower. When he heard a knock at his door, he thought he was being saved. Instead he gave some unsuspecting Sum 41 fans quite an eyeful. We all threw on sunglasses and did our best to keep it together for the media (we didn't do very well). While this sounds like your average "rock stars do the craziest things!" story, the Mystic Blue Powder changed me. It changed all of us. That whole experience did something to my mind and I have never been the same. It opened the door to a panic and anxiety disorder that I have struggled and fought with ever since. It's hard to revisit this story without a lot of discomfort and my heart rate accelerating.

We started out 2003 with our first arena tour of the UK, bringing our friends American Hi-Fi and the Mighty Mighty Bosstones with us. Both bands had helped us out in our early days and we wanted to repay them. Having friends with us made the tour feel like a fun family vacation. Well, a family vacation with lots of famous people. We had reached a point where stars now wanted to hang backstage at our shows. Steve-O from *Jackass* met up with us in Manchester. Bruce Dickinson and Adrian Smith from Iron Maiden brought their kids backstage at London's Wembley Arena. The stars wanting to meet us was surreal enough, but things got even more unreal when I got a call from Greig Nori. He had just gotten off the phone with Iggy Pop's manager because Iggy wanted us to work with him on his new record. I was in disbelief, certain I hadn't heard him correctly: "The Real Iggy Pop? He wants to work with us?" I was shocked and confused, sputtering my questions: "Why? How? Us?" Greig replied, "Yes, he wants to know if you would write a song with him and if I'll produce it." My first thought was to say no. I mean, I didn't feel good enough or worthy enough to work with a legend such as Iggy Pop. Greig had plenty of issues, but he could be the kindest, caring, and most understanding person when he wanted. Luckily, at this moment, he wanted to. He gave me a pep talk that filled me with confidence. He told me who I was and what our band meant. He made me feel like I was a great songwriter and the fact that Iggy wanted me to write with him proved it. So I took a deep breath and said: "Fuck yeah! I'm in."

My nerves flared up again a few weeks later when I called Iggy. I had no reason to be nervous. He was so friendly and charming and we ended up chatting for forty-five minutes. He grew up in Detroit, which is close to Toronto, and shared stories about Toronto back in the sixties and seventies and playing shows with his first band, the Stooges, across Canada. Chatting with him felt like catching up with an old, cool family member. At the end of the call, we decided that I would sketch out a song, send him a demo, and we'd see where it went. Like most of my songs, I started with a riff and wrote a quick little verse and chorus—just chords and melody—with gibberish lyrics. He loved it and we made plans to record the track.

Iggy and I met face to face for the first time at Cello Studios in Los Angeles at the end of April 2003. This was right after he performed with a reunited Stooges at Coachella, and he'd gone so hard at the show that he walked into the studio on crutches. We were in awe, but, of course, refused to show it. After chatting for a bit, Iggy, Greig, and I sat down to write the lyrics and figure out the song's structure, so we could teach it to the band. The lyric writing was quick and easy, and the outline of "Little Know It All" was done in about an hour. Once we got into the control room and the band was playing, Greig's insecurities started to flare up. I knew what it was like to feel unsure in front of Iggy Pop, so I tried to boost his confidence the same way he had boosted mine. Things only got worse, though. When it came time to do the vocals, Greig kept making Iggy sing the song over and over even though he had already delivered an incredible take. I felt bad for Iggy and embarrassed for Greig. Iggy never said a word, but you could tell he was unhappy. While *All Killer* producer Jerry Finn had taught me a lot about what to do as a producer, Greig showed me what *not* to do. You need to know what you want, and know when you have it.

Twenty years later, almost to the day, I saw Iggy perform in Las Vegas. When I went backstage after the show to say hello, he leaned over to me, and said, "You know, I really didn't like your manager Greig." I burst out loud laughing—it had been twenty years! Iggy reiterated it, "No, really. I really, really didn't like him!" I wasn't surprised that he felt that way, but he had never mentioned that in all the years since we recorded that song, and we'd been around each other a fair amount.

While he may have disliked Greig, Iggy seemed to be a fan of the band. "Little Know It All" was slated as his new album's first single, so we flew to Miami to shoot a video together, at his favorite dingy hole-in-the-wall rock bar in Little Haiti called Churchills Pub. Then we essentially became his band, traveling with him as he performed the single on Letterman, at the MTV Awards, on the CASBY Awards in Toronto, and more. After the Toronto show, I had an after-party at my new house. Iggy came, but things took a turn when a drummer from one of our friends' bands started hassling him. I was pouring a drink when I heard Iggy growl, "Listen, you fuck, if you don't quit bothering me I'm going to punch your fucking lights out." I thought, *Holy shit, Iggy doesn't play!* I quickly jumped in and defused the situation before fists were thrown in my kitchen.

By this point, all the money from album sales, publishing, and touring was starting to add up. We were finally making real money and able to buy our first homes and decent cars. We were sloppy about a lot of things, but money wasn't one of them. I had been saving since earning my first dollar, but I finally decided to buy a few things. Cone bought his condo in downtown Toronto first, and since we were all such best friends I bought a condo next door to him. I barely lived in mine before upgrading to a big house in Riverdale, which is an upscale neighborhood of Toronto. It was almost exactly a million dollars and I paid cash. I leased an Audi S4. I also purchased some drums, guitars, and better recording equipment and built a little demo studio in the basement.

Now, Stevo and I always had a healthy but competitive relationship. When I bought my condo, three days later he bought one that was bigger, had a higher ceiling, and actual 24-karat gold flecks in the plaster. When I got my Audi, the next day he went and got a BMW. If I partied hard, he partied harder. Okay, so not always *healthy competition*, but you get the point. We were all enjoying life and enjoying each other's company. Back then, we would spend months on the road together, finally return to Toronto, and the same night call each other and say, "Let's meet up!"

Going out in Toronto wasn't easy for me, though. Somehow the place where I grew up was the hardest place for me to be out in public. There was no "hometown hero" welcome whatsoever. In fact, it was the complete opposite. Drunk people at bars would spit at me. They called me names and shouted homophobic slurs when I walked down Queen Street in the middle of the afternoon. They started fights with me at clubs or local shows. It was heartbreaking to feel hated in your own city, and it made it difficult to leave the house. It didn't stop me, though. I still went out and did what I wanted to do, knowing I would have people hassling me. It felt like high school. I had my cool group of friends, and everyone else were just fucking losers to me. Still, Stevo and Cone never got any of this negative attention. People bought drinks for them, while I got drinks thrown at me. While lead singers usually get most of the attention, good or bad, I've always had a look that made people want to start something with me. I just had a face that people wanted to hit.

Luckily it was easier for me to go out in L.A. Sometime that year we were in Los Angeles, to perform our new single, "Hell Song," on Jimmy Kimmel, and our Hollywood party friends Heidi and Mike took us out to a club called Joseph's on Cahuenga Blvd. As soon as we walked in, I made eye contact with a beautiful blond girl who I recognized but couldn't place. She clearly recognized me, too, as she came straight over. "Hi! Remember me? We met a couple years ago at the MTV thing you played." I realized that it was Paris Hilton. She wasn't a household name yet, but she was still Paris Hilton and I definitely remembered her. "How could I forget you?" I said with a smile. "You were so cold and rude to me." Her eyes widened and with an embarrassed laugh she said, "No I wasn't! Was I? What did I say?" I laughed and said, "You looked at me and said in a stuck-up pretentious voice, 'So . . . what cool band are you?'" Luckily she had a good sense of humor about me calling her out; she cracked up and apologized. "I'm sorry. I was just nervous and uncomfortable," she said. "That guy just grabbed me and my sister to introduce us to a band but he never said who." I chuckled and admitted that the meeting was just as awkward for us. We laughed it off and she invited me to her table, introducing me to the celebrities and kids of famous people sitting there. "This is so-and-so's daughter, this is blah blah blah's son, this person is part of the royal family," and so on and so on. We sat and talked, did shots, and pretty soon, Paris and I were making out at the table. She was funny, cool, sweet, clearly wild, and liked to party. Right up my alley.

When the bar closed, we ended up at some weird old mansion in the Hollywood Hills. It apparently belonged to an old out-of-work movie producer from the seventies, but we were greeted at the front door by a barely twentysomething girl wearing lingerie and seemingly stoned on heroin. She showed us around the enormous house while the mysterious producer stayed in his bedroom. While I was still scarred by the whole Mystic Blue Powder incident and had sworn off drugs for a bit, I figured I was never going to be in a *Once Upon a Time in Hollywood*-like situation like this again. I did one bump, which turned out to be the purest, most amazing blow I'd ever had in my entire life. It wasn't edgy, it wasn't speedy, I didn't feel my heart racing at all. I just felt fucking incredible. It was already 3 a.m. and the band had a show in Anaheim the next day, so I couldn't stay long. We kept making out as I left the party, and soon we found ourselves living out some eighties dream, high on coke and making out on the hood of the movie producer's vintage Porsche. Her top came off and it was getting intense. The only thing that wasn't part of the dream was the guys from the band at the end of the driveway yelling at me because I was taking so long. I told her, "Fuck, I have to go, everyone is getting pissed." She promised to come down to Orange County for the show the next day. I couldn't wait to see her.

This began a whirlwind six-month relationship based on sex, drugs, booze, and partying. It was wild and fun and neither of us thought it would last, but we were determined to enjoy it while it did. After coming to the Anaheim show, Paris followed us on tour through California. When we weren't together, we talked constantly, spending hours on the phone every night. Whatever little time off I had, I spent in L.A. at her place.

While I had spent a lot of time in rock bars and strip clubs, I knew nothing about the Hollywood club scene. I never got used to strolling past the hordes of people lined up in the hopes of getting inside or walking up to the velvet ropes that were opened for us like we were royalty as the paparazzi blinded us with their flashbulbs. I didn't know about table service and the bottles of champagne and vodka that would arrive for free. We were having so much fun together that Paris started traveling with me outside of the U.S., too. She came to England to attend the Kerrang! Awards. She hung out with me before we played with Metallica at the Reading and Leeds Festival, partying and doing blow backstage with Lars Ulrich. The guys loved having her around. I remember being on one of those giant Ferris wheels at the festival, high on blow, and hooking up with her as the wheel turned. When we hit the top of the rise, I looked out at the scene below while Metallica's "Enter Sandman" blasted from the PA. I thought, *Now I feel like a fucking rock star!* It wasn't all partying, though. We had mellow nights where we'd just stay in or go to a movie. I got to see a sweet and vulnerable side of Paris that many people never witness.

In those days, when we were filled with the invincibility of youth, the guys in the band all felt like we could do anything we wanted, stay up all night on whatever drugs, and then wake up and play a show as if nothing had happened. But one night I seriously fucked up. I had one week off before our Canadian tour and I spent it in Los Angeles with Paris. I was starting to get cocky and had booked my flight to Toronto at 6 a.m. on the day of the first show. This is a stupid mistake, because if possible you should always fly in the day before, in case the travel gets fucked up. Like I said: I was cocky. The night before my flight, Paris's friend was having a big house party up in the Hills. I had the passing thought that maybe we should stay in and chill, but we decided that we would just stop by for a drink. (Yeah, like that ever fucking happens.)

Soon enough Paris and I found ourselves in a back bedroom of a Hollywood Hills mansion with my friend Byron from the band Pennywise and some guy I didn't know. We were sitting around a small round table doing lines of blow and talking at each other. I started chatting up the stranger, and while he was pretty fucked up and slurring, I gathered that his band had just been signed to a major label and he was excited about their new music. I was high, but still genuinely happy for the guy. I loved my life as a successful musician and hoped this guy could experience it, too. As we kept talking, I heard him say the name Duff, and then he mentioned his guitar player, Slash. Who the hell was this guy? Then it fucking hit me: He was Scott Weiland from Stone Temple Pilots, and he was talking about his new supergroup, Velvet Revolver, with him and members of Guns N' Roses. He looked so different from what I remembered from the nineties. He was so skinny and didn't have his trademark goatee and red hair. Right as I was putting these pieces together, someone burst through the door, yelling, "The cops are here busting people for drugs!" I fucking panicked, jumping up to flush the drugs or hide or something, while Paris calmly cleared the mountain of coke into her bag. Scott Weiland sat there seemingly completely unfazed, talking about the legality of drug laws or some shit. I continued freaking out because now Paris had a ton of blow in her purse, there was no way out of this back room, and the cops were about to bust in. Also, we were super fucking high. That's when I came up with what I thought was a brilliant plan. "All four of us should jump in the bed, get under the covers, and pretend like we're having an orgy, so when the cops come in they'll think we're gross sex freaks and leave us alone!" I said. Everyone (they were also high) thought it was a perfect plan. We jumped in bed and Scott started rubbing my chest and undoing his pants. I shouted, "Whoa whoa whoa what the fuck are you doing?" He replied in a really stoned voice, "What? I thought you said we were having an orgy." I shouted back, "PRETEND! I said pretend we were having an orgy!" He must have heard me through his blow-induced fog, because he stopped undoing his pants and we went back to laughing and talking under the covers. After about fifteen minutes of our pretend orgy, we heard music playing and people talking. Someone had just panicked when the cops showed up for a noise complaint, and we were safe.

It was around 3 a.m. when I realized I had forgotten something really important: I was supposed to be in a cab on the way to the fucking airport. I started making frantic phone calls, but there was barely any cell service that deep in the Hollywood Hills. Then it dawned on me that even if I got a cab right then, there was no way to make my flight. I ran outside and down the hill to find better cell reception and called our tour manager, Jeff. He didn't answer, so I left a message explaining that I was going to miss my flight, which meant I was going to miss the show. "Jeff, you need to cancel the show and get it moved to another day," I said in a panic. "Also, I need a new flight home now, too. Bye." I walked back to the party, relieved that I had gotten it all sorted out, so I could continue with my night.

The four of us stayed in that back bedroom till the sun came up and then Paris and I crashed in the bed. Well, we tried. We were so wired from blow that we couldn't sleep. Luckily, Greig Nori had taught the band a "clever" trick: take a Xanax to come down from blow. When he recommended it to us, I pointed out that it was really bad to take downers with uppers. Isn't that what killed Elvis? He confidently (and incorrectly) replied, "Yes and no. Xanax is one of the only ones that's okay, everything else is bad." I thought, *What an amazing trick! Thanks, Greig!* To be clear, this is terrible advice. Xanax and cocaine can kill you. Still, Paris and I took some Xanax as the sun came up, then didn't wake up until 7 p.m., over twelve hours after my missed flight.

As we drove back to Paris's house and back into cell range, my phone starting blowing up with voicemails. I started listening to them, but as they got angrier and angrier, I had to stop. Turns out that thanks to the bad cell reception, the message I'd left for our tour manager was just broken up gibberish and he couldn't understand any of it. No one knew I wasn't going to make the show and no one believed I would fuck up so badly as to miss it entirely. The amphitheater was sold out, the fans were packed in, the opening band played, and then it was time for Sum 41 to go on. The whole band was waiting at the side of the stage, guitars on and ready to go. They were convinced it was some elaborate prank, that I was going to surprise them at the last second, say "HAHA! GOTCHA!" and play the set for the sold-out crowd. Nope. I wasn't even in the country. I was conked out in a Xanax coma next to Paris Hilton in some random person's house in the Hollywood Hills after partying with rock stars all night. When it became clear that this wasn't an elaborate prank and I really wasn't showing up, the venue announced that the show was canceled. Understandably, the crowd started booing and throwing whatever they had at the stage. The next day, the front page of the local newspaper was emblazoned with the headline: "BOO! SUM NO SHOW!"

It was really bad and I knew it. I always took the band seriously. We had obviously partied in the past, but this was not like me. I loved my job and I didn't want to fuck it up. Stevo was the most pissed about it and rightly so. They were convinced it was some elaborate prank, that I was going to surprise them at the last second, say "HAHA! GOTCHA!," and play the set for the sold-out crowd. Nope. I wasn't even in the country. I was conked out in a Xanax coma next to Paris Hilton in some random person's house in Hollywood. This was a new low and it was all on me. Dating Paris was a lot of fun, but I knew that this short, wild ride needed to come to an end.

Near the end of our time together, Paris heard rumors that her ex was going to release a sex tape of her. She was doing everything she could to stop it from coming out, but six or seven months after we broke up, the shit hit the fan. We had stayed in touch after we split, and after the tape came out, I reached out. We had some sad conversations and I listened to her cry about having to tell her parents about it. She's a smart person, though, and it was great seeing how she was able to turn that invasion of privacy into something that worked for her in the long run. Her advocacy is admirable, too. She definitely knew how to be the Mac. And most importantly how to stay the Mac.

AVRIL, CHUCK, THE CONGO, AND L.A.

The first time I ever heard the name Avril Lavigne was in 2001 when I got a call from her manager asking me if I knew any musicians from Ajax who looked like us, played like us, and wanted to be in her band. I did actually. I suggested Matt Brann, one of our best friends from childhood, who had been the drummer in Cone's original band. I also recommended Mark Spicoluk, who had been through Sum 41's revolving door of bass players. They both got the gig, along with a few other guys we knew.

Even before Avril and I met, people would tell me that she and I would make the perfect couple. Turns out, they were right, at least for a time. We first met in Vancouver in 2002, on the last night of the *All Killer No Filler* tour, while she was rehearsing with her new band ahead of the release of her first record. Although it took years for anything to happen between us, there was a spark from the second we laid eyes on each other. Needless to say, we hit it off. Since our friends were now part of her band, we all hung out and partied together, and she played me the singles she would be releasing soon. From the moment I heard her voice on "Complicated," I was blown away. That song was a smash hit right from the first hook. As for "Sk8r Boi," in all honesty, I hated it when I first heard it. It just wasn't for me, but then she played me "I'm With You," and I knew she was going to be a massive star. "Get ready, because this is going to be so fucking big," I told her. "You're probably going to sell five or six million albums." Fuck was I wrong! It sold three times that, and by the next year she was the biggest new artist on the planet. After that night in Vancouver, we went our separate ways, but watched each other's career from afar, bumping into each other occasionally as we toured.

We didn't really reconnect until we both happened to be off the road at the same time near the end of 2003. She had just finished her second record, and I was writing new songs for what would eventually be the *Chuck* album. Avril had bought a townhouse in Toronto, just two doors down from Greig Nori and not too far from my place. She hosted a New Year's Eve party, and Stevo, Cone, Greig, and I all attended. At the time, Avril was dating her guitar player, but the attraction between us was building. Soon after the new year began, we started hanging out more and more, and by my twenty-fourth birthday that March, we were officially dating and I was practically living at her house. I would spend all day working out of my home studio and then head to her place for the night. It was tricky with Greig living more or less next door, though. If he found out about us, I knew he would blow a fucking gasket. To avoid a confrontation, I always had to sneak in and out of her place, but I could never tell her why I was doing that. She thought it was so odd that I had to check and see if he was out front before I got in the car, but I didn't know how to explain my situation with Greig. I still didn't know her that well and wasn't about to tell her my deepest, darkest secret or lay out all that I had been through with him over the past few years. My relationship with Greig was extremely complicated, humiliating, and embarrassing. Instead of telling her the truth, I played it off like "If Greig knew I was hanging out with you, he would be pissed that I'm not working on the record."

The truth was, Greig and I were at our worst at this point. If we spoke at all, we argued or he made me feel like shit, so I avoided him as much as possible. And I especially avoided him coming out of Avril's house in the morning, because I had been in this situation years before and I was still scarred by his reaction. At a party, I had been hanging out and just talking with the singer Esthero, when Greig burst in through the bedroom door, freaking out and yelling at us. I didn't know if he was jealous of her or of me, but his reaction was disturbing and horrifying and I didn't want anything like that to happen with Avril.

For whatever reason, Greig had taken an instant dislike to Avril. In hindsight, I think it was because he knew it wouldn't be long before we hooked up, and he was scared both of losing me to her and because he knew it would be a massive story for the press. He had done the same thing when I was hanging out with Paris, saying I was losing cred and tarnishing the Sum 41 name and telling me that everyone was laughing at me behind my back. Greig was also very good at pitting the band against me, telling them that I was "going Hollywood" and ruining the band's reputation.

I knew his game, but the rest of the band hadn't seen his dark side yet. And the truth was, I wasn't ready or willing to go to the guys and say, "Hey, Greig is an evil motherfucker who has been stealing half of my songwriting royalties, and also groomed and pressured me from a young age to be in a sexual relationship with him." I knew Greig was trying to make my life miserable and turn the band against me and against any future relationship I wanted to be in, but I couldn't say this because I didn't even understand it that clearly yet. I always just buried all the bullshit and tried to stay focused on the most important thing to me, which was Sum 41. But because they didn't know the truth about Greig, he was able to manipulate the band, planting seeds against first Paris and then Avril, and I watched it all unfold in real time. The band was against Avril before they even knew her.

It was hard for me to keep my relationship with Avril a secret from everyone. She thought it was fun and exciting to sneak around, but I thought it was torture. I had fallen madly in love with someone for the first time and I wanted to freely express it. I had been so focused on making Sum 41 a success that I willingly sacrificed everything else, so I hadn't been in a serious relationship since Crazy Amanda Bunk Face. Being with Avril

The Whibleys in 1966, right after moving to Canada. My grandparents are in the top row, and my mom, aunts, and uncle are also here. My grandfather still says that's the best car he's ever owned. Papa (John), Nan (Mary), Uncle Chris, Aunt Dylis, Mum (Michelle), and Aunt Caroline.

I was about two years old and my mum would've been eighteen. This is when we still lived at my grandparents' house. I remember that house very well. My nan always had a garden, and I remember she had a big strawberry bush in the back that I would go in and pick the best ones for her to bake with. Nan also had an aggressive cat that didn't like me and often attacked me around this time. I don't like cats now.

Me at age three on the first-floor balcony at our Tuxedo Court apartment. This was my mum and B.D.'s first apartment. My mum was nineteen years old when we moved here. I have very happy memories as a child, but the thing I remember most about this building complex was the constant smell of urine in the hallways. I never knew where it came from.

Out of all the jobs I had in my youth, being a clown on the side of the road holding a sign for roses was probably the worst. This was 1993, and I was thirteen years old. I made five bucks an hour while people drove by, yelled insults at me, and gave me the finger.

Fishing off the dock when I lived at the Indian River Lodge in 1990. I couldn't wait to get up early and try to go catch a few fish before I went to school. There wasn't much other than sunfish and some perch off the dock, though. We took the boat out deeper into the lake for the bigger fish like bass and trout.

My great memories of my childhood are times like these: my mum and me as a little team. Once my stepdad B.D. was out of the picture, we just had fun together, watching movies and eating junk food for dinner. Growing up, you always think your parents look old, so it's crazy to look back these and see how young my mum really was raising a child on her own.

Early 1998, somewhere outside of Toronto, opening for Treble Charger. We had finally convinced Dave to come and play with us. This show was a sort of "testing the waters" for Dave. I had been pressuring him to join our band for a while now, and I thought if he played a show with us, he might see how good it could be. This show was soon after we had returned from our failed New York trip, shopping our three-song demo to record companies. Dave is playing a heinous, weirdly shaped Jackson flying V. It sounded like shit and couldn't stay in tune. He ditched it soon after he officially joined the band.

We always had a video camera with us in the early days. Sometimes we borrowed one from family and friends. I believe we rented this one to document our early demo session at Metalworks Studios in 1999. We never spoke about it, but we all instinctively knew that one of us should be filming at all times.

My pin-striped "Mafia suit" I used to wear to school and around Ajax when I was fifteen to sixteen years old. People already thought I dressed strange at school, it didn't bother me to show up to class and have everyone look at me. In fact, I kind of preferred it.

My job at the gas station in Ajax. I worked there for a few months when I was fifteen. My mum was always worried I was going to be robbed during the night shifts because of my age. I felt like an adult at this point in my life, but looking back at the photo, I clearly see she had reason to be worried. I often brought my guitar and wrote songs all night between customers.

Me and Greig Nori in January 1998 recording a three-song demo at Twitch's house to try to get us a record deal on our trip to New York the following week. This is the recording equipment I kept on using in my bedroom for the next year and a half to record all my own personal demos for early *Half Hour of Power* and *All Killer No Filler* ideas. This particular demo tape did not sound very good or get us a record deal, but it was fun taking our first shot.

July 27, 1996: the day that started it all for Sum 41. My stepdad drove Stevo, Gary, Jon Marshall, and me to the Warped Tour that morning. We got there at 11 a.m. and stayed for the entire day. We showed up as the band Kaspir and left as a new unnamed punk rock band, hoping to one day play with the bands we saw that day, NOFX and Pennywise.

Top row: Twitch (bass), Dave (guitar), Stevo (drums), and Ed Krautner (engineer). Bottom row: Marc Costanzo (producer) and me. We had just finished recording our first demo in professional studio called Metalworks Studios. That studio would become our home for the few years of demos and first three albums. Right before this picture was taken Marc looked at me and said, "Staring contest. Go." It caught me off guard and I was trying my best not to laugh. Soon after this recording I signed a publishing deal with EMI Music Publishing.

My very first band, Eternal Death. Me (guitar), Jay Thompson (drums), and Steve Payne (vocals) playing a loud mess of thrash grunge music in my basement at the Monarch Mews townhouse. The unfinished basement was always cold and damp but we didn't care. We had a place to jam! Steve is singing into one side of a pair of small headphones taped to a rusted tent pole for a mic stand plugged into an old stereo amplifier.

Cone's first show with us in 1999 was in a tiny bar in a small town outside of Toronto called Bolton. There were only about fifteen people in the audience and half of them were part of the other bands that were on the bill. Cone was technically just filling in for us because we had no bass player at the time and needed to get through a few shows. A few shows turned into more and more throughout the rest of the year, and by the fall he became our permanent bass player.

early days of Sum 41, 1996. Me, Stevo, and Jon Marshall outside the back of the Chameleon Cafe before a Sum 41 show there that night. The entire back wall was covered in graffiti by a local artist that I don't know the name of. This building stood out to anyone passing by because it was the only cool looking building near the train tracks.

This is us loading our gear in for a show in some small town outside of Toronto in 1999. I can see that Dave has one of our mini trampolines in his hands and Stevo is holding a good old Canadian PC Cola. We used to drink ten of those a day back then. One of my favorite things to do in high school was drink half of one before bed, leave it on the table, and chug the rest of it warm first thing in the morning when I woke up. Ah, youth.

The first time we ever got to play a show on the Warped Tour was in the summer of 1999. In a bid to impress us as an unsigned band, the Canadian indie label Aquarius Records pulled some strings and got us in the Montreal and Toronto shows on the side stage. Needless to say, we were impressed and ecstatic that we finally got to be a part of the tour of our dreams. A few months later, we would make sure that Aquarius was a part of our record deal in Canada when we eventually signed to Island Def Jam.

Walking the streets of Toronto in 1999, taking photos and shooting random footage for our Electronic Press Kit to sent out to record companies. This was taken right before we did a choreographed dance for unsuspecting patrons in front of giant movie theater called Colossus.

Kaspir show at a club called the Eclipse in 1995. One year later, I would see Treble Charger play on this very stage and meet Greig Nori for the first time. The piece of paper taped to my mic stand was our setlist. I don't remember what most of the songs were called, but one was "Wet Cow." The girl with the dark curly hair is Sofia Makrenos, the girl who turned me on to bands such as NOFX, Pennywise, and the like. My guitar wasn't working that night, so I had to borrow one from the singer of another band on the bill named Clap Trap.

The end our first long tour, dubbed the Beast in the East Tour, in summer 1998. This is our van after it had been fixed up post–car accident in St. John, New Brunswick. The mechanics initially told us the van was totaled. Since we were stuck out on the East Coast of Canada with all of our gear, Dave's dad opted to pay for a new rear axle so we could make the twenty-two-hour drive back home. We continued to tour with that van for another year. It had no air conditioning and the heat didn't work. The floor was falling apart due to rust and you could see the road while we drove. But still, it was our home for many years.

Me and Dave catching a little bit of sleep on our way to a show somewhere outside of Toronto. We rarely played in the city in these days and usually had shows out in the suburbs two to five hours away. This was before we had built an actual bed frame in the back that would allow us to sleep above our gear. Here, we'd just thrown a mattress on top of our equipment. We were either so tired from staying up late partying the night before or coming home really late after a show.

Stevo and me in the old blue Econoline, driving to a show in 1997.

It was very typical for our van to break down. This is yet another time we needed to get a jump from someone. Twitch grew up fixing cars and was always the designated mechanic whenever something went wrong. This would've been in the summer of 1998, somewhere outside of Toronto.

In 2001, once "Fat Lip" and "In Too Deep" had become worldwide successes, our schedules filled up exponentially. We were getting booked for multiple appearances in a day, and it was physically impossible to get from A to B without taking a private jet or helicopters. This was the first time we ever got our own private jet. Dave, Cone, and I were twenty-one, and Stevo was still twenty years old. We were in Europe somewhere and had to get to the UK for a TV appearance. Most likely *Top of the Pops*, which we used to perform on a lot back then. If you can't tell by the look on my face, I was extremely excited. We'd made it!

Myself, Stevo, Cone, and Dave signing our record deal at 360 Restaurant at the top of the CN Tower in December 1999. We got hammered on cosmopolitans, and Stevo was eventually cut off by the waiter for being too drunk. We all went out at strip club afterwards, minus Stevo who was still underage and drunk as hell.

This was taken in very happy times, sometime in 2006 after Avril and I were married. We had fully settled into life at the Mulholland house in Los Angeles and were loving spending that year off together.

his would've been in 2005. Avril and I
ere constantly taking pictures of ourselves
hen we were together. This was taken
mewhere on her tour, I believe.

When I proposed to Avril in Venice, Italy, we spent a couple of days sightseeing, taking
gondolas and boats around to private lunches and dinners. This photo was taken on our
penthouse balcony suite in the afternoon. Later that night, after dinner, I surprised her with
a ring on that same balcony.

Although we were young and wild and we
partied a lot, Paris and I also had normal
moments. It's widely known that Paris
loves animals. I like this candid photo
because you can see the sweet, human
side of her that people don't get to see
that often.

Reaction Studios in Toronto, 2004, recording the guitars and bass for the yet untitled *Chuck* album. The working title we were using was at the time was "Hot Blonde Shooter Sandwich." Dave is playing my 1968 Fender Telecaster. Behind us is the wall of different amps we used on the recording. They were all plugged in and ready to be patched in at any time.

This was one of our first moments of feeling "safe" on the U.N. compound after we got out of the armored tanks. Chuck came up behind me and gave me a big hug, letting me know the worst was over. At least, we thought so. While we were on the compound, the fighting was still only a few hundred feet down the road, and there were stray bullets coming through the camp occasionally. You could hear the whistle of them as they flew by or when they hit a tree close by. We had to be evacuated to the airstrip a day later through the city and the fighting. None of it was safe, and I didn't feel relaxed until we touched back down in the United States.

Chuck Pelletier and the band. Soon after this, we were brought by armored tanks to the U.N. compound. All of us are seemingly shell-shocked while Chuck is cool as a cucumber, almost looking like he just had a good time.

Lying in the hospital bed in 2014, completely sedated. You can see all the bruises on my arms from where I had pulled out all of my IVs when I woke up in a panic in the middle of the night not knowing where I was. I was like this for over a week before I came to and had no idea what had happened to me.

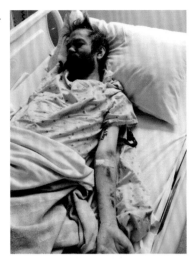

I had been in a hospital bed hooked up to IVs and machines for four weeks. I was getting close to being released from the hospital. The doctors had said I should do a walking test to see how bad the muscle atrophy was. I couldn't make it one step. My legs were too weak and the pain in my feet from nerve damage was too much to bear. I desperately wanted to see the sun, so my mum and Ari wheeled me outside for about twenty minutes of air on a private balcony at Cedars Sinai. I felt so humiliated, ashamed, and sad as I got outside. Reflecting on the gravity of what I had done to myself, I watched the sunset thinking, *I almost lost the chance to witness something as simple as a sunset ever again.*

This is me sitting in my backyard soon after I was released from the hospital. I look terribly strange, but I felt so happy to be out of the hospital bed, not hooked up to all the wires and getting constant needles in my arms every day anymore. I still couldn't walk whatsoever and had to be helped wherever I went. But I was happy to be alive and spent most of the days sitting in the sun, trying to figure out how I was going to put the pieces of my life back together, one step at a time.

May 2019. Ari and I had been through hell and back in our personal lives. We had also been trying for a few years to have a baby, which was proving very difficult for us. On this trip to New York, we sat talked about our future and how nothing was going to change the fact that we loved each other and wanted to be together forever. With or without a baby, we knew we were meant for each other. We walked around the city every day for a week and would end our nights together out here on the balcony, reflecting on what we'd been through and where our life was headed. We knew as long as we had each other we would be happy.

Ari took this photo in our backyard in Los Angeles in 2019. We were on totally solid ground by this point in our lives. The band was doing well. Our relationship was strong. We felt like we'd come through the other side and were better for everything we'd gone through. Now we were just enjoying life sober, happy, and healthy.

After we had Lydon, I really wanted to have a girl. We were lucky enough to be blessed with Quentin Arlo. This is me, holding my baby girl at three months old. She has a smile that lights up every room she's in. Strangers can't get enough of her. At one year old, she's the star of the show everywhere we take her.

From the moment he was born, Lydon has been by my side in the studio. He's been obsessed with music since before he could talk. Ari and I always said that we don't care if our kids want to play music; we just hope they like it, because they're going to be surrounded by it their whole lives. So far, both of our kids seem to have the music gene deep in their souls.

Me with my first guitar in the kitchen of the Monarch Mews townhouse. My uncle Tim bought this for me to practice. This guitar was hard to play and you really had to fight with it. To learn how to play guitar on this particular acoustic, you needed to be determined to practice because it was not a fun guitar to play whatsoever. I played that guitar for about a year before I moved on to an electric. I still have that old El Degas guitar to this day.

made my life feel complete at that time. Even as great as I was feeling inside, I was still terrified of being ostracized by my best friends and worried about my manager mentally torturing me. On top of that, I was still having strange aftereffects from the Mystic Blue Powder that were not helping my mental state, either. Ever since that night I would get a feeling in my brain like I was going crazy or on the edge of losing control. I would become dizzy, tight chested, and start breathing shallowly, and when I closed my eyes, I would see the images of snakes and monsters from that night in Tokyo. It felt like I was having a lucid nightmare. And it seemed to be getting worse. I was convinced my brain was completely fucked and realized I had to see a doctor. Livia Tortella was head of marketing at Island Def Jam, but served as a sort of "Band Mum" for us, so I asked her if she knew any doctors that dealt with idiots who had permanently fucked up their brains from drugs. She did. The doctor told me that what I was describing were anxiety and panic attacks. Turns out that powerful hallucinogens can open up a door to anxiety and panic disorder. "Most people with the disorder experience their first panic attacks around their early twenties and it can come out of nowhere," the doctor said. He recommended I talk to a therapist to help. Once I started talking to the therapist, I realized not only that I had not permanently destroyed my brain from drugs, but that anxiety and panic were manageable. I started taking the steps that would eventually make it easier for me to handle. With her help, I also felt less frightened of Greig and the band finding out about Avril. Being able to finally talk to someone openly about my life and all its issues took a huge weight off my shoulders.

Somehow through all the good times with Avril and the mental fuckery with Greig, I successfully wrote the mandatory twelve songs we needed for the next album. We were heading to L.A. to start recording it, and luckily for me, Avril also had to be in L.A. to do some promo work. Not that anyone knew we were together yet.

Sum 41 was spending two weeks at Sound City Studios in the Valley to record the drum tracks for the album, but right on day one, Stevo was a disaster from staying up partying instead of sleeping. I don't even know how the drums ended up getting recorded, because after a couple of days of barely getting through a song, Stevo was so frustrated and angry that he kicked us out of the studio. Since the end of the last tour, he and Greig had been partying way too hard, staying up all night, drinking and doing blow. When a tour ends, I hole up to write songs for the next record, but the rest of the band guys have time off, and Stevo frequently spent it partying. I never drank during the writing process, because it always made things much harder. Plus, I'd given up drugs for good at that point. I was doing a lot of work trying to get my brain back to normal and drugs seemed counterproductive. So while Stevo worked through recording his drums, which in the end sounded great, I just hung around my hotel, working on lyrics in the day and spending as much time with Avril as possible at night.

Soon we were headed back home to Toronto to continue recording. We laid down all the bass and guitars at Reaction Studios in Toronto. We were making our heaviest record to date, but it also had the most slow songs we'd ever put on an album. Dave and I decided to switch it up and lean into our strengths when it came to putting down guitars. Brownsound had become an incredible metal guitar player and was writing all his own solos now. I didn't want to interfere and ruin it, so I would play all the rhythm guitars and stuff that added color and texture, and Dave would play all the leads and main riffs. There were some exceptions, of course, with Dave playing all the guitars on some songs like "The Bitter End," me playing all the guitar on "Pieces," and then some hybrids, like on "88," where I played the first half of the song and then Dave came in to play the metal section near the end. It was a cool change of pace for us. I loved recording this album together. Whenever the band was in a room together, we laughed the whole time. Even though his drums were done, Stevo was there this time, too. He didn't want to miss out on the fun, and besides, what else was he going to do? We were each other's only friends. While Greig was producing the album, along with our friend Matt Hyde, he would either not show up to the studio or show up late and then sit on the phone or his computer the whole time. Granted, he was still our manager and was doing work for the band, but he wasn't paying much attention to the recording. To prove he was still the producer, every so often he'd walk into the room, tell us to change this or that, and then he'd leave. Even though we'd make the change, Matt Hyde and I would look at each other afterwards, because it had sounded better before he made us change it.

When it came time to record my vocals, things became difficult, because it was just Greig and me in the studio and he was in full producer mode and not in a good way. After we had been repeatedly photographed together, Avril and I were no longer a secret, and ever since Greig found out, his attitude towards me had been worse than ever. As I tried to record my vocals, he was constantly belittling me and putting me down. I would record something, and he would stop the take and say, "You call that being a professional singer?" Worse, he would stop the song and, not saying anything at all, just start the song over from the beginning, because it was apparently so bad he had no words.

I would scream my fucking guts out on songs like "I'm Not the One" and "Open Your Eyes," directing all my rage and anger at him through the microphone. The whole thing was sad, too, because when we made our first demo seven years ago, he'd been amazing at making me feel confident, and now it had all come to this. In retrospect, the worst part was that the whole time, I was blaming myself and saying this was all my own fault. I felt like somehow I had caused all of this, maybe by leading him on when I was a teenager. I wondered, *Am I a bad person? Am I incapable of actual love? Do I really only care about myself like he's been saying? Should I have tried harder with him?* I pushed all of this aside because at the end of the day, we had a fucking record to make! *Only thing harder than being the Mac, is staying the Mac.* I told Greig that it might be better if I recorded my vocals on my own. He agreed, and I finished the album just recording myself. I liked this method so much that to this day, I still record my vocals by myself.

Both Avril and I had new records that were soon to be released, but we had a little time off and were enjoying the calm before the storm. For the past year, the band had been talking to the charity organization called War Child, who work to protect, support, and educate children displaced by war. Sum 41 met with their Canadian branch to discuss ways we could support their important work. We wanted to be hands-on and do real work on the ground. They were open to that and gave us a list of countries where they were currently active. We settled on doing something in the Democratic Republic of Congo, where two decades of war had displaced millions and put millions of children at risk of starvation. This cause seemed like the perfect fit for us. There were children in need and in danger, and because much of the fighting was over rare minerals used to make cell phones and computers, it was the Western appetite for technology that was responsible. We decided to visit, meet the children, and make a documentary to raise global awareness about the causes and effects of the war. At the time, there had been a ceasefire for a full year and the U.N. was there, so the people at War Child felt it was safe enough for us to go. We planned a two-week trip for late May in 2004 to interview the survivors, former soldiers, victims of sexual violence, and the volunteer peacekeepers, and put it all on film to get the word out.

A small prop plane dropped us off on a dirt runway in Bukavu, a city on the banks of Lake Kivu. The natural beauty was incredible; from the sky, we saw nothing but miles of beautiful native forest and rivers, but that feeling of peaceful tranquility quickly dissipated on the ground. As we drove into town, we passed under an archway over the road with a sign that said "Bukavu, the Tourist Capital of Congo." It was riddled with bullet holes. It seemed clear that even though there was a ceasefire, the Congo was still a very dangerous place. We met more representatives from War Child at the hotel that served as our home base and were briefed on the various places we would see over the next two weeks. They were very clear that these kids, who were between the ages of four and seventeen, had been through hell. Most of them had lost their parents because when opposition forces came to a village, they killed the adult men, raped and then killed the adult women, and took all of the young boys and girls as captives and forced them into mining and sex slavery. Despite the unfathomable trauma they had endured, somehow each of the children we met had retained the innocence of being a child. It was incredibly humbling to witness and a huge testament to the work that War Child was doing.

On the tenth day of our two-week stay, the yearlong ceasefire abruptly ended, pretty much right outside our door. It was the evening when we heard the gunfire start. Just a few shots, then a few more, then an unmistakable barrage. On one side of the hotel compound were the rebel forces, and on the other, a battalion of the DRC national army. They exchanged gunfire and mortars and launched rocket-propelled grenades at each other, and there we were, stuck in the middle. Most of the structures in the hotel were plaster and wood, and bullets could easily whiz through them. An explosive would level one of the bungalows, no problem. We were exposed and trapped and terrified. We didn't know what to do, so we got down on the ground like everyone else and crawled away from the windows.

That first evening, the fighting lasted for about an hour and then stopped. That is when a few officials from the U.N. camp nearby came and told us everything was going to be all right. They confidently told us it was just a skirmish and wouldn't continue, so we decided to stay the full duration of our original trip. They left and we never saw them again to tell them how very wrong they were. During the next three days, our hotel compound continued to be hit with stray bullets, misguided mortars, and RPGs. The shooting would go on for an hour or so at a time, then die down for a few hours. It would get eerily quiet and peaceful and we would hope maybe it was over for good, before it suddenly started up again. Since the hotel was mostly a collection of small stand-alone, one-room cabins, we had to keep running to different rooms to escape the fighting. It seemed that every time the fighting resumed, it was right beside us, and we were constantly running to find new places to hide. We'd camp out in a room and huddle in the bathroom, in the hopes that the tub was bulletproof. Eventually we all gathered in the only brick building on the compound, because it offered the best protection. I know at some point the fighting died down enough that we got food from the kitchen, but I don't remember eating anything or sleeping more than a few minutes for the three days we were trapped there.

There are two reasons we got out alive. The first is that a high-ranking U.S. ambassador happened to be visiting that day and was one of the forty people trapped with us. He was important enough that the U.N. had to evacuate him, and they needed to take the rest of us, too. The second, and most important, reason we made it out alive is because of Charles Pelletier, Chuck to his friends. He was a former soldier and a volunteer U.N. peacekeeper who happened to be at the hotel when the fighting broke out. We had met him earlier in our stay and had chatted a while because Chuck happened to be Canadian. He had a shaved head, goatee, and some tattoos, and was really nice (*go figure, eh?*).

Nice Guy Chuck disappeared once shots were fired, transforming so completely that at first I didn't realize he was even the same guy. He was now in fatigues and combat boots, wearing Kevlar body armor, a blue U.N. helmet, and carrying a wooden club. He also had a stubby cigar in his mouth, which really completed the look. Chuck was highly trained, uncannily calm, and immediately took control of the situation. He divided us into numbered groups and ferried us from one bungalow to another to keep us as far as possible from the gunfire. When there was a pause in the fighting, he would leave the hotel and go down the road to assess the crisis and then decide his next move to best protect us. Every time he left and the gunfire resumed, I thought we'd never see him again, but he was trained for this and, to be honest, I think he kind of enjoyed it. He'd come running in telling us to get in our assigned groups, directing us to where we'd move next. When he shouted our numbers, we'd run to the next building and dive to the ground, hoping the rest of the group would make it okay. Nobody questioned him, because it was clear that Chuck was the only one with any clue of how to make it out of a hot zone alive.

Since Chuck was part of the U.N. peacekeeping force, he was able to arrange our exodus. Each time he rejoined us, he'd have more information and bits of a plan that eventually materialized into a convoy of several armored tanks to drive us to the relative safety of a nearby U.N. refugee camp. The only problem was that the tanks couldn't get into the compound, so to get into them we would need to run from the hotel into the street where the fighting was thickest. It was time to go. The tanks were about a hundred yards away, but the distance was daunting. I felt hopeless. We'd spent ten days interviewing former child soldiers, U.N. peacekeepers, and people all too familiar with how war was conducted. We knew what the insurrectionists did to people, and I was convinced that I was going to die there. I was way too young for my story to end, but was completely sure that in a few hours it would.

After two days of no sleep and little food, running a hundred yards to the tanks felt like the last miles of a marathon. My legs were heavy as lead and I didn't think I would make it. I remember holding the doorframe of the hotel looking at the line of tanks and feeling like they were a mile away. But the tanks were freedom, and all I had to do was get to them as fast as possible with my group, which included Cone, while Dave and Steve were in another one. Chuck called my group's number and we took off running. I was fighting off the biggest panic attack of my life and Cone was in tears as we ran as fast as we could, not *as if* our lives depended on it, but *because* our lives depended on it. We finally made it to the tank, the finish line, to the light at the end of this hell, and . . . nothing happened. The door was locked! I expected to jump in like a POW being liberated by Rambo, but we had to just stand there waiting, expecting gunfire to take us out at any second. My panic attack grew to a boiling point. I started aggressively banging on the sides of the tank and twisting a random latch hoping something would open. Finally, there was a loud "pffft" from the airlock, the rear hatch opened, and they let us in. It was a minute that passed like an hour.

The journey didn't end there. The U.N. compound was close enough that we had been walking there throughout our stay, to do interviews. Now it was inaccessible without an armored vehicle. Our tank rolled in and our group of forty joined about fifteen hundred other people displaced by the fighting. We pulled up to a patch of grass, feeling lucky to be alive, but uncertain of what was next. When we regrouped at the U.N. compound, we learned that after we left, the rebel soldiers had broken into a room at the other end of the hotel, and shot a woman who worked for War Child in the leg and raped her.

It took us another day and a half to make contact with the pilot who had dropped us off, because he wasn't scheduled to come back for us until the end of our trip. Rescheduling our flight was the least of our problems, though, because the airstrip was over an hour away, deep in territory now held by the rebels. There were a number of people who needed to get to the airstrip, so our tour manager worked with the U.N. to make arrangements. At first we were told our immediate group—the band and the film crew—would be flown to the airstrip in a U.N. helicopter. Twelve hours later the helicopter was swapped for an armored car, then an armored SUV with bulletproof glass. Twelve hours after that, the SUV was swapped for a bus that would transport us and twenty-five other people. It was not an armored bus, it was the U.N.'s version of a party bus: long, slow-moving, and all windows. This was to be our ride through the thickest zone of conflict. I hadn't relaxed much in the U.N. camp, but this sent my fear reflex off the chart.

Before we pulled out of camp, a U.N. staffer told us to duck down in our seats for the entire ride. Bags were to be put next to the window to offer some protection in case stray bullets flew into the bus. "Keep your bags up as protection because if the glass is hit with a bullet it will shatter and the glass shards could blind you," the staffer said. *Sure, the glass could blind you,* I thought, *but what about the bullets?!* I was sure this was how we would go. We'd made it through all the shit, but we would be killed on the way to the fucking airport. On the ride we heard shots and lots of shouting, but I saw nothing because I didn't dare look up.

The scene at the airstrip was straight out of a movie where there's been a coup and people are trying to escape. The rebel militia was in fatigues and armed with AK-47s. They were angry, screaming, and ready to fucking kill. It didn't look like anyone was moving in or out of the place. The DRC is the largest French-speaking country in the world, so the rebels were shouting in French, and since everyone in our band is Canadian, a few of us were able to translate. (Not me, though, because out of rebellion and hatred for school, I had refused to learn the language.) My bandmates confirmed what I already thought: The guys were fucking pissed and didn't want to let us out. I don't know what happened next, because I returned to staring at my feet, hoping that I wouldn't be systematically killed on a U.N. party bus parked at a dirt airstrip in the middle of a jungle. I'm not sure how long we stayed there, but we ended up getting out, probably because somebody paid off the rebels. The next thing I remember is getting on that same prop plane to Uganda, leaning against the window, shaking from head to toe. My hands were trembling so much I couldn't hold anything. Chuck warned us that we would all be leaving with PTSD, but I couldn't even grasp that concept, let alone appreciate that it was happening to me. Still, I knew I was in severe shock when I looked at my limbs quivering as if they belonged to someone else.

In Uganda, we regrouped for a day or two as we arranged flights home. It was safer there, and we stayed at a Marriott or a Radisson, someplace with a pool. We decided to spend the day like we were taking a day off on tour. We would mellow out by the pool, have some drinks, and let ourselves return to normal. That proved to be impossible. We had all been friends for so long and never lacked for things to say, but the quiet that afternoon was painful. There was nothing we could do, no joke we could make, to lighten the mood. The hotel had hosted a party the night before, and when a few leftover balloons floated into a fence and popped, all of us lost our shit. We threw our drinks and ran, thinking it was gunfire, thinking we were back in danger.

All I wanted to do was see Avril. When we were finally able to book flights, I bought a ticket to New York City to meet up with her. I boarded a plane in Uganda to take me to Heathrow, where I'd have an hour to catch my connecting flight. Once we landed, I realized I only had thirty minutes to make my connection and I was nowhere near my gate. When I thought I might not make the connection, I felt an intense terror. I ran as fast as I could, dragging my rolling bag, bumping into people, thrashing through the airport as if my life depended on it. Completely out of breath and almost hyperventilating, I got to the gate as the flight was doing its final boarding. I ran onto the plane, stowed my bag, and took my seat. And that was when a feeling crashed over me that was unlike anything I'd ever experienced. It was nausea, shock, and elation all at once; an overwhelming heightening of my senses. I started crying, weeping in my seat, and then I began to feel incredibly sick. As people were buckling their seatbelts, I ran to the bathroom and projectile vomited, completely missing the toilet. I was shaking, crying hysterically, and gasping for breath. I was finally in a safe place and my body was finally physically reacting to all that I'd been through, which is how PTSD works. I'd never projectile vomited before and I've never done it again, even at the deepest depths of my drinking. I'm thankful for that, because wiping up that bathroom is definitely not on the list of cool shit I've done in my life.

PTSD AND THE NEVER-ENDING
SUNSHINE

*N*one of us were the same after that trip and how could we be? During the worst moments trapped in the hotel, when Chuck was our only lifeline, I told him that if he saved our lives we'd name our third album after him. We lived, so we kept our promise, and in October 2004, *Chuck* was released. The man himself came to a bunch of our shows, and when the album went platinum we gave Chuck a commemorative plaque on stage in front of a sold-out crowd.

The documentary of our experience was released by War Child on DVD in November 2005 and it aired on MTV worldwide. At the time MTV was in more homes around the planet than CNN, so we had high hopes that we would get the message out about what was happening in the DRC. We really thought it would cause the world to take action, but it came out, people saw it, nobody cared, and it faded away. We continued to do everything we could to spread the word. For the next two years, all of us brought the experience up in interviews, but still, nothing happened. I was and still am really disappointed about the entire thing, but it was a life lesson. As confused as I was that the documentary didn't make an immediate impact on the world, someone wisely told me, "At your age you're old enough to want to change the world and young enough to think you can do it."

Our journey and the lessons learned had a profound effect on us. Not only because of what we witnessed and all of the people we met, not only because we were nearly killed, but because the experience was an undeniable turning point for the four of us. We never spoke about PTSD or the trauma we brought home, but if you look at what came next, it is clear that each of us dealt with it in very different ways and was about to go through big changes personally and professionally.

By the time we got back to Toronto, Island Def Jam was going through major personnel changes, which meant most of the core team that had signed us and had been with us since the beginning were now either gone or leaving. It was upsetting because we had all taken a chance on each other and built something successful together and in the process had become like a family. The worst thing to happen to a band or artist putting out a new album is to have a team that doesn't care about the artist, doesn't understand the artist, or is simply shuffling in and out at the label. And that's exactly what happened throughout the *Chuck* album cycle. Our record was done, mixed and mastered and ready for release, with the song "No Reason" slated as the first single. Everyone had felt strongly about that song, until the new boss took over the company.

When Island Def Jam's people at the time heard the album, they decided that not only was "No Reason" not a good first single, but, in fact, they didn't hear anything that could be a single at all. I had to write a new song immediately. I was devastated. Not only was I creatively tapped out after writing those twelve songs, but I had only been home from the Congo for a week and was still shellshocked. Unfortunately, I had no options. They weren't going to release the record unless I wrote a new "hit song" and fast. Looking back now, I can see it for what it was. The IDJ team came into the process when our album was already finished. They needed us to have a new song that was written on their watch, so they could take some credit for the success. I hate it when I hear people say "oh to be young again." I say fuck that, I wish I had been older and wiser in those days, because everything is so obvious now!

I was still reeling from the trauma of the events we had just lived through, but I had a job to do, so I picked up my guitar and quickly wrote the bulk of "We're All to Blame." I wanted the song to have the feeling of what we'd just gone through in the Congo, calm one second, crazy and intense the next. Since we needed this song done ASAP, and I was struggling with the verse and bridge sections, Greig suggested bringing in Ben Cook, the young singer of No Warning, the band he was working with. Ben had some great ideas, and we managed to get the song finished, recorded, and sent to the label for approval. L.A. Reid said he loved it and we had our first single. For the third time in a row, the last song I wrote for an album became the first single. (And another top ten!)

Avril and I had only been together a few months, but after my near-death experience in the Congo, we decided to officially move in together. We started looking in all the nicest neighborhoods of Toronto, but as hard as we looked, we never found anything that could compare to the beautiful old Spanish homes of L.A. that we both loved. There was no denying it, our hearts were in California.

The weekend of July 23, 2004, Avril and I moved into a big, beautiful seven-thousand-square-foot Spanish Mediterranean mansion at the top of Mulholland Drive, in a gated community overlooking the whole valley. When we first walked into the grand foyer with soaring high ceilings, we instantly felt that we had found the right home, without even seeing the rest of the house. By the time we made it to the backyard, the deal was done. The house was like a resort, surrounded by palm trees, bird of paradise plants, bamboo trees, and hidden flagstone walkways with fountains and flowers. It even had a basketball/tennis court. Since we both toured constantly, every time we came home now it would feel like we were on vacation.

Of course, I had bittersweet feelings. I was devastated leaving my mum and knew I would miss being able to see her as often as I'd like. Now that I was in my early twenties and was more stable, she didn't have to worry about my career or where my life was headed. Now we had a new kind of relationship where we could just enjoy each other's friendship. The same went for Kevin as well. We had both grown up a little and become close and respectful of each other. It was hard to leave them, and I could tell my mum was sad, too, even though she acted so happy for me. After all, her only child would now be twenty-five hundred miles away. Still, I needed a new chapter. Toronto had become too dark for me. I wanted to escape from Greig Nori, but he wasn't the only one I was happy to leave behind. Everyone I knew outside of the band was either a drug addict or a drug dealer. Plus, I felt unsafe and harassed everywhere I went, and now with all the extra attention on my relationship with Avril, it had gotten even worse. I wanted all of it out of my life.

We moved in on a Friday, and by Monday I was back on the road for a promotional tour pitched by MTV for the upcoming release of the *Chuck* album. It was called something like Fourteen Shows, Fourteen Cities in Fourteen Days Around the World with Sum 41. None of it made sense. Not the travel, the logistics, the name, or the cost. Still it went on sale and sold out. Then MTV bailed on the idea after they realized the final price tag, leaving us stuck with having to do the tour without them or the benefit of the TV promotion. It would be grueling to pull this off. We'd have to perform our show and then head straight to the airport, fly to the next city, trying to grab a few hours of sleep on the plane (or in the van or backstage), wake up, and get ready to do it all over again. Every day for two straight weeks. The last show was in Singapore, a performance that was filmed and aired on MTV the week of our album release. It now lives on YouTube.

From there we went straight to Japan to play the Summer Sonic festival. Avril and Sum 41 were actually on the same bill for the first time. It was an odd bill for her, because she was set to go on right after us and right before Green Day, sandwiched between two fast, hard-hitting rock bands. I was having major inner turmoil, because our objective was always to do the best show possible and make us a really tough act to follow. But now, my girlfriend, who I just fucking moved in with two weeks ago, was on stage right after me! The guys in the band weren't exactly fans of Avril, but even they recognized that I was in a tough spot. Stevo hesitantly asked me, "So, how are you gonna approach this one? Take it easy out there tonight?" I paused for a minute and went through all the different ways this could turn out. I knew I needed to follow what my heart was telling me to do, so I looked at Stevo and said, "Well, I'm afraid . . . we're going to have to blow her off the fucking stage!" Everyone burst out laughing and we all picked up our shots of vodka and toasted to the best show of our lives.

I felt guilty but figured, at the end of the day, we were both professionals and putting on the best possible show was our job. Even though we were all burnt out and exhausted from the fourteen-day around-the-world tour, the guys were energized. Yeah, I may have moved to L.A. and was now living with my famous girlfriend in a mansion in Beverly Hills, but I was still the same fucking guy I'd always been. Nothing comes between me and my music. I rushed out on stage, guns blazing with all the energy I could muster on a late summer afternoon in Tokyo and was met with a thunderous crowd. I was worn out, jet-lagged, performing in the sweltering hot humidity, and felt overwhelmingly sick due to the clash of energy, emotion, adrenaline, and exhaustion. Somehow it all energized me, though. The crowd started roaring from the second we started "Mr. Amsterdam" and kept going long after we'd walked off the stage. They were still chanting our name even as Avril was starting her show.

The onstage me felt like we had just fucking killed it, but the loving and caring boyfriend part of me felt fucking horrible for Avril as I walked offstage and saw her and her band looking nervous to go on. This was a hard rock crowd, and I knew it was going to be tough to follow us with her kind of music. I felt even worse after her set when she walked offstage to complete silence. No cheering, no booing—just nothing but an eerie quiet. Needless to say we all felt bad. The truth is, her performance wasn't bad, it was just the wrong bill for her. Nowadays it wouldn't matter, but back then it was a punk rock show and she was a pop star and the crowd wasn't having it. It was so hard to watch that even Fletcher from Penny-wise pulled her aside and told her not to worry because she'd done a great job. Yes, even Fletcher from Pennywise, the biggest, scariest, truest punk rocker, has a heart.

I left Japan feeling victorious, but that good feeling didn't last for long. Soon I was back in Canada and arguing with Greig Nori over publishing splits again, this time for the *Chuck* album. As usual, he was adamant about taking large percentages of songs that he had nothing to do with. This time, though, I wasn't backing down. I was willing to give him credit and percentages where he had contributed—and he had contributed some—but he always wanted so much more. This time I even pointed out that I had written songs for both Treble Charger and No Warning and was never given any publishing credits whatsoever. He laid on the guilt by saying I was so greedy for suggesting I get a piece of the little income they received. We fought so long and so bitterly that it was holding up the release of the album. In the end we agreed to compromise, and I gave him more than I wanted to, but not as much as he was demanding. The whole thing left me completely broken, drained, and sick of this whole relationship, personally and professionally.

When he came to L.A. a few weeks later for the "We're All to Blame" video shoot, I barely spoke a word to him, and if I did have to talk to him, I looked at the floor. This relationship had once felt like the most amazing gift in my life, and now I couldn't even look him in the eye. At one point, I had thought our bond was unbreakable. Now it was apparent that he only saw me as someone he could manipulate and cash in on. Was it always his plan from the beginning? It couldn't have been, because I was just sixteen and he couldn't have seen this kind of potential in me. It was all such a mind fuck. I was so upset that day, I got completely ham-mered just to handle being on set with him. In the last shot of the video, if you look closely, you can see that the dancers are practically holding me up to make sure I don't fall off the stool, because I could barely see straight at that point.

I knew that my professional relationship with Greig could not go on like this. We needed to figure our shit out one way or another before things fell apart even more. I asked Greig to come up to the house and have a talk. I was terrified of how he would react to this huge new house in the exclusive Mulholland Estates community and was prepared for the worst. When he walked through the doors, he looked around at the giant foyer with a fountain at one end. Then he surprised me. He was so happy for me, saying, "Congratulations! I'm so happy for you guys. Look how far you've come." I admitted that I was surprised that he felt this way, and he told me that he was coming around to Avril and me being together and now only wanted the best for us. I was stunned and elated that he felt this way. I told him that I wanted nothing more than to go back to being friends, the way we used to be before it all went to shit. He said he genuinely felt the same, and for the first time in years I actually felt like maybe I could trust him. I had hope that our future would be even stronger, because of everything we had overcome. That lasted all of five minutes.

Turned out Greig had his own reasons for wanting to talk that day. He had an idea: He wanted me to tell Avril that Greig should produce her next record and that I would write the whole thing. I laughed, because there was no way. Avril was going to do what she wanted to do, because it was *her* record. Greig immediately changed back to the Greig I had gotten so used to. He was angry, raising his voice, and yelling that I was going to tell her what to do and she would listen. I was both disgusted and frightened with how loud he was yelling at me about this. More than anything, though, I felt sad for him, because his anger not only revealed his motives, but showed me just how desperate he was. In that instant, my entire image of him as some great, confident man who knew so much, was finally shattered. The spell was broken. Either he had been a fraud all along or he had lost his way because of our success, his jealousy, or drugs and alcohol. Being kind and wishing me and Avril well was all just another attempt to manipulate me. He didn't care about anyone but himself. We went back and forth for a few more minutes, but he just sounded like an out-of-touch chauvinist who thought controlling women was our right as men.

He finally took off, and I was left feeling nauseated. I could not work with him anymore. I called a band meeting. On top of all the personal feelings I had about Greig, which the band didn't know about (and I wasn't going to tell them), he also wasn't a great manager anymore. In the beginning, we never could've made it without his help, but now, he had become destructive. We were constantly getting complaints from the label and agents that he was either unreachable or took days to get back to people. We were constantly missing opportunities or waiting for answers on time-sensitive issues. He even showed up at one of our shows in the U.S. straight from the airport and high on some ecstasy that he'd taken before he left Canada. He was bragging about how high he was talking to the customs agent and shocked they let him into the country. It was too much. This had to end, for the sake of our business. But my argument that we had to fire Greig fell on deaf ears with the rest of the band. Even though they all agreed with the issues I raised, they felt loyal to him. They thought Greig was "our guy," with us since day one, and we couldn't just drop him. They wanted to give him one more chance. So I was overruled and Greig was still our manager. I warned the guys that it was going to end badly for all of us.

Despite the issues with Greig and the ever-revolving door of staff at the record company, Sum 41 still had a lot of momentum going for us. Momentum is key in the entertainment business. In some cases momentum can be more important than the artists themselves because it opens every door in front of you. It just keeps pushing the next album, the next song, the next video forward, creating more fans who want to see more tour dates, more festival gigs, more videos, more music, and on and on. Fortunately for everyone involved, we still had momentum on our side, and with the wind at our backs, "We're All to Blame" and "Pieces" were both top ten singles in multiple countries, "No Reason" and "Some Say" were popular fan favorites, and a few more million albums were sold. The Sum 41 machine was still charging along.

Although we had a brand-new record, it felt like the press really only wanted to talk about my relationship with Avril. It's not like most of the press ever acknowledged our music on previous albums anyway. When we first came out with *All Killer*, they called us a flash in the pan and treated us like some little kid band that would only last the year. When *Does This Look Infected?* came out, with songs about teenage suicide and HIV, the press at the time barely noticed and still wrote us off as teenagers writing songs about getting dumped by our girlfriends. (For the record: Not one song had ever been about a sad breakup.) With *Chuck* they were just lumping us in with every other band from the emerging pop punk scene and, as usual, not focusing on the growth and evolution in our music.

Part of the problem was that our sense of humor, antics, and jokes had overshadowed some of the seriousness in the music right from day one. Just because we (and especially Stevo) were funny didn't mean we didn't have important things to say or that we weren't serious about music. I got pretty bitter about talking to the press at this point in our career. I felt they rarely had anything good to say about us. I had tried to open up and be honest in interviews and tell our story, but sometimes when we let journalists spend time with us, they would pretend to be our best friends and then write sarcastic, condescending articles about us, twisting stories or flat-out making things up. To this day our Wikipedia page says we started on teen television in Toronto and that we were initially a NOFX cover band, neither of which is true. This is all to say that I was sick of doing press and didn't want to talk about my life with Avril, so I started to have a much more adversarial approach in my interviews. I didn't like being that way, but I always felt on guard, giving them as little as possible in hopes they wouldn't have much to use against me.

Withdrawing from the press wasn't the only problem, though. I knew the band hated the fact that Avril and I were dating, so I was hesitant to talk about my personal life with them, too. I had heard from friends that they were shit-talking us behind my back, and whenever Avril came around they acted weird and uncomfortable and didn't make much of an effort to make her feel part of our club. Granted, Avril can be strange and shy when she first meets people, too, like a lot of us are. She grew up sheltered in a small town and hadn't learned the social skills necessary to fall into easy conversations with people she barely knew. Avril was savvy enough to pick up on the fact that my band didn't seem to like her, and she would often ask me if they hated her. I didn't have the heart to tell her that my manager had poisoned them against her and that she had never stood a chance. Instead, I just said, "Of course the guys like you! They're just tough to get to know at first, but they'll come around." On top of that, while we loved being together, it seemed our fans didn't feel the same way. I got a lot of flack for dating a pop star. Sometimes at our shows, people would bring signs that read, "Avril Sucks!" When I signed autographs after the show people would flat-out say, "Why are you with her? Her music is shit." Similarly, her fans thought I was ugly and not good enough for her. All of this made us retreat into our own relationship. Us against the world, fuck 'em all.

Dating another musician can be really tough. We tried coordinating our tours to have time off at home together as much as possible, but it was still hard to see each other as often as we wanted. The second we were done touring, we would dive headfirst into domesticity. We were really good at balancing being young and wild, and taking advantage of the nightlife L.A. had to offer. But we'd also go months living extremely healthy without drinking, too. Being in a serious relationship, taking care of a big house, being a romantic boyfriend, and putting someone else first was all new to me, but I loved it. Our families were getting to know each other, too. Having a big house meant we could bring both of our families down for Christmas, spoiling everyone with huge gifts. Being from Canada, they got a kick out of sitting outside and having breakfast under palm trees on Christmas Day and running into our famous neighbors, like Brian Wilson from the Beach Boys and Charlie Sheen. Another perk of success was that I was able to send my grandparents back to England on a first-class trip to see friends and family they hadn't seen in years. Things were going well both professionally, with three albums selling well and multiple hit singles, and personally, since I got to live in the never-ending summer of Los Angeles with this amazing girl. My life wasn't done surprising me with just how great it could actually get.

The only dark spot in all the light was still Greig Nori. Ever since the band said they wanted to keep him as our manager, I'd kept my mouth shut and never mentioned firing him again. However, as Avril and I got closer, I felt ready to open up to her about some of the things that had gone on with me and Greig. I told her about the manipulation, his desire for control, how he took credit for my songs, the pressure to have a sexual relationship, how it all started and where it led. It was so hard to talk about any of it, but I needed to finally tell her. Avril's immediate reaction was "That's abuse! He sexually abused you. He's fucking disgusting! That's so fucking wrong." I couldn't wrap my head around it, saying, "No, it's not abuse. I don't think of it like that. I allowed it to happen." She was adamant that it was abuse and that I needed to get rid of him as our manager. I explained that I couldn't because the guys still wanted him, and I had never told them any of this shit—and didn't feel like I could. Later, I lay in bed thinking. Was it abuse? Could it be abuse if I went along with it? I did tell him that I couldn't and didn't want to do it anymore but . . . I didn't think it was abuse. It was my own fault. I was not a victim. I refused to allow myself to think that I was a victim of sexual abuse.

Surprisingly, after that night, I never really thought about any of that again for years. Saying it out loud to Avril was enough at the time. I think I was also afraid of her being right, that maybe it was abuse, and I was afraid that I might someday have to deal with the issues associated with being a victim. I blocked it out and we never spoke about it again.

It was easier to put it out of my mind because by the end of the *Chuck* album cycle, it had become apparent to the rest of the band that Greig needed to go. They had finally become aware of how many opportunities were being missed because of his disappearing acts and lack of focus. Or maybe it was the many stories of our manager and accountant constantly doing blow together that was the real nail in the coffin. Either way, on the final day of the *Chuck* tour, we called Greig and told him, "Don't bother coming to our last show because you're fired." The four of us were all on the phone, but I did the initial talking. I didn't take any pleasure in saying the words "you're fired," I just felt terrible that it had come to this. Greig was instantly livid and yelling, "I made you! You're nothing without me! I'm going to sue you!" There was no self-reflection or apologizing for fucking up or even asking for another chance. Nope, we were a bunch of assholes and we were doing this *to* him. Typical narcissism.

I went home with a strange mix of feelings. I was happy that his darkness was gone from my life, but deeply sad that our once-great friendship ended so badly. I was also a little frightened that he might be right. What if we were nothing without him? The only way to know was to keep going. We hired Nettwerk Management, which was the same management company that Avril was with at the time. They were a hugely successful company that would take care of the band, and on the personal side, having the same management meant it would be a lot easier for Avril and me to plan our schedules together.

I had proposed to Avril in Venice, Italy, earlier that summer. I surprised her by booking a secret trip at the end of her European tour. She thought I was just being romantic, showing up at her last show in Stockholm and taking her on a getaway after a long tour. I rented us a private jet to get there, we stayed at a beautiful hotel near the San Marco Square, and after a gondola ride and an incredible private dinner, I proposed on the balcony of our penthouse suite. We spent a couple days being tourists and then went back to our tours and finished out the rest of the year on the road.

By the end of 2005, Avril and I finally had some real time off together and we wanted to plan our wedding. We had the time, because I didn't want to rush the band's next record. Even though I felt creatively spent after the last album, of course, I couldn't help but pick up a guitar and start messing around with some song ideas soon after the tour ended. This time the ideas weren't as dark as the ones on *Chuck*. They were leaning a little more pop punk and upbeat. I don't know if it had something to do with all of my recent life changes, being happily engaged, living in the L.A. sunshine, and getting Greig out of my life, but I didn't question it, I just kept writing. Some of the early ideas I wrote became "Underclass Hero," "Walking Disaster," "Speak of the Devil," "Dear Father," and "With Me." None of these early pieces of music came out as full songs, though, mostly just as riffs and a lyric or two here and there. Just enough to get the ideas started.

Before I dove into another record, there was some stuff I wanted to talk about with the band, stuff that had been bothering me for the past couple of years. Stevo and Cone were partying a lot more than usual and a lot more than me at that point, and I was worried it was becoming an issue. Worse though, Dave had been distancing himself from the band. It had started during the recording of the *Chuck* album and it had only gotten worse throughout the touring cycle. He wasn't traveling with the band to and from airports and hotels, or even to the shows anymore. He would rather smoke weed and hang out with the crew, opting to stay behind after shows and drive back to the hotel with them instead of us. I felt we needed to get together as friends, not as a band, to talk about the future. I was not going to do all the work of putting together another album if everyone's heart wasn't in it anymore.

Early in the new year of 2006, we all met in Las Vegas. The idea being that we hadn't really hung out just as friends since the late nineties, before we got signed. I thought if we hung out just as old friends, then maybe we could be open and honest with each other about the future. The first night, we went to dinner and discussed the issues. Dave explained that he was having a lot of problems at home, which is why he was retreating inwards. He swore he was still 100 percent into the band. Stevo and Cone agreed their partying had become too much and both pledged their dedication as well. That was all I needed to hear.

I went back home three days later excited to start writing new music. I also needed to find a new producer. My first choice was Rob Cavallo, who had wanted to sign and produce us back in the late nineties and had produced all the Green Day albums. I reached out and we had a great meeting. I played him some of my early demos, and he liked them enough that he wanted to make the record with us. The problem was that he was still under contract with Warner Bros. and technically wasn't allowed to produce bands who weren't with the company. He suggested we stay in touch as friends and he could give me some friendly feedback on the songs, and then when his contract was over, he would produce the record.

Soon after that meeting, in April 2006, Iggy Pop asked if we could perform with him at a Grammy event where he'd be accepting a lifetime achievement award of some kind. We jumped at any chance to play with Iggy, so we all flew to Miami. At the last minute, the organizers asked me to write and read my own speech before giving him his award, which was a bit terrifying but also a huge honor. Despite his assurances in Las Vegas, Dave was definitely still off and distant during those few days in Florida. He flew home as soon as the show was over, while the rest of us stayed and hung out on the beach for a couple of days. I had no idea that this would be the last time he would perform with us. A few weeks later, I got a call while Avril and I were at a food tasting with our wedding planners. Dave was quitting the band. He called us all individually to break the news. I hung up and went back to tasting different kinds of fucking cheese pretending like my call was no big deal. Stevo and I weren't shocked, but Cone was blindsided. After the Vegas retreat, he thought we were a solid unit again.

Although I was not surprised by Dave's decision, I thought it was fucking crazy to leave a successful band made up of your best friends. Dave told us that all the touring was too much for him and he needed to be at home with his family and off the road. I could understand that. We worked constantly, with very little time off. When he told me he was leaving, I asked him if he was 100 percent sure, before we went through the whole process of finding someone new. I'll never forget how quickly and confidently he replied with "Trust me, I won't be coming back." I remember it so well because it stung.

About a week later Dave sent us a statement he had prepared for the public that he wanted us to approve, which was very respectful of him. We all signed off on it and soon it was public. One of my only regrets during this time was that I didn't push for him to stay and try to figure out a way to make it work. I just let him go without a fight. I can admit now that I was angry inside. I was pissed that he was leaving our band, mad that he had been so distant, and felt like he hadn't been taking this seriously for the past year and a half. So I just thought, well, good riddance then. Now I see that was just my own ego talking. I don't know if I could've said anything that would've made any difference, but I regret not making an effort, because I believe that was the moment where it all slowly started to unravel for us internally. His departure shattered the sacred bond we once had, making it easier for people to leave in the future.

Dave's departure also created new band dynamics. With Greig out and Dave gone, I started looking to Stevo for help in decision-making, which made Cone feel like a third wheel. Band dynamics are a funny thing. In our case, we were a band when it came to performing live, making videos, and picking group photos, album artwork, and how the group presented itself. It was important to us to allow our individual personalities to come through equally. But all the business and big-picture decisions were between me and management. The musical direction and the songwriting was my department, too, usually with a producer overseeing elements along the way. It's not like the guys never made contributions to the music, but the process had always been that I wrote the songs and came in with full demos complete with riffs, vocals, harmonies, drum parts, and fills exactly the way I heard it in my head to the best of my ability. I then gave the guys a "demo-quality" version of a finished album with every song I'd written to that point. From there, if anyone had an idea for how to improve the song, we tried it in the studio, and if it was good we made the change.

That said, I write pretty simple songs and 99 percent of the time the demos didn't change from there to what ended up on the finished record.

When Dave left the band, it seemed the credit for the songs and riffs and even some guitar solos I had written went with him. Fans were not happy, and I kept reading comments and blogs saying, "I can't believe the man responsible for all the riffs like 'The Hell Song' and 'Fat Lip' just quit the band. These guys are over." Or "Well, this band is gonna be shit now that guy who wrote everything left the group." It went on and on like that, which felt like a punch in the face after all the work I had put into the music. Nobody knew how the albums were made, of course, but it felt like all the hard work, panic, and self-doubt, all the torturing myself under pressure, and all the accomplishments and success, were being thrown out the window when Dave quit. But how could I blame anyone really? Our fans didn't know that the day the tour ended was the same day I started writing the next record. They didn't know the grind of having no days off between touring and writing and recording and touring again, with the cycle repeating over and over again for years. No one knew how much I had poured into the music.

Then, like each record before, I just said fuck it and set out to once again make the best record of my life. Besides, I still had a lot to be extremely happy about. I was getting married in a couple months and Avril and I had a great life together. I settled into a pattern of balancing home life with work life. I was the best fiancé I could be during the mornings, nights, and weekends, but worked my ass off in my studio from noon till 8 p.m., Monday to Friday. I hoped that structure would bring me focus, but I found that being on a schedule made both my home life and work suffer. I was forcing myself to be in the studio even when I wasn't inspired, because it was on the schedule. Then when I was at dinner, I wasn't present, because my mind was still thinking about music. Really, the biggest problem was that I was burnt out from constantly touring and making records. It was another one of those things that I couldn't see clearly at the time, but now in hindsight, maybe Dave had the right idea. Maybe we all should've just taken a break back then. The problem with taking a break was that even though the band had done well up until that point, it didn't feel like we were on solid enough ground to walk away yet. It felt like we were still proving ourselves with each album. In other words, we needed to *stay the Mac*.

My usual anxiety over writing was getting worse, and all the changes in the band weren't helping. I started thinking too much about writing the "best Sum 41 record" instead of writing what I was feeling. I do like a lot of songs and specific moments on the *Underclass Hero* album, but it's hard for me to listen to, because it reminds me of the most uninspired period of creativity in my songwriting. It was forced, distracted, and although unintentional, some of the work was unoriginal and reminiscent of things I had written before.

One thing about that record that I *am* proud of is that it was the first time I'd really opened up in my lyrics. In the past I usually just wrote without thinking about the words, just letting it all come out. Now I was picking a topic about my life and sticking with it. Like not knowing my father in the song "Dear Father," or in "Walking Disaster," which is about the period in my life as a teenager when I couldn't live at home anymore and spent all my time hanging on people's couches doing drugs. This new lyrical openness was brought out by having Rob Cavallo as a ghost producer throughout the writing process. While he couldn't come on board officially, I had taken him up on his offer to help me out as a friend. Since we lived close by, we got together once a week to hang out and listen to my progress. His excitement got me excited, the same way it used to be with Greig, being a coach pushing me forwards from the sidelines. Rob and I spent a lot of time talking, and he helped me navigate my life and pushed me into becoming more of a leader within the band. As things got rolling and songs were getting completed, we both got more and more excited about how the album was shaping up.

It was one of those rare times when things were going well professionally and personally. Avril and I weren't planning a huge or extravagant wedding, but it was going to be really nice, with only close friends and family. The wedding was at a beautiful private estate in Montecito, California, in mid-July. Even though Stevo didn't really care for Avril or our relationship, I still wanted him to be my best man. He was the closest thing to a brother in my life, and I didn't want anyone else up there. A week or two before the wedding, the date and location were leaked, and we were warned that it would be a paparazzi circus, and sure enough it was. There were so many helicopters hovering overhead to take photos that it was hard to hear our own wedding vows. We had hired police for the day and they had arrested a photographer who had snuck onto the property the day before and fully dug himself into the ground to take pictures. When he was spotted, he couldn't run anywhere, because he was, well . . . in a hole. Stevo and I went over to have a laugh at this guy when they were digging him out. I commended his efforts, but was happy to watch the handcuffs go on. It was kind of the only light moment of the day for me.

I was happy to be getting married, but the whole day was full of stress with the paparazzi and worrying about it being "the perfect day." It felt awkward getting married in front of people who didn't approve of our relationship or who felt like it would never last. To add to the stress, after the ceremony, I learned that my grandmother was being rushed to the hospital for unknown reasons. My heart sank. It ended up being dehydration, but it gave us all a huge scare and added to the stress of the day. I just couldn't wait for it all to be over—and that included the honeymoon. Not because I didn't want to commemorate the occasion, but because Avril wanted to spend a week floating down the Amalfi Coast on a huge 120-foot yacht.

As luxurious as it sounded to float around in a mega-yacht in the Mediterranean, stopping for lunches and dinners from Positano to Portofino, it still meant we had to be on a fucking boat out in the fucking water. I knew I was not going to be comfortable doing that. Still, we flew to Italy after the wedding, and once we got on the boat, I had to admit, it was fucking gorgeous, and being out there in the middle of summer was stunning. I ended up having more fun than I thought I would—maybe even more fun than Avril! Still, boats suck. Whenever we docked in a new city to get some food, we had a hard time walking thanks to a major case of sea legs. It felt like we had vertigo everywhere we stepped, walking through the old Italian cobblestone towns. Plus, after a couple days we, and especially Avril, started to feel trapped. There was no trouble in paradise—yet anyway—we were just sick of the boat.

We were solid in our relationship and really felt like we would have an amazing life and future together. How could we not? We had so much in common. We were both close in age, both from Canada, and we grew up relatively near each other. We were both singers who had success in the same era and could understand the demands, the pressures, and the requirements of our careers. We both loved our privacy and didn't want to be an "it" couple that had a reality show (which we were offered). We didn't want to do red carpets together or be in front of paparazzi. We hated all of that shit and were totally aligned with each other. Sure, there were some differences, like she didn't like to watch movies or TV or listen to music at home. While I was bummed that I couldn't listen to Elvis Costello or Frank Sinatra when I woke up anymore, everything else appeared to be perfect between us. We talked about having children after making a few more records. We discussed how long we'd live in L.A. and where we might move next. With all of the touring we both did in Europe, it seemed to make sense to have a second home in London. A real estate agent had even talked us into considering buying a castle in the countryside. It's a very British musician thing to do, and I thought it sounded like some Jimmy Page shit. In the end, we didn't buy one, because it seemed like a hassle. I did enjoy a day of castle shopping, though.

Despite being happy and in love, I couldn't wait for the honeymoon to be over, partially so I could get off the damn boat, but also so I could get back into writing for *Underclass Hero*. Avril was working on her own album, *The Best Damn Thing*, with a new and up-and-coming producer named Dr. Luke, and they were killing it writing song after song. I was the opposite. I had fallen back into an uninspired, self-doubting writer's block. The worst part was, Greig's voice was rattling around in my head.

He always used to say that songwriters inevitably lose their gift. And that someday it would happen to me. I was worried that day had come. It felt like pulling teeth to move any of my songs to the finish line. I've never really been one for spending money on material things, but I was getting really into buying vintage guitars. Something about these old guitars felt different; they had songs in them. When I was struggling with writing, I would pick up a different guitar and all of a sudden I would come up with a new riff or finish a song. It became an expensive writing trick, but whenever I got stuck on something I would go down to the Guitar Center in Hollywood or Norman's Rare Guitars on Ventura Blvd. and buy a '57 Les Paul Junior, or a '62 SG/Les Paul Standard. I took home a beautiful '67 Gibson Hummingbird acoustic guitar from Norm's one day, and when I started strumming it, I finished writing the song "With Me" in just a few minutes. The sound of that guitar was so inspiring and conveyed the emotion I was feeling at the time, which, in essence, was pure joy and love. I couldn't help but just start writing that song, which to me isn't about a person, it's about an emotion. That is why I think it connects with people so well. There's not a single night that we play that song that I don't see multiple people in the audience crying, both men and women. That song seems to hit deep, and it all came out just by strumming a couple chords on that guitar.

When it came time to record both of our albums, Avril and I wanted to be near each other, so we rented out rooms next to each other at Ocean Way Studios in Hollywood. We started our records the same day, driving to and from work together, and able to pop into each other's studio throughout the day.

I had no intention of producing *Underclass Hero* on my own, but Cavallo couldn't get out of all of his contractual obligations in time. Instead, he gave me the confidence to produce the album on my own and suggested I use his engineer Doug McKean. We were still in the days when the music industry had huge recording budgets, and we decided that we wanted to take our time. We set aside a month to record drums, working on just one song a day. It was easy to find the time, because Stevo now lived in Los

Angeles after I had waged a campaign to get him, Cone, and our childhood best friend Diddler to make the move. While Stevo and Diddler packed their bags, Cone, who is a major creature of habit (remember how he got his nickname?), opted to stay in Canada.

This, of course, caused more unintended change to the band dynamic, which started to show when it came time to record the new album. It felt like Cone was trying extra hard to stand out on the *Underclass* sessions. He had come up with wild bass lines for every song that were so busy and all over the place. I had to keep telling him to go back and simplify his parts. He always came back with a different variation that had the same issue of being too busy, with the wrong rhythm and notes that didn't work in the scale. Both Stevo and I agreed it was not right for the music we were playing. One morning before Cone got to the studio, Stevo printed out a little stop sign and taped it on the twelfth fret of Cone's bass, because his bass lines were getting out of control and way up the neck of the bass. He was firmly into solo Sting territory, aka not the good Sting. This went on and on and started driving me crazy. I wanted him to thrive, but I just felt it wasn't right musically. I had so much on my plate to deal with and this back-and-forth was adding another layer of stress to the process. Finally I told him to just play the root notes of the chords so we could move on. Later I found out he had been working out all of his bass parts using an acoustic guitar, so it made sense why he thought some of these weird notes could work. On a guitar, it sounded like it could be a cool lead riff, but converting it to bass made it sound like bad jazz.

Despite all of this, we still had a great time in the studio, and having my wife in the next room was awesome. There was a lot of drinking during the sessions, not to the extent of the *All Killer No Filler* partying, but we were having a great time. With Avril, Dr. Luke, and our whole team all in one building, the evenings usually got tipsy, and we often ended up back at our house or out at some club in Hollywood. Dr. Luke was also working with a then young and unknown Katy Perry, who started hanging out with our crew as well. It was all carefree and fun.

HEARTACHE, GOOD SEX,
AND SOME BAD TATTOOS

*E*arly in 2007, Avril and I were still in our newlywed bliss. We had just moved into a new house, the Bel Air mansion where Travis Barker and his then wife Shanna Moakler lived in *Meet the Barkers*. We were both wrapping up our records and feeling confident about the next chapter in our lives, but it wasn't all sunshine and roses. Right before Sum 41 hit the road, our management had been notified by the FBI that I was receiving credible death threats for being with Avril. Normally, they ignore these things, but these letters were a bit more sophisticated, and had no fingerprints on them. They suggested that the band bring on professional security that dealt with this kind of stuff. We brought in a guy named Kenny Gabriel who had toured with Britney Spears and had dealt with a lot of crazy stalkers. Kenny became my right-hand man, taking care of me and the band, babysitting everyone, and saving me from more than a few attacks out on the road. I once saw him take on a whole group of drunken idiots trying to kick my ass while I was stuck on a ferry with nowhere to escape, in Toronto of all places. This drunk, rowdy guy had started hurling insults at me, gotten too close, and when Kenny blocked him, all his friends jumped in. One by one Kenny took each guy out, throwing these dudes around like rag dolls and punching like he was Jason Statham in an action movie. I was terrified in the moment, but after that night I was confident that I was in good hands.

Before we could leave on tour, though, we needed to fill Dave Brown-sound's spot on lead guitar. We held auditions in L.A., jamming with about five different people, but it never felt close to being right. Our dream guitar player was Allison Robertson from the band the Donnas and we almost asked her, but there was no way we would ask her to leave her own band. The next person on the list was our old friend Tom Thacker, who played in a Canadian punk rock band we loved called Gob. I'd looked up to Tom as a teenager and loved Gob's record *Too Late . . . No Friends*. We flew him down to L.A., and after a few songs we all knew he was the guy. We were already friends, and he knew this kind of music inside out, was an incredible guitar player and singer, and most important, he was Canadian!

By the time *Underclass Hero* was ready for release, our A&R guy, Rob Stevenson, was the only person left at Island Def Jam who had been there when we signed our record deal. We were his first successful band, and he went on to sign more huge acts, like the Killers and Fall Out Boy. He understood us, but it didn't feel like anyone else at the label did anymore. We had a brand-new marketing person who took our new record and said, "I don't really know much about you guys, other than you're supposed to be the Canadian blink-182, right?" That was bad, but the fact that no one at the label could agree what the first single should be was worse. It was down to either "Underclass Hero" or "Walking Disaster," and our entire team was split down the middle. The indecision went on for weeks, until our agent just said, "Pick whatever song you want, because they're both going to be top ten singles anyway." Based on our past success, he didn't seem wrong.

Rob had been pushing hard for "Walking Disaster," but in the end I went with "Underclass Hero," because it was short, catchy, and felt like old school Sum 41, which I thought our fans would like. I should've listened to Rob. "Underclass Hero" failed to break the top thirty and everyone, including me, went into a panic. For whatever reason, we weren't getting any love from radio this time, and MTV was moving away from music and towards reality TV. The label tried to save the record by switching out the singles and swapping in "Walking Disaster" instead. That only made things worse. Some radio stations were playing "Walking Disaster," other stations were playing "Underclass Hero," and the rest of the stations weren't playing either song until one of them went up the charts, and given the situation, it was impossible for either song to do anything but go down.

In an instant, all of our momentum was gone and the entire launch was over before the album even came out. When *Underclass Hero* was released in July of 2007, we managed to debut at number seven on the *Billboard* charts, which was our highest to date. It eventually went on to sell over a million albums worldwide, but there was no way to deny it, the whole thing still equaled a failure. To pour salt into the wound, many fans seemed to hate the return to the lighter pop punk sound and reignited the argument that Dave was the only good part of Sum 41. This killed me inside. I also knew that Greig Nori would be taking a lot of pleasure in knowing that the first record out from under his wing was a flop. I was embarrassed and confused, because I thought the record was great and I'd assumed it would be a huge success. I wasn't used to failure yet. Still, I'm always an optimist and thought there was a chance this record would have its moment. So we did what we always did and planned a world tour to play our hearts out every night on stage and show people why we still mattered.

We started out doing whatever promo shows and radio festivals we could book around the U.S., before kicking off the world tour in Canada. But when the tickets went on sale, not many people were buying them. It was another major blow to my self-esteem and overall mental health. I couldn't figure out why our career was falling apart so quickly. We had been selling out arenas around the world for years and then it's all over because one song didn't work for radio? My mind was spinning. Was it because Dave left? Was Greig right, that we were nothing without him? Was it because I pissed off our fans by marrying Avril? I had no answers.

Four weeks into the tour, we hit the Calgary Saddledome. It was totally packed and the crowd was amazing, which was a desperately needed boost. The final song of the night was "Pain for Pleasure," where Stevo sings and I play drums. I sat down at the drum kit and instantly felt the sharpest, most excruciating pain I've ever felt in my life. It shot through my whole back and cut off the function in both of my legs. I went into total shock and was having a hard time even breathing, but the show must go on. I played the song drumming with just my hands, no feet, trying not to burst into tears from the pain and, most of all, fear. I was convinced I had broken my spine or something equally severe.

The song finally ended, the lights went out, and the band cleared the stage. I stayed on the drum kit yelling for Kenny to come get me. By the time he got over to me, I was hyperventilating and almost passed out from the pain. I barely got out the words "I can't walk. I can't move my legs. I'm in so much pain." He picked me up and carried me offstage, then put me on a road case to wheel me through the halls to the medics. As he wheeled me, every tiny bump caused me to scream, "HOLY FUCKING GOD, FUCK ME. THIS HURTS SO FUCKING BAD!"

The medics weren't sure what it was, and I was taken to the hospital. After an X-ray, the doctor seemed to think it was a muscle spasm, which none of us believed. I was in too much pain. It had to be something far more serious. Luckily, the promoter had connections to an NHL doctor who treated the Calgary Flames. He got me in for an MRI the next morning. Those results showed I had herniated a disc in my L4, L5 vertebrae. Likely caused from years of traveling and jumping around on stage with a heavy guitar. I'm convinced those fucking trampolines that we used on stage in the early days didn't help either. This kind of injury required months of recovery, and surgery wasn't really an option. It was suggested that I see a physical therapist and work on strength rather than having medical procedures done, but recovery was going to be slow. Our tour—and the chance to promote the new album—was over, just as it was starting.

I went home in a wheelchair to an empty house, because Avril was away on tour. Her album had exploded, and "Girlfriend" was her biggest song to date. As down and out as I was, I couldn't have been more proud of her and happy that at least one of us was killing it. I wanted her to be out there taking over the world, and I was determined to learn how to manage on my own. Luckily, the house had an elevator. When we moved in, we'd thought it was extremely excessive, but holy fuck did that come in handy when I was stuck in a wheelchair in a huge house.

Physically, I knew I had a few weeks in the chair before I could start any physical therapy. Emotionally, I was still reeling trying to figure out what the fuck had just happened to my life and career. I felt like a total loser. The saving grace was that I could retreat to my studio. Not only had I been collecting vintage guitars, but I was also buying recording equipment and building my own professional studio in the house. Now I finally had the time to learn how to use it.

Slowly, my back started to get better and I got out of the wheelchair. I was able to start doing physical therapy to get me moving again. Avril had come home from tour and we could go out for dinner or for drinks. I started to notice a shift in the way people treated me out in public. If I was with Avril, they either looked down on me or ignored me entirely. Whenever online press used a photo of us, they didn't bother mentioning Sum 41, and snarky writers started calling me "Mr. Lavigne" or "Avril's troll of a husband." Paparazzi would taunt me with Avril's success, trying to get me to react on camera. As if my life could get any worse!

As 2008 rolled in, I got a phone call from Rob Stevenson at IDJ. He wanted to know if I had seen how well our song "With Me" had been selling on iTunes. I had not. Rob told me that the song had been used in *Gossip Girl* and had been in the top ten on iTunes for eleven weeks and wasn't slowing down. My first reaction was "Holy shit that's awesome, but what the fuck is a *Gossip Girl*?" Rob explained that he thought we should make a video for the song and release it as a single, because it was clearly becoming a hit on its own. This was that fucking moment I had been waiting for. I just had a feeling this album would eventually catch on, and with this news I wanted to get back out on the road and finish what we'd started.

My back was finally strong enough that we could perform. In February, we played the song on *Jimmy Kimmel Live* and then headed to the UK and then back to Canada to pick up where we'd left off. I was taking it easier on stage, but I felt strong. While touring in Canada, we shot the video for "With Me" and Stevo directed. It turned out amazingly. The label hadn't officially released "With Me" as a single yet, but Rob had a lot of clout there. We were getting closer to releasing this song that we felt would be the hit we needed off this album. Then I got a phone call. Rob Stevenson had been fired from IDJ with no explanation. He was the last person from our original team and was our only champion at the label. When I finally met our new rep, I asked about releasing "With Me" as a single, but I got nothing but hollow industry talk. IDJ didn't care about us or the single. I wanted this to work so badly that I even made a desperate plea to CEO L.A. Reid, offering to pay for everything myself. They still said no. I don't blame them for not letting me pay. If it were to become a hit song on my dime, Reid could lose his job. By the summer of 2008, the album was completely dead. The strangest thing about that album is that over time it has become the record I hear fans talk about as their favorite. When we'd play songs from *Underclass*, they would be some of the most sing-along moments of the show, and I would regularly see people drop to one knee and propose when we'd break into "With Me."

At that time, though, the lack of support for "With Me" was the final straw. When the tour was over, I couldn't take it anymore. I went straight from the last show on the Sum 41 tour and jumped straight onto the road with Mötley Crüe, to spend a week hanging out with Tommy Lee. I got shitty drunk all day; at night I watched the Crüe perform, ate good meals, and partied with one of the greatest drinking buddies you could ever ask for. This may sound crazy, but out of all the people I've ever met in the music business, the one person I can honestly say has never let me down and who I've always been able to count on is Tommy Fucking Lee. It started when he said yes to joining us for the MTV twentieth anniversary show. When I needed to be cheered up after the *Underclass* cycle, he made me laugh and smile again. Later on, when I was getting sober and needed support, he said yes, I'm here for you. When we were shooting a documentary and asked people to be in it, he was the first person to sign on.

Even though hanging with Tommy for a week lifted my spirits, I wasn't ready to face reality. On top of the struggles with my career, home had become a struggle, too. For reasons I didn't understand, whenever Avril came home from her tours, it felt like something had changed in our relationship. She had become very distant, physically because of all the touring and traveling, but more emotionally. I couldn't figure it out. There was no single moment or situation that I could point to that caused things to turn. It wasn't like it had been going downhill for a while and turned into a bad relationship. We never fought and always seemed totally in lockstep with each other. In the past we couldn't wait to be back in each other's arms again. Sitting in our backyard drinking Coronas by our pool or going to our favorite restaurants. Now she just seemed less interested in me and our relationship altogether. I tried to brush it off as a passing moment that we'd eventually get through, since we were both always exhausted from touring and spent so much time apart. I figured we just needed to spend some time together and it would all go back to normal. So, I hopped on a plane and joined her tour, figuring we could find that spark again. I was wrong. I felt unwanted, like I was in her way and being a nuisance. To stay out of her way, I would hang out with her band and dancers, getting drunk with her drummer Rodney and jamming with the guys in soundcheck. I was worried, because the way she was distancing herself reminded me of Dave Brownsound through the *Chuck* years, and I was desperate to not repeat that situation.

One day while I was jamming with her band in soundcheck, one of the guys suggested we play "In Too Deep." It sounded great, and when Avril heard it, she said we should play it for her encore. I was a little apprehensive to say yes, because I knew my band would be really unhappy the second they found out about me singing a Sum 41 song with Avril in front of her pop audience. I eventually agreed, though, because I wanted her to be excited about me again. I'd been worrying that the reason I was getting the cold shoulder from her was because of how badly our album had bombed. Between that and my injuries and people making fun of me in the press, I worried I had become a failure in her eyes. I was desperate to get us back to the place we used to be, and if playing a Sum 41 song at her show would help, then I was going to do it. When it came time to walk out on her stage, I was terrified. What if no one cared? What if no one sang along? Would I look even worse in her eyes? None of those worries came true. The crowd went crazy and sang just as loud or louder than for her own songs, and it became a highlight of the show. She wanted me to keep it up for the rest of the tour. I have to admit, it felt amazing performing with her and for her audience. I finally felt good on stage again, for the first time in a long time. I had heard that my band knew about the performances and thought the idea was lame, but they never spoke a word about it to me. I wouldn't have cared if they were mad about it anyway. I was trying to save my marriage.

The good feelings didn't last much longer than the tour, though. When we got home, we went back to living separate lives. For me that meant hanging out in the home studio working, and for her that meant going out with friends to clubs and restaurants. Sometimes we'd have our own friends over at the house, but since it was so big, we would be in our separate spaces with our separate friends and barely even notice each other. By the end of the year, reports of her cheating were starting to circulate. I chose not to believe the rumors, but it was embarrassing to be asked about it by close friends and family members, and it was just more fodder for the paparazzi. I would see pictures of her coming out of clubs with other guys or read articles about her cozying up to this person or that, but I didn't have any more proof than the public did. I was finding out and hearing about these stories just as everyone else was. When I confronted her about it, she said it was all bullshit lies. Sure, there seemed to be a lot of smoke, but I never found any fire. I wanted to trust my wife and was hoping we would get back to the way we used to be. Now, when I look back, it's not lost on me that this was a similar pattern to the way I had handled things with Greig Nori. Burying the obvious truths and ignoring my own pain. I'm fiercely loyal, and sometimes that's a flaw.

By 2009, I knew I needed major damage control in my life and career. I hired a new manager named Ron Laffitte. He had been a music executive at Capitol Records, but switched to management because he wanted to get back to representing talent and making great things happen for artists. In his early days he had managed the band Megadeth and worked with Sharon Osbourne. He also had a long history with Metallica that dated back to their earliest days. As cool as that all was, the most important thing was he understood the band and where we needed to go. He had something special, and I'm happy to say he's still our manager today, through all the ups and downs. It is one of the most important relationships in my entire life.

When I first met Ron, I was planning on putting Sum 41 down for a while and trying a solo record or a side project, but Ron's arrival energized me to jump back in the ring. By this point, Avril was hardly ever around. Based on the thousands of paparazzi photos, she was traveling the world with girlfriends, hanging out in Europe or New York or wherever they fancied. It was hard to watch it all in the press, but her absence gave me time to work on music. I was still completely in love with Avril, or at least thought I was, and was trying to repair the relationship, but the way things were going and how they were playing out publicly also brought out a certain anger in me. That translated into writing music that was much darker. In the same way that marital bliss and sunshine had brought out my pop-punk side, now I was writing songs like "Holy Image of Lies," "Skumfuk," and "Sick of Everyone." I was alone, pissed off, confused, and unhappy, and living in a cavernous twelve-thousand-square-foot mansion on a canyon in a secluded gated community. I always tell people that it doesn't matter how big the home is, if it's not a happy one, it's fucking miserable.

The only solace I found was in writing music, and for the first time in my life it was easy. Full songs and lyrics were pouring out of me within minutes, and they were all great. Sure "In Too Deep" and "Still Waiting" had come to me quickly, but this was different. I decided that I would adopt a new rule for this record: If I didn't come up with a song within a few minutes of working on it, I would walk away and try again or scrap it altogether. I didn't have a deadline for writing this album, so I would only write if I was inspired. I had nothing to lose.

I asked our guitar player, Tom, if he had any ideas kicking around, and he sent me a track with just music, no vocals. I listened through once and thought it was great. On the second listen, I hit record and started singing along and wrote most of the vocal melody on the spot. I quickly wrote down some words, and the song "Screaming Bloody Murder" was done in under fifteen minutes, named after an album title I'd been kicking around for a while. I was elated with the material and was stunned by the speed of my writing.

Avril and I kept living separate lives until I couldn't take it anymore. Motivated by the lyrics of Tom Petty's "I Need to Know," I decided to confront our problems and gave her an ultimatum: We had to fix what was broken or I was moving on. I was done being humiliated in the media and hurt by the photos and articles that kept coming out. I didn't want to waste any more time if this was going nowhere. I was ready and willing to fix whatever was broken between us and was hoping that this ultimatum would serve as a wake-up call. Like when I gathered the band in Las Vegas, I wanted to create a space to talk about the issues, move on, and get stronger because of it. When she was finally at home for a few days, I laid it all out for her. "We have to go back to the respectful loving relationship that we had, or we need to just call it quits," I said. "This isn't working and I can't live like this anymore." Avril told me her decision. There was no crying. There was no big fight. There wasn't even much of a discussion. It was just over. I went upstairs, packed a few things, and left the house.

It was about a two-minute drive from our house to the big gates of the Bel Air Crest community. I was stunned by what had just happened and shocked that our marriage had ended so quickly, so I gave myself those two minutes of driving time to either change my mind or get a call from her. Neither of those happened.

As I drove out through those gates and onto the main road, I actually smiled for the first time in a long time. A huge weight had been lifted off of me. I headed straight to a neighborhood where six months before I had seen a "for sale" sign at a really great house. The house stuck out in my mind, because things had been going so badly between us for so long, that I told myself, "I wouldn't be surprised if I end up in this house one day." To my surprise, the house still hadn't sold, so I called my friend who was a real estate agent and asked if we could go see it. I put in a fair, but low offer on it, and the owners took it immediately, because this was the middle of the housing crisis. Since it would take sixty days to clear all the escrow and inspections, I ended up crashing on my old friend Diddler's couch for a few weeks. It was on his couch in his run-down shitty studio apartment where the gravity of what had just happened hit me hard. My marriage was completely over. I was so sad that it had been a failure, but I was elated the pain was over. I hadn't told anyone except for Diddler and Stevo, because I was embarrassed and in no mood to confirm my marriage's ending to people who thought they'd seen it coming. Stevo came and kept me company. We drank, went to lunches, and hit the Body Shop strip club on Sunset, but the latter only made me feel worse and was a one-time jaunt.

After two weeks spent down and out, I knew I needed to stop feeling sorry for myself and get my shit together. Spending each night on Diddler's couch was depressing me, and since I still had to wait for the sixty-day escrow to clear on my new house, I got myself a nice suite at the London Hotel behind the Viper Room on Sunset. I hadn't spoken to Avril since I left the house. It had been a few weeks, so she reached out and wanted to talk. When we got on the phone, I told her I'd bought a house. I don't think she'd expected that or liked it very much, because right after that call she put out a statement that we had broken up. Informing the press was the last thing I cared about. In my opinion, I didn't owe them or the public anything. The news of our separation broke, and the press made it sound like she had dumped me. I mean, I guess that was true, since she had taken off around the world for the past year and a half, but to me, the actual split was mutual. Once the news broke, my life got exponentially worse, because suddenly the paparazzi were all over me. I had multiple cars chasing me around and people hounding me trying to get some kind of "sad, lonely Deryck" picture. I became terrified to leave my hotel, and holed up there for over a month, never leaving my room, ordering room service for every meal, and rarely seeing people. I even stopped going to the rooftop pool or any of the hotel restaurants, because people were whispering and staring at me. I was a paranoid wreck, not shaving, showering, cutting my hair, changing my clothes, or even letting housekeeping in to clean the room. I just sat there in my filth playing my guitar, working on songs, and watching movies.

After about four weeks of hiding out, my friend Archer showed up. "This isn't fucking healthy, man," he said. "I'm taking you out tonight. I don't care what you say, you're leaving this room." He wanted us to go to a spot called Teddy's inside the Roosevelt Hotel. There was no way. I immediately started feeling a panic attack coming on, saying, "It's too soon. I can't be seen. I'm not ready. The paparazzi are going to pounce on me." He kept assuring me that everything would be cool. Then he played his last card, saying, "Avril is being photographed all over the place having fun since you split and you're hiding in a fucking hotel." He won.

I made myself presentable and we headed out to the Roosevelt in Hollywood. He had a table set with my favorites: a bottle of Jack Daniel's and a bottle of Grey Goose. I saw Benji from Good Charlotte that night, along with a few other friends I hadn't seen in a while. No one made me feel uncomfortable, no one cared about the breakup, everyone was just happy to see me. I was having a great time and was so thankful for Archer forcing me out of the hotel. Through the crowd of people dancing, a beautiful dark-haired rock 'n' roll girl came walking straight towards me like she was on a mission to talk to me. I assumed maybe she knew Benji and was coming over to talk to him, but our eyes were locked the whole time as she made her way over to our table. She introduced herself to me as Hanna Beth, and even though it was a loud club, we started chatting like we'd known each other for years. I admit, I was struck by her beauty, but I was nervous to be talking to another girl in public, like maybe it was disrespectful to Avril or something. When the club closed, we all decided to head back to my hotel suite to continue the party. Archer was sober and got behind the wheel of my Bentley Continental Flying Spur, which is a big car but felt cramped with all of us piled in and Hanna sitting on my lap. As we tore down Sunset Boulevard, blasting "Street Fighting Man" by the Rolling Stones through the open windows, Hanna started kissing me. I didn't know what to think. On one hand it felt wrong, like I was cheating on Avril, but on the other hand I couldn't deny that the kissing made me feel alive again. If this really cool attractive girl wanted to make out, maybe I was not as much of a loser as I'd thought. When we walked into my hotel room, she pulled me into the bathroom to keep making out. It was getting intense, and I started to feel really guilty and had to put a stop to it. It was all too much of a head fuck. I hadn't kissed anyone other than Avril in almost seven years, and even though it was feeling great, I felt like I was doing something wrong.

Hanna ended up staying the night and I woke up feeling very anxious, like I had made a mistake. I could feel a panic attack brewing as we lay in bed—the sweat, the beating heart, the lightheadedness, heavier breathing. I needed to get her home and hopefully not have a mental breakdown in front of a complete stranger. While part of me was happy, my mind was racing between guilt and panic and filling with questions like *Technically I'm still married, what if Avril finds out? Do I even care if she does?* I finally snuck Hanna out of the hotel and dropped her off at home. Back in my hotel room, it all hit me again and I was consumed by a full-on panic attack. I decided that I needed a woman's perspective on this, and I called Lexi Ben Meir, who worked in our management office with Ron. She calmed me down, pointing out that this was going to help me move on and I had done nothing wrong. It was a relief to hear.

My friends were right. It was time to get back out there and stop being a hermit. I decided a change of location would help, so I moved over to the Sunset Marquis Hotel and started going out at night. With the encouragement of my friend Todd, I asked the hostess of the restaurant we were at to come meet us at a club when she got off work. After all, I was newly single and needed to start dating. Later she texted, asking if I could meet her in the parking lot of Mel's Diner on Sunset. I thought it was odd, but Todd reminded me this is what adult dating life is all about. When I met her, she was smoking weed and got really stoned, talking about outer space and galaxies and shit. All of a sudden, she decided to kick off her shoes and run barefoot into the Hollywood foothills behind the diner. Instantly, she stepped on a broken beer bottle and her foot was completely cut open, bleeding profusely. The memory of my severed hand came to mind, and I shouted, "Oh fuck! We need to get you to hospital right away!" She had no insurance and was afraid that her parents would freak out. Instead, she begged me to take her to my hotel room, pour alcohol on it, and bandage it ourselves. Next thing I know I'm carrying a beautiful blonde twenty-four-year-old girl with blood pouring down her leg through the lobby of the Sunset Marquis Hotel. The front desk clerk didn't bat an eye. They just said, "Welcome back, Mr. Whibley." Being the premier rock 'n' roll hotel of Hollywood I guess they were used to this kind of thing. I spent the rest of the night tending to her open wound and cursing the name Todd Morse. I was ready for a new chapter, but dating wasn't it.

OPEN WOUNDS AND BLOOD IN MY EYES

A t the tail end of 2009, the band came to L.A. to start preproduction for the *Screaming Bloody Murder* album. We were working with the producer Gil Norton, who had done the early Pixies albums, the Foo Fighters' *The Colour and the Shape*, and the Distillers' *Coral Fang*. I was desperate to heal the open wound that was *Underclass Hero*. I had originally reached out to Rick Rubin to see if he was interested in producing us again, but he wouldn't even take a meeting. It was another reminder of how far we had fallen. A few years ago, Rick had signed on to produce a song before we had even committed to recording it. Now he wouldn't return our call. Gil Norton is a great guy and a great producer, but we didn't quite gel. He didn't seem to speak the same musical language and didn't seem to know when we had a good take or not. It reminded me more of working with Greig Nori than with Jerry Finn. I think we were making different records in our minds.

By this point, I had taken ownership of my new house in Sherman Oaks. However, because I didn't have a studio setup and I needed to be close to the action, I rented a house in the Hollywood Hills that had a recording studio built in. Not only was it a great house and studio, but it was in a prime Hollywood location, close to the music and to the Hollywood nightlife. I was deeply sad and dejected after Avril and I broke up, but now, three months later, I was making a record, living in two different homes, on either side of the Hills, and tearing up Hollywood. I was having the time of my life. I was going out every single night and, on most occasions, would bring the entire club back to my house in the Hills. My friend Todd Morse from H2O and the Offspring had been dumped by his girlfriend, so he was single, while she was gallivanting around the world as one of Avril's new besties. It only made sense that Todd move in with me. We loved being free and single with no one to answer to anymore, and the house was the quintessential bachelor pad thanks to its 180-degree views of Hollywood, with a pool and jacuzzi.

At this point, I knew so many club promoters, restaurant owners, door people, and other celebrities that wherever we went, we were treated like royalty. The best tables at every restaurant, an invite to every event and party, and never-ending bottles of Jack Daniel's and Grey Goose at every club from L.A. to Las Vegas. Even in New York I was set up everywhere. I had a good friend who worked at Homeland Security, and although he was completely sober, he liked to hang out and be a part of the fun. He would pick us up, take us around to clubs or parties, never stopping for red lights or waiting in any Manhattan traffic, just flashing his lights and sirens. He was my personal government escort. Everything in my life was so easy all of a sudden. My personal life was amazing, I was writing songs with ease, I could stay up all night, wake up without a hangover, and do great work during the day. And as much as I was drinking at that time, I still wasn't addicted. I was fully functional, felt in control, and was convinced that I could stop whenever I wanted. My doctor even gave me a clean bill of health at my checkup. I started to feel invincible. That's what made it dangerous. This was something I learned a little later. But we're not there yet.

At the time, though, everything was fucking awesome. Well, everything except my relationship with Stevo. I started to detect some envy coming from him, because I was living free and having fun while he was married and living out in the desert, in Palm Springs, which is basically a retirement community. I think it goes back to the healthy competition we'd always had with each other. Our lives usually mirrored each other's. If I bought a car, he got one; when I bought a house, he did, too. When

I moved to L.A., he was right behind me. And when I got married, he did soon after. I'm not saying that he was copying me or anything, but we had always been on parallel tracks. Now, for the first time since we were fifteen years old, our paths had diverged. It reminded me of the *Seinfeld* episode where Jerry and George make a pact to get married, and when Jerry's engagement is called off, George is left with a fiancée and saying, "Wait a minute we had a pact!"

Stevo openly talked about how he never enjoyed the process of making an album, even on *All Killer*, so being in the studio with him wasn't always pleasant, but this was different. It felt directed at me personally. And when I thought about it, it may have been brewing for a long time. Even when we first started having success, he seemed to be a little envious of the attention I got as the singer of the band. It's no secret that Stevo was an attention seeker, and he was good at getting it. The reality is, the singer of any band gets more attention, and as hard as we tried to showcase our individual personalities, there was just more focus on me because I was the one at the front of the stage. Stevo had been making cutting comments that weren't quite jokes, and definitely made me feel shitty, all the way back around the *Does This Look Infected?* record. As time went on, they got louder and more personal. We all knew how much he hated Avril and that relationship. He had outright blamed it for a lot of the failure of the *Underclass Hero* album. I don't remember what we were arguing about, but in a moment of anger, and drinking, he once said, "We're not doing as well anymore because you dated Paris Hilton and now are with Avril Lavigne." Now that my marriage was over, I thought maybe he would be stoked, but as soon as I started my newly single lifestyle, he adopted a holier than thou posture towards anything that I did. It felt like I just couldn't win, but also I wasn't sure if I cared what he thought or had to say. In my mind he was just kind of an asshole now, and I didn't mind that he didn't want to stick around after work.

Juggling two houses while making a record was getting difficult. I was overseeing the construction of a studio in my Sherman Oaks house, but had to spend all day at the Hollywood house working with the guys on *Screaming Bloody Murder*. I needed to hire an assistant to help me out. That's when I got a call from an old family friend, who I had known since I was a kid. We hadn't seen each other much recently, because Mike had been working odd jobs around the Vancouver suburbs. He had gotten fired from his last gig and had nowhere to go, no money, and was too embarrassed to tell the family back home. He had been sleeping on the floor of his friend's house with no prospects or future. I told him to come live with me and be my assistant. I gave him a weekly salary, not one, but two roofs over his head, and the keys to my Maserati. He was ecstatic at my proposition and so was I. Since I didn't have a real brother, he was about as close as I could get, and I had known him since before he could talk. He was a few years younger than me, though, so once I hit my teen years, we didn't see each other as often. Still, he was basically family. Now I had an assistant I knew I could trust.

When he got to L.A., he quickly became part of the entourage and the life he once knew was a thing of the past. He was in awe of everything and so excited about his new world. He organized my whole life, drove the Maserati as my driver, started dating a Playmate, and was hanging out at the Playboy Mansion with me. Paparazzi started taking his photo, thinking he had to be someone famous, too. He once asked me if I had ever seen the show *Entourage*. I hadn't, but he told me to check it out. "Your life is exactly like that show," he said. "I'm your Eric, Archer is your Drama, and Diddler is your Turtle, and the craziest thing is, you're friends with Jeremy Piven in real life and he's part of our crew!" The first time I actually ever saw the show was when Piv invited us to watch a taping. We got kicked off the set in about ten minutes by the producer Doug Ellin for drinking and making too much noise. I eventually watched the series and definitely saw a lot of parallels to my own life—and there definitely is a little of Ari Gold in the real Piven, which was always good for a laugh.

Once preproduction for *Screaming Bloody Murder* was over, we moved over to Capitol Studios to record drums. The drums took two torturous weeks, and Gil Norton thought we needed two more for the bass, and that was enough for me. Gil and I were just on different pages. I called management and said I couldn't work with him anymore. We went back to the Hollywood house to do it ourselves. Jerry Finn had sadly passed away from a brain aneurysm not long before we started making this album, but he had recommended an engineer named Ryan Hewitt, who helped finish the album. He's incredible in the studio and we had a blast getting cool guitar sounds and reminiscing about Jerry. As for production, I would produce it, because I wanted this album to be recorded the same way I wrote the songs, easy and spontaneous, not labored over. No overthinking, just hit record and whatever happens, happens. My philosophy was that records are like a Polaroid, caught in time, and I wanted to capture exactly who I was at that moment.

Stevo and Tom had already left town, and Cone was done with his bass parts and was on his way back home just a few days later. That meant my friends outside of the band and I could pick up where we'd left off, which is what I wanted. My bandmates and I were living in different worlds and just couldn't comprehend each other's life anymore. They were all married and taking it easy, while I was living as if it was my twenty-first birthday on New Year's Eve in Las Vegas every single night. I worked all day, but when I was finished recording, we would go out to clubs in Hollywood, invite a ton of people back when the bars closed, and party all the way into the next morning. We were always finding random people passed out in the house. They would be asleep outside on the deck by the pool or crashed out on the floor under a table. Sometimes I'd find out a woman's name for the first time when we were waking up in my bed together. I was always terrified we were going to find somebody dead in the pool, but thank god it was only ever filled with furniture, which seemed to happen every night for some reason. There's a documentary on YouTube called *Sum 41—Don't Try This at Home* that shows what it was like living in that house for those few months.

Towards the end of February 2010, I took a small break during recording, to shoot over to London to attend the premiere of Tim Burton's *Alice in Wonderland* because Avril and I had worked on the theme song for the movie. Tim Burton is one of my favorite directors and I was thrilled to meet him. I wanted to move on from my ex-wife, but first we had a bunch of music we needed to finish. It wasn't just this song, either, but songs I was still in the middle of producing for her upcoming album, *Goodbye Lullaby*. We had started working on her album a year before our split and had a few loose ends to tie up. Creating music with someone I was in the middle of divorcing was one of the hardest things I'd ever done, but I looked at it the same way I look at producing my own work. I compartmentalized it, removing the person from the artist. At the end of the day, it's about the music. It's a job that I was hired to do and I want to do it to the best of my ability. We had barely spoken since the separation and I was unsure how this trip would go. Turned out the trip was great, because it brought me closure. I really didn't feel anything good or bad about Avril at that point, she just wasn't on my mind anymore. I quickly returned from London because I wanted to get home to finish my album and go back to living my new life. I was finally able to move into my new house in Sherman Oaks, too. Todd was ready to move out on his own, so it was just me and Mike living in a five-thousand-square-foot house. I was also seeing much more of Hanna Beth at this point and even though I still wasn't ready for a real relationship, she and I had fun together. She made me realize that Avril wasn't the only one for me and that I would find love and happiness again. I knew Hanna was ready for something real, but I just wasn't. I still needed to figure myself out. As cool and fun as it was, it was never going to work.

By spring, we were 90 percent finished with *Screaming Bloody Murder*, but we couldn't complete the album, because we had tours we'd lined up thinking the album would be done by then. Before we left for the road, Stevo called a meeting about finances and cuts he wanted to make on the upcoming tours. It started out a little hostile and I quickly realized where this was headed. Not only did he want to cut all production from our shows, like the lighting and sound, but he also wanted to get rid of as much crew as we could. We already had a bare bones road crew, so I knew that it could only mean getting rid of my security guard, Kenny. I swear he said it with glee, too, as if it brought him joy to take something away from me. I told him that I felt uncomfortable not having security because just a few weeks earlier, our drum tech Dan Moyse had been randomly attacked at a bar. Stevo immediately raised his voice, saying, "You're wasting our money. You're not with Avril, nobody cares. You're not getting death threats anymore, get over yourself. If you're worried about people beating you up when you go out, then don't go out." I couldn't believe he was serious. I was supposed to hide in a fucking hotel room, while everyone else got to live a normal life? When I balked, he fired right back, shouting that it wasn't his fault I had chosen to be the singer, and he was done paying for my security. Cone didn't say much, but he sided with Stevo and I was outvoted. I said, "Fine, I'll go along with this, but I promise you, what happened to Dan Moyse is going to happen to me. It's not a matter of *if*, it's a matter of *when* I will be attacked." Neither of them agreed or cared and the meeting was over.

Our European tour was a lot smaller than we were used to, playing to around three hundred people in major cities. In the U.S., we were only offered the side stage on the Warped Tour, just like when we started out. We took it because we had no other offers in the U.S. It was humiliating to see the lineup and watch young no-name bands perform on the main stage. Still, we went on stage and fucking destroyed day after day, eventually pulling huge audiences, making the side stage look bigger than the main stage. As shitty as it was, it felt amazing to draw that many people away from the main stage bands. But it was yet another reminder of just how far we'd fallen since the *Chuck* album.

The one glimmer of light was heading over to Japan to play the main stage at the Summer Sonic festival. Our first night was in Osaka, and when we landed we headed straight for our favorite tiny little rock bar called Rock Rock. That bar is usually packed with whatever bands are in town, but for some reason it was pretty empty that night. That didn't stop us from having a good time or getting rowdy. Stevo, Tom, and Cone were completely trashed and jet-lagged and wanted to head back to the hotel to pass out. My assistant, Mike, had come on tour with us, and he and I wanted to stay, but first he wanted to make sure the guys got into a cab okay. He left to take them outside and I went to wait in line for the bathroom. Then I heard someone yell, "He's talking to my friend's girl!" And out of nowhere I felt like I was hit by a train.

I went straight down to the floor, hard, and suddenly multiple people were punching and kicking me. I went into a turtle position trying to block my head and face as best I could (I'd been in fights like this before, when I was younger). Luckily, Mike and Cone heard the melee and came running back in to break it up. As soon as I could, I stood up and punched one of the guys hard in the face, hoping to knock him out. He fell back, but it didn't knock him out, it only made him even more violent. He came running, screaming "I'll fucking kill you!" I got thrown into a back room for protection by Cone and the manager of the bar. That barely stopped the guy, though, and he kept banging on the door trying to break it down. I was confused, terrified, and realizing I was in a very familiar kind of excruciating pain. I feared this attack might have herniated my disc again or, even worse, herniated a new one.

I hunkered down in that room with Cone, until the guys who'd attacked me left the bar. Mike came in and said, "What the fuck happened? Those guys want to fucking kill you." I explained that I was just waiting for the bathroom and these guys attacked me from behind. I had no idea who they were and Mike didn't either, but we knew they were American and had made some reference to "finishing this" at the show. We went back to the hotel, but I couldn't sleep from the excruciating pain.

Early in the morning, our manager Ron and Stevo came to my room to see if I was going to be able to perform that night. By this point, the pain had gotten much worse and I couldn't stand up. First order of business was to get an MRI, and once we did, our fears were confirmed. I had reinjured that same old herniated disc. I couldn't face canceling the shows and going home, so I just said, fuck it. I would take a bunch of Advil, drink enough Jack to take the edge off, and go out there for these two festival shows. When we got back to America, I would need to cancel the next few weeks to recuperate.

Ron wanted to find out who these assholes were, and he walked around the backstage area with the promoter to investigate. It didn't take long to learn that they were a couple of touring musicians who played for the artist Everlast. When confronted, they played it off as "just drunken bar shit" and "no big deal." Ron explained that it was a big deal. "My singer just got out of the hospital and can barely walk right now, so to us it's a huge fucking deal." One of the guys took off his sunglasses and presented his black eye and said something like "Well your singer got me pretty good, so I'd say we're even." When Ron came back to our dressing room with the info, we decided there was not much we could do. Ron said, "What are you gonna do, sue the guy and take his fucking bike?" I've never sued anyone or called the cops in my life and wasn't about to now.

On the way back to L.A., the singer Everlast was sitting near us on the plane. Halfway through the flight, he came over to Ron and me and started getting into the whole thing. Telling us he was at the bar, too, but when he saw it was a total "Dick Farm" he left and that I should've, too. Ron told him to chill out and that thirty thousand feet in the air in the business class section of a 787 plane was not the place to start a fight with an injured guy who could barely walk. He left us alone on the flight, but picked up the same conversation in the customs line at LAX, getting right in my face. Ron came running over once again. "Seriously, dude, you're doing this in customs now? You gotta be kidding me. If you wanna talk, let's talk once we get through customs, but there's a better way to handle this." Everlast muttered something like "Next time you see forty dicks in a bar, you leave," but we never saw him or his band ever again, thank fucking god. I didn't want to fight anyone and certainly not Everlast. I'm assuming he has that name for a reason!

I went home once again to figure out what the fuck I was going to do next. Having been through this before, I knew I did not want to cancel the rest of the year's touring schedule. I was scarred from the *Underclass Hero* cycle, and I didn't want that history to repeat itself with this album. I started doing some of my physio exercises, but they weren't helping quickly enough. I went to doctors, but all they wanted to do was prescribe me heavy painkillers that were going to make me loopy. I had heard that these drugs were horribly addictive, too, and that people were getting really fucked up on them. I don't even remember what the drugs were, but seeing what opioids have done to people, I'm glad I didn't go down that road. So I handled things myself. I would be in pain all day, but if I had a drink or two and popped some Advil, by the evening most of the pain would just disappear. I figured that instead of being on heavy addictive drugs, I would just have a few drinks when the pain was too much. I continued self-medicating my pain as soon as we were back out on the road. Night after night, the combination of Advil and alcohol worked. The shows were great, and I was confident I could get through the whole album cycle like this. Whenever pain flared up, no matter what time of day it was, I would just ward it off with a glass of Chardonnay, a beer, or shots of Jack. My tolerance had always been so high that it didn't really make me feel drunk, just good.

When I came home, I used the break to work on finishing the record and to hang out with a few different girls. Not for any actual relationship, but because I needed constant company. I couldn't bear to be alone at night, but I also didn't want to commit to anything. I tried to be up front about that when meeting women, and most of them were okay with it. From the moment I stopped feeling dejected from my divorce and started feeling free again, I don't think I spent one night alone in my bed for years. It wasn't always sex; sometimes I just needed to hang out and sleep next to someone. Maybe it was all a subconscious reaction to feeling rejected at the end of the marriage. I don't know. What I do know is that other than the back pain, I was having a blast.

My friend Diddler started having some difficulties in his own life and broke off his engagement to his fiancée. So, sure enough, he moved in with me and Mike, into what we were now calling the "Lonely Hearts Hotel." Diddler wasn't much of a ladies' man. In fact, way back in high school, he had picked up his nickname because he would always rather diddle himself than get laid. Living in a bachelor house was somewhat lost on him, but we still had a great time. We were glad he was there to keep an eye on the house while Mike and I were out on tour, and we were on tour a lot.

Whenever we got a short break, I was desperately trying to finish the last few songs for *Screaming Bloody Murder*. One song in particular, called "Blood in My Eyes," was giving me the most trouble. I felt very strongly about it, though, because it captured the disillusionment and collapse of my relationship with Avril. I had written all the music, the melody, and some of the lyrics really quickly back when the marriage was falling apart, but couldn't for the life of me seem to write any more words now. I was just blank. The record label was more than impatient by now.

By that point, we had grown into having an adversarial relationship with them, and I could tell they just wanted to fill their monthly sales quotas and didn't really care about Sum 41 as a band anymore. They wanted me to forget the last few songs and just release the album as it was. I had been getting calls, texts, and emails every day from our A&R guy urging me to forget "Blood in My Eyes" and "wrap this cookie up." I was so pissed that I had Ron tell the label to never contact me directly again. I'm trying to make the best Sum 41 record I can, and this clown is calling it a fucking cookie? Fuck that guy! On top of that, they had been pressuring me to write poppier songs, pointing to the success of Fall Out Boy and Good Charlotte for what we should try to emulate. All power and respect to both those bands—and I think they're both great—but that just wasn't where our heads were at. We wanted to be a heavier hard-rock band and didn't care about radio or what was a "financially viable" music genre. We had lost so much ground by not having a radio hit on the last album that I made a conscious decision not to live and die by radio ever again. I wanted to build a long-lasting fan base by making music that we believed in and proving our worth on the road. Come hell or high water, "Blood in My Eyes" was going to be on this fucking record.

After yet another frustrating morning of getting nowhere with the song, I went out to lunch with Todd. I told him that I didn't understand why I just couldn't finish these lyrics when it had once been so easy. He asked me what the song was about, and when I told him it was about my breakup, he pointed out the obvious: "It's because you're not in that dark place anymore. Look at your life now. You're happy, you're killing it. Everything is good for you now." He was right. Of course I was having trouble writing a song about my divorce, pain, and anger when I was so far removed from it now. I went back to work after lunch, realizing I needed to somehow get back in touch with that angry, hurt guy who had started this song. I decided to study my old self, so I went online and pulled up every bad article, every tabloid photo of Avril with other guys, all the humiliating press about myself, until I got extremely sad, angry, and most importantly, motivated. I picked up my pen, and the rest of the song poured out of me. It worked so well that it kind of freaked me out. It's a trick I hope I never have to repeat. It was all worth it in the end, though. "Blood in My Eyes" went on to be nominated for a Grammy at the 2012 awards, for Best Hard Rock/Metal Performance. It was the first time we'd ever been recognized by the Recording Academy. Figures that the hardest song of my life was the one the label didn't think needed to be on the album and was also the one to get nominated for the highest musical honor.

I don't believe in the secrets you keep
But I do wanna know,
How do you sleep at night

And I'm over you, congratulations
And thank you for all the pain
'Cause it made it be so much more fun

There's nothing to say now
The feelings are already dead
And I don't believe there's a way now
All that is said has been said
I'm waiting for another day, another way
And I don't believe that you can make all the pain go away
So I'll leave it all behind, but I'm leaving with blood in my eyes

Seen through the lines, while believing the lies
For too long a time
And I still don't know how I did

Now war's declared, drawing the battle lines
And I can't see straight anymore
With all of this blood in my eyes

There's nothing to say now
The feelings are already dead
And I don't believe there's a way now
All that is said has been said
I'm waiting for another day, another way
And I don't believe that you can make all the pain go away
So I'll leave it all behind, but I'm leaving with blood in my eyes

I'll be honest, I was devastated when we lost the award to the Foo Fighters, not because I thought we deserved to win over them, but because personally I had put myself through hell for that song. I thought winning that Grammy would be the ultimate validation for my effort. What was far more upsetting than the loss was my band's seeming disinterest in winning, losing, or even being nominated. They just said, "Who cares about getting this stupid award anyway? We were never going to win." I don't know if they were just acting cool or being serious, but I was hurt. Then Lexi from our management team said to me, "Why would they care? They don't put the same thing into the songs as you do, so they don't care about getting the same things out of them as you do." I had never thought of it that way, but of course she was right. All of the music by default is much more personal to me. In some ways, I'm glad we didn't win, because by 2012 I was really starting to lose control. I was so drunk at the awards show that if I had gone up to accept, I would've made a huge fool of myself. Instead, regrettably, I thought it would be funny if I heckled the Foos from our seats at the back when they went up to collect the little gold gramophone. (God, I hope they didn't hear me! I really do love that band.)

The grind continued, and on March 29, 2011, *Screaming Bloody Murder* was finally released. The label gave us no video budget, no marketing budget, and no promotion whatsoever. They spent as little money as they possibly could to make as much money as possible from the Sum 41 super-fans who were going to buy the album no matter what. I was heartbroken, but also not surprised. I felt this was my best work and was extremely proud of the record, but I couldn't force Island Def Jam to promote it. Our only option left was to once again go out and prove ourselves on the road.

The constant back pain on top of the nonstop working, touring, and partying was starting to take a toll. On our Australian tour, I went into the hospital with pneumonia that I am pretty sure I picked up from a woman who coughed on me for the entire eighteen-hour flight. When we landed, I told everyone that I was definitely going to get sick. Sure enough, it hit me hard a few days later. I ended up in the hospital with what the doctors told me was a rare, acute form of pneumonia. They gave me a fifty-fifty chance of survival. They almost had to put me on a ventilator. After a week of being in the hospital on all the IVs and medication, under the care of amazing doctors, I felt great again and was ready to get back to the tour. Unfortunately, we didn't even get to play a single show in Australia on that run, because the tour was over by the time I got out of the hospital. I basically flew there, spent a week in hospital, then left the country. We flew to Spain the next day to resume the tour.

The crazy thing is that I just went straight back into my normal life-style, like I hadn't almost just died from pneumonia a week ago. It didn't occur to me to slow down or ease back into it. The first show back, I was hammered and smoking cigarettes backstage like I hadn't just had a lung infection. The band, and particularly Stevo, were getting more and more angry with me. After we played a particularly bad show in Spain due to my drunken condition, he destroyed the dressing room while screaming about my behavior to Tom and Cone. I wasn't there to hear it, though, because I was already out partying with Mike and some girls. I definitely heard about it later, however, when our agent and manager told me about the damage and informed me that My Chemical Romance had been right next door for the whole thing and now considered us too volatile to tour with again. Stevo's anger at me was the correct response, but it also didn't feel like anything new. To me Stevo was just always angry about something all the time now. While a lot of times it was directed at me, sometimes it was at tour managers, our own management, travel agents, booking agents, or some of the girls I was hanging out with. Everything was coming down to money with him. I understood that people need to make a living, but we were at the lowest point in our career and needed to rebuild. There was nothing but pennies for us at that time. It felt like he was trying to squeeze a dry lemon and getting pissed that there was no juice coming out. Not to mention, I felt like he and Cone were being hypocritical; a pair of drunks telling another drunk to stop drinking. We were all bad! I mostly just blocked it out and kept on doing what I was doing, because I was still in that dangerous mindset of feeling invincible. Not even pneumonia could keep me down!

We were in L.A. performing on Jimmy Kimmel and *Lopez Tonight* and some other shows to promote the album. Before we headed back on the road, Mike and I had to hit the clubs. My friend Buster was a club pro-moter and he had been telling us about this group of models he wanted us to meet. I kept telling him no, because I was not interested in meeting more models. They were usually vapid, vain, and self-absorbed party girls that I had no interest in being around. He swore these girls were different. I did not believe him. Mike and I were at a club called Tru (the old site of the Cathouse) and we ran into Buster, who was hanging out with the models. One of them instantly stood out to me. She was over six feet tall in heels and absolutely stunningly gorgeous. She was really cool-looking in kind of an alternative/punky way. After talking to her and her friends for a while, I could admit it, Buster was right. We hung out, drank, chatted, and as per usual, ended the night back at my house. This girl and I talked all night in my kitchen, while the party raged on without us. She was fun, beautiful, and cool, but also really smart. I had no idea how she was feeling about me, though. Around 4 a.m. the party had dwindled to just a few people and I was afraid that she might be leaving soon. I really wanted her to stay, but I wasn't going to ask her to spend the night with me, because there were no signs that she was interested in me like that. Out of the blue, she decided to jump in my pool, fully clothed, even though it was pretty cold outside. As she swam around alone in my pool, looking beautiful, I leaned into Archer and said, "If I want any future between us, I probably gotta jump in that pool, don't I?" He said "Yeah, I'm afraid you do." So I jumped into the freezing cold water with all my clothes on and within a few minutes we were wrapped up in each other's arms, kissing, and I asked her to stay the night.

She had to leave early for work the next morning. When I came downstairs, I realized I had forgotten her name and failed to get her number. I told Mike that I really liked this girl. She was totally different than anyone I had ever met in my life, but I forgot her fucking name. He grinned at me. "Well lucky for you I found her license on the floor in the kitchen." He gave it to me and I saw that her name was Ariana Cooper.

CHAPTER 14

THESE GIRLS WILL BE THE DEATH OF US

These girls will be the death of us," Mike said to me before we left to tour in Japan. I laughed and said, "What does that even mean?" He replied, "I don't know. I just feel like it's the end of our lives as we know it. You like Ari, and I like her friend Rhiannon." I wasn't sure I agreed. I had no idea where these relationships were headed. Sure, we had a couple great nights in L.A., but we might never see these girls again. That's the way of life for a touring musician. You come home after a few months and shit has changed. In your absence, people have moved on, forgotten about you, gotten into other relationships, or left town. We had a record to promote, and the next year and a half was going to be all about touring. This tour was on top of the almost full year of touring we'd already done before the release of *Screaming Bloody Murder*. It was turning out to be the longest tour we'd ever done.

On day one, when we got to Japan, I woke up and just instinctively felt that it was time to take a break from drinking. I told Mike, "I don't want to party on this tour. It's two weeks long, Japan is always a ton of work, and I could use the break." He was impressed with the decision and with how easy it was for me to just choose to not pick up a drink. I still didn't feel any addiction to alcohol yet. I relished the thought of putting booze down for a bit. I had been going hard for nearly two years straight without a single day off from work *or* partying. Every day was busy and every night was wild, and I was averaging only about three or four hours of broken sleep a night.

Feeling happy, healthy, and confident, we hit the stage for our first show in Sapporo. The Japanese crowd had always been crazy for us in the past, but this trip was very special and meaningful to them (and us). We were the first international band to visit the country after the 2011 earthquake and tsunami, which caused irreparable damage. The show was going great, but halfway through, something started feeling wrong. I don't know if it was due to exhaustion, or the fact that I'd stopped drinking so suddenly, but halfway through "The Hell Song" everything started going into slow motion. It felt like my voice, the music, the audience were being pitched down, like a machine was manipulating the sound in my in-ear monitors. Putting a pitch alternating machine in people's monitors is an old-school tour prank, so at first that's what I thought it was, just a prank that the guys were playing on me. I pulled out my in-ear monitors and quickly realized that wasn't it, because I could still hear it. Something was happening in my brain. I looked out at the crowd, and the audience's faces looked like they were distorting, too. Almost as if I were high on the dreaded Mystic Blue Powder. I felt really dizzy and faint and I knew I was about to collapse. To avoid doing that on stage, I stopped singing and stumbled over to the side, where I dropped facedown with my guitar still strapped on, making a horribly out-of-tune feedback noise. Dizzy and disoriented, I picked myself up, threw my guitar to the ground, and ran backstage. The band was still out there playing "The Hell Song," not knowing what was happening. Mike and our tour manager, Marko, came running after me into the dressing room, where I was on the floor and having a full-blown panic attack. I didn't know what was going on and I wanted to go to the hospital, but I could barely speak and struggled to tell them, "I dddoon'tt knnnow whatttt happp-ppeneddd. I cccaan't gggoo back ooouutt there. I cccaann'tt . . . ddooo thisss." All the while, the band kept on playing the same section of "The Hell Song" over and over in a loop waiting for me to come back out. Finally, Mike went out, told them to stop the music, and brought them backstage.

Cone and Tom were quiet and genuinely concerned about my health.

Stevo was angry and blamed it on having too many drinks. When he realized that I hadn't been drinking at all, he said it was just a panic attack
then and acted like I should just get over it. I admitted that yes, *now* I was
having a panic attack, because I was terrified of what had just happened.
"I've had panic attacks before," I explained. "And whatever was happening
to me on stage, that was something different." I had never felt that kind of
neurological meltdown before in my life and it scared the shit out of me.

I wanted to go to the hospital, but the promoter told us we hadn't
played long enough and we wouldn't be paid unless we went back out and
played some more. I said I didn't care about the money, I was worried
about my brain. Stevo sternly replied, "Well, I do care about the money.
This is why we're fucking out here. Some of us have families. Just because
you don't care doesn't mean we have to suffer the consequences." The rest
of the guys put the pressure on me, too. They thought I should just man
up, have a shot of vodka or whatever it took to get over it, and go back
on stage so we could get paid. So I knocked back a few strong drinks, and
once I was buzzed enough not to care about my health, I went back out
and delivered a really great second half of the show. Afterwards everyone
except me was happy. I left the venue and went straight back to my room. I
was so pissed at them. When they needed me to perform, they encouraged
me to drink. I complained to Mike, "They just pick and choose when my
drinking is a problem or when it works for them. They can drink, do drugs,
fuck songs up on stage, get wild and get in trouble and everyone just laughs
it off. But if I do, it's a problem. I'm so fucking sick of their hypocrisy."

That night was the beginning of the end in my opinion. I saw how
they looked at me and now I saw them differently. It felt like they didn't
give a shit about me and hadn't for a long time. "All I've ever been to
them is the guy who makes everyone money. No one cares about me or my
health unless we're on the road and we're in jeopardy of not getting paid.
When we are home, no one has ever once asked about my back pain," I
told Mike. "They blame me for everything bad that has happened to our
career, but I see their true colors and from now on it's me against them."

After that night, it was clear they didn't care about me, so I wouldn't care about them. I was done with this camaraderie shit.

One bright spot at the time was Ari. She and I had stayed in touch while I was away, and she was constantly on my mind. Whenever we were home between tours, we would hang out. I was always worried that sometime I would come home from tour and she would have a boyfriend. I needed to do something about that. So one night we were at a house party that the band Muse was throwing and I asked her if we could make it official and if she'd be my girlfriend. That was something I never thought I would ever do again after my divorce. I felt like I could be single forever living in my bachelor pad and running around the nightlife with Mike. Now things had changed, I wanted to be with Ari, and Mike wanted to be with her friend Rhiannon. I could see what Mike meant, these girls *would* be the death of us, or at least the single version.

Aside from Ari, my life had become nothing but drinking and touring, drinking and touring, and medicating myself for the never-ending back pain. I was starting to run on fumes (well, mostly Jack Daniel's). When summer hit, we were on the Warped Tour again (still on the side stage), but after only a few shows, my back gave out once more. It happened when we were playing our last song, jumping around to "Fat Lip." I hobbled back to the bus on pure adrenaline and then collapsed on the floor crying, saying, "I can't do this anymore." I went home exhausted and unable to walk. We canceled the rest of the shows that year so I could focus on getting my back in shape for the heavy schedule of touring coming in 2012. As much pain as I was in, I was actually happy at home. Ari and I finally had time to really get to know each other. She stayed and took care of me every day. We drank a lot and talked even more, telling each other every secret about ourselves. We got to know each other so well during that time that it was like we had been dating for years.

Tour was looming, though, and I was horribly anxious about seeing the band again. I hated the idea of being in the same room with those guys, let alone traveling with them for months. We hadn't spoken much since

I went home injured, and I just assumed they had all been on vacation for the last few months. I also had to admit that I hadn't dealt with my back injury properly during that time off either. I had been self-medicating for so long that I had forgotten what it was like to not be in pain or filled with anxiety about it, or remotely sober. I didn't want to cancel more shows or let what happened on stage in Sapporo ever happen again, so I drank. If I felt back pain creeping in, or any other bad feeling for that matter, I would just drink. I knew I was probably drinking too much, but I needed to do whatever it took to get through this album cycle. I would take care of myself when it was all done.

Our first tour run of the year was through Southeast Asia. Ari was coming with me for the first time, and I was glad to have her there, because tensions in the band were incredibly high. I was dreading seeing them, and I assumed the feeling was mutual. We were professionals, though, and were going to do what we needed to do. We had an album out and like it or not, we had to go out and tour. I figured I could drink my way through it like I had always done in the past. When it came time to leave for the airport, I was a complete walking disaster. Normally before each tour I rehearse for days or weeks on my own, getting my voice in shape and getting my stamina up. This time, I hadn't rehearsed or practiced a single song since last year, I didn't even know that I was leaving for tour when it was time to go to the airport. When we got to LAX, I went directly to the bar even though it was the middle of the afternoon. I was already so drunk I had to be reminded that we were not at a nightclub and were actually getting on a plane soon.

When we got to Japan for the first show, I just kept drinking. In the past, I usually kept my drinking in check before shows. As I've mentioned, I always had a huge tolerance, but for the first time alcohol was affecting me differently. I was getting really sloppy and lethargic after only a couple of drinks. My theory for this is that my liver had been working overtime for so long that it wasn't processing alcohol the same way anymore, so I was getting drunk after only two drinks. But hey, I'm not a doctor so who the fuck knows.

The shows started bad and got worse as the tour went on. I had entered into my Jim Morrison period. I was bloated, belligerent, and incoherent. We were flying to every city, waking up early and going to bed late. I wasn't the only problem on tour. We had rented equipment that didn't work and a new crew that didn't know our show. At our show in China, the government had preapproved our set list, but on the day of the show they were demanding we change the songs to ones we hadn't rehearsed or played since we recorded them in the studio. On top of all that, the band relationship was at an all-time low and tensions were simmering.

At dinner one night, we were at a large round table with the whole band, our crew, and the Chinese promoters and their whole team. In Asia, almost everyone still smokes cigarettes, and that night the entire restaurant was smoking, including 90 percent of the people at our own table. Ari was a smoker back then, but was refraining from smoking indoors out of politeness. She leaned into me and said, "I really want a cigarette so badly but I'm afraid to." I laughed and said, "Afraid of what, getting more lung cancer tonight? This entire room is smoking, don't worry about it." The second she pulled out her pack, I saw Stevo eying her. When she lit up, he jumped up and shouted, "Put your fucking cigarette out. I don't want that shit around me!" I was shocked, not because he had just yelled at my girlfriend in front of everyone, but because everyone in the room was already smoking. I shot back, "The whole fucking table is smoking, why are you being a dick?" He fired right back, "They live here, it's different. They're allowed." Ari was mortified and told me not to worry about it.

We went outside so she could smoke, and I told her I was so sorry that Stevo was an asshole and that the rest of the guys followed when it was him against me. Ari was devastated thinking the band hated her and didn't want her around. I tried to explain that it was just stupid band politics and it had nothing to do with her. We went back in after about fifteen minutes, which was apparently enough time for Stevo to have a couple drinks and start smoking himself. I couldn't help but say, "Oh, so now it's okay for you to smoke?" Like always it became a joke to him and

the guys. He smiled and said, "Ah, you know me, once I have a few . . . ,"
as the band all laughed. They all thought it was funny, but it only drew a
deeper line in the sand for me.

The next day, when I saw them all in the lobby, the sight of them
started making me really anxious. Once my anxiety kicks in, it just snow-
balls, and on the way to the airport things were snowballing fast. Hoping to
stave off an impending panic attack, I went to the airport bar and downed
a couple glasses of wine, but they didn't help. I had some really low-dose
Xanax in my bag that I always carried for panic attack emergencies. I had
never actually taken it for its medically prescribed purpose before, but
figured it was necessary. For the first time since the cocaine days, I popped
a half one, and then passed out in my seat on the plane before it even
kicked in. I woke up thirteen hours later in a hospital in Malaysia. I had
no recollection of how I got there. Apparently I was unresponsive when
the plane landed and medics carried me off on a stretcher, put me into an
ambulance, and brought me to a hospital where none of the doctors spoke
English. I remembered nothing. The funny part was that I felt surprisingly
great, like I had finally caught up on all the sleep that I'd needed.

Even lying in that hospital bed, I didn't understand the severity of it
all, or realize that this should be a huge wake-up call. Not only was my
drinking out of control and my back pain worsening, but I also had a
major anxiety and panic disorder that I wasn't dealing with properly. I was
self-medicating through life yet somehow thinking that I was keeping it
all together. I actually thought the whole thing was surprising, because I
had taken full Xanax bars so many times to come down from hard drugs
and was always fine. I didn't think half of a low-dose pill plus two glasses
of Chardonnay would do much. Obviously I was hugely mistaken.

We played the last show and headed home. The guys were rightly
fucking pissed and worried, although whether that was about me or their
paychecks, I didn't know. No one talked to me for the rest of the trip,
which in some ways was a blessing. Ari and I just kept to ourselves, hung
out in the hotel room, drank on our own. She was concerned that I had

gone into the hospital, but she had her own alcoholic demons that were starting to take over. I just wanted to get home and away from the band and enjoy the short break before we headed back out. When we landed and got our luggage, Stevo grabbed his bags quickly and bolted without saying goodbye. I just thought, *Fuck that guy. It's just a matter of time before I quit or find a new band anyway.*

Mike picked us up and drove me and Ari back to the house. He was taking a weird route even by L.A. standards and kept texting people while he was driving, so I knew something was up. He was in a good mood, though, so it didn't seem like something bad was happening. I thought, maybe it was a welcome home surprise party? Or he was taking me to some cool event? We just pulled up to my house, though. We walked in the front door and down my long hallway into my living room and then I realized what was happening. A group of all my closest friends and colleagues were sitting in a semicircle with one empty chair waiting for me. Surprise, it's an intervention!

At least now I knew why Stevo had left the airport so quickly—because he needed to be at my house before I got there. It was just like I had seen on television. Everyone took turns telling me how they felt and reminding me that if I kept drinking I was going to die. I was honestly touched by some of the things that were said. However, I couldn't help looking at the group and thinking, *Some of you are enablers, some of you are just as bad as me, but in different ways, and some of you have been sober your entire lives and would think I needed rehab if I only drank one beer a day.* A lot of blame was directed at Ari, too, as if somehow she'd been forcing me to drink. If anything, I was the bad influence on her! Mike couldn't help but point a finger her way (while also building himself up), saying, "When I was with you all the time, I got you to every meeting, helped you get songs recorded, made sure you were always on time for everything. Now she's in the picture and you're a mess."

When it came time for Stevo to speak, I almost laughed out loud, because he had a whole host of his own issues that needed to be addressed.

I did my best not to crack up as he quickly read through his paper in an "annoyed to be here" monotone. He sounded so disinterested that he reminded me of Chris Klein's character in the movie *Election* when he reads his "Metzler You Bet-zler" speech in the school gymnasium. For a moment, I almost forgot this was a serious event and honestly thought he might be making an inside joke that only he and I would get, like we used to do in the old days. Nobody else laughed, though. I listened calmly to what everyone had to say, and at the end I didn't disagree with them or get combative. I wanted to take it all in and think about it, but at the end of their speeches, they said there was a rehab waiting for me to check into right that minute. I understood confronting me about my drinking and I understood telling me that alcohol had become an issue for me, but this was literally the first time anyone had ever mentioned that my drinking was a problem. Sure, they had been angry at me in the past, but they had never pointed at me and said, "You have a problem." They hadn't even given me a chance to try and fix it yet. Or to fail yet. I told them, "I understand where you're all coming from and I appreciate your concern, but I'm not going to rehab tonight. I'm not saying I won't go at all, but I need a moment to process all of this and see how I feel."

When I finished saying my piece, most of the group seemed disappointed and took off. Stevo and a few others hung around in my backyard and the mood lifted a little. I figured that this was a good opportunity to let Stevo know that we should also take some steps to fix our relationship. "I agree that my drinking has gotten out of control and I honestly want to fix it. I may even go to rehab, but I need to just think about the idea for a few more days," I said calmly. "Regardless of any of that, Stevo, you and I need to work on our relationship because we've gotten to a bad place as friends and as a band and it's not good for anyone." He didn't take it well. In front of everyone still there, he jumped up and started screaming at me. "I haven't done anything wrong," he yelled. "How is this my fault? Oh, so you're blaming me now or something? Tell me what I did. What have I done? What do you mean we're in a bad place? This is all you. Not me."

And without giving me a chance to speak or even respond, he stormed out of my house, leaving everyone stunned by his reaction. All I could say was "What the fuck was that? Isn't that how *I* was supposed to react at my own intervention? Did I say something out of line?" Diddler had seen the whole thing and replied, "No, that needed to be said at this point." It was clear that no matter what I did to sort myself out, Stevo and I were still going to have major problems on the other side.

Since I didn't go straight to rehab, I could tell by the deflated looks on everyone's face that they were upset and didn't think I was taking this all seriously enough. My friend Archer had jumped out of his chair and said "I knew it. I fucking knew he wouldn't go!" and then walked right out my front door. I always want to be a team player, so a couple of days after the intervention I agreed to go take a look at the rehab facility up in Malibu. I went to check it out with Ari and Diddler, and when we got there, they gave us an incredible sales pitch. This place was unbelievably gorgeous, tucked in a canyon with beautiful views and incredible gardens. They offered yoga, meditation, and massages. They said I could bring a guitar if I wanted to, but I just wouldn't be allowed to use a phone or computer, and visitors would only be allowed once a week. It felt like this could be the perfect uninterrupted vacation I'd always wanted. No, not just wanted, deserved. I was actually excited and thought it could be kind of interesting to learn about how alcohol affects the body and the brain. I wanted to dry out, get my anxiety and panic under control, do some yoga to help my back issues, and most of all sit out in the sun and work on some new music. So I said, "Yes! When can I start?" They said they could take me in one week and I should do my best to wean myself off booze to avoid intense withdrawals once I checked in. I told them I'd had two glasses of wine after the intervention and hadn't had a drink since and wasn't planning on starting back up.

I came into rehab stone-cold sober, but due to protocol I was put in a detox room for two days. I was so bored. I didn't have anything to detox. It had been over a week since my last drink, and like every time in the past,

I had just stopped drinking with no issues. No shakes, no withdrawals, no cravings whatsoever. On the third day, they woke me up at 6 a.m. and I had to go to a group meeting almost immediately. I wasn't expecting that, but thought, *Okay, I'll get through this morning meeting and then get back to playing my guitar.* But that didn't happen; the meetings never stopped. They just kept going all day, one after the other. We'd start with a communal breakfast followed by group cognitive behavioral therapy, or maybe individual therapy, topped with some family therapy. In between these meetings and therapies everyone would take five minutes to chain-smoke as many cigarettes as possible before the next one started. There were other meetings, too, but they all blended together in a sea of boring. I asked someone, "When do we go back to having some free time?" They said, "Free time? Never. This is it. Those two days you had were for detoxing. Now it's meetings like this all day every day." There would be no time for playing music, no time for relaxing or working on my back. When I asked about the yoga and the meditation, they said it was all part of the program but on a schedule and just once a week. I instantly regretted my decision, but like everything I do, I was going to try and see it through. I figured worst case, maybe I'd learn something.

The problem was, I started thinking that my issues were nowhere near as bad as everybody else's in rehab. So many other people at rehab were really fucked up and having a hard time. People who were coming off major narcotics or much heavier drinking than even mine. People who had OD'd several times, lost their families, had multiple DUIs, or been in and out of prison. I felt like an idiot in meetings when it was my turn to share and all I had to say was, "Well, I've been touring in a successful rock 'n' roll band my whole life and I really like to party, my back hurts, and I get anxiety." The counselors would ask me how many times I'd tried and failed to get and stay sober. They were shocked when I would say, "Never. This is the first time, and I stopped on day one." It just felt like I was there way too soon; I hadn't hit bottom yet.

One of the things I really enjoyed was my solo therapy sessions, which happened a couple of times a week. I quickly realized the only thing I talked about in therapy was my relationship with my band and particularly Stevo. How we used to be such best friends, but now it had been deteriorating for years. In therapy, I was able to trace it back to the early days of our success and how it felt that the more attention I got, the worse our relationship would get. I couldn't sit there and say "that was the cause," but sometimes the obvious answer is the right one. I also started to realize that I was really resentful about their hypocrisy around drinking. The truth was, we all drank too much, which made the whole thing feel wrong. It was like someone who has twelve drinks a night telling a guy who has fifteen drinks a night that he's the one with the problem.

The fact that the arguments always revolved around canceled shows and not getting paid—especially after the incident in Japan—made it feel like drinking was an issue for me, but not them, because I was the money-maker. They wanted me to stay clean and sober so the money machine could keep rolling. Everyone else could go wild, as long as I showed up and delivered.

Other than being able to finally talk to someone about my band issues, I felt like rehab was bad for me. I knew that I had been drinking far too much, and even though I didn't want to stop completely, I felt I should definitely slow down. Rehab wasn't right for me because it gave me yet another excuse. I could look around and say, "I'm nowhere near as bad as anyone here, so I must not really have a problem." After two weeks, I was done; I couldn't take any more, so I left and went home. In hindsight, I just think it was too early for rehab. I wasn't there yet with my alcoholism. Unfortunately, I also think going to rehab was the tipping point that made me go even harder later. Let me be clear, I believe rehab is great and it's possible I would've ended up there eventually. It just wasn't a good first step for me, because I hadn't hit rock bottom yet. Instead I came out of there stupidly feeling invincible again.

When I left rehab, I was enjoying being healthy and sober. Like I said, I knew I had been drinking too much and I was willing to work on that. I stayed sober and organized a series of group therapy sessions with Cone, Stevo, and our manager, Ron, to work on our problems. Tom has been in the band for a few years but was never part of the inner drama. I had gotten a lot out of therapy in the past, back in 2004 when I was sorting through the aftereffects of the Mystic Blue Powder nightmare, and hoped that if we had a professional in the room we could get to the root of our band issues. I was wrong. What I didn't realize was that therapy only works if the people involved want it to work. Stevo and Cone came in and sat on the couch next to each other, facing me on the other side of the room, making me feel like they were aligned against me right from the start. I came in wanting to expose the guys for being hypocrites and treating me like shit. Stevo came in with a chip on his shoulder and acted like he was only there to fix *my* problems, not *ours*, and certainly not *his*. He didn't seem to think he shared any responsibility for the place we were in. We didn't really get anywhere with the therapy, but it wasn't only Stevo's fault. We were all bad in therapy. All three of us had our own agendas and just couldn't get anywhere with it.

With nothing fixed and still very much broken, we had to hit the road again to fulfill the rest of the year's touring obligations. I was done with my bandmates, so this time, I just said, *Fuck it, I'm doing this for the music and for the fans that we have left.* The one good thing about this tour was that none of us went out drinking heavily. We never made a collective decision or said anything out loud, but I think we all knew we drank too much and should tone it down a little. Instead, we would drink a glass of wine before the show and maybe one or two afterwards, and no hard liquor. It felt like we were all making an effort, at least at first. The tour was long, though, and slowly the temptation to drink started mounting. The band problems, the grueling schedule, the anxiety, and of course, my back pain were pushing me towards self-medicating, and soon I was back drinking heavily again on tour. I believe this is when my body started to become physically addicted to alcohol. I had crossed an invisible line. And started to become dependent. In rehab I learned that the way the brain works is, when you take time off drinking, your addiction doesn't get weaker, it's actually getting stronger and waiting for your return. You always come back worse than you were before. And that's certainly what happened with me.

By the end of the year we started a full tour of the U.S., which we hadn't done in eight years, since the *Chuck* album. It was the tenth anniversary of *Does This Look Infected?*, and to mark the occasion, we were going to play the album in full. I was psyched, because I heard the tour was selling really well, but what I didn't know until we got to the first shows was that the venues were small. They were more suited to up-and-coming acts, not a band that had been around for sixteen years and sold millions of albums. These were small bars and shitty clubs that held only a few hundred people. I had no idea it had gotten this bad for us. The realization pushed me towards heavier drinking than ever before.

I was looking worse than ever at this point. I was puffy and bloated and starting to feel what I now know were early onset symptoms of alcohol-related neuropathy in my legs and feet. The neuropathy led to pain and weakness that made me lose my balance. Well, the neuropathy and being drunk all the time. Strangely enough, on that tour the shows were still pretty good and I managed to keep it together enough to perform. When we went home for the Christmas break, I was drunk the entire holiday. I have no recollection of having my entire family staying with me at my house for a week over Christmas. I've seen photos, but they don't bring back any memories whatsoever.

We were set to play the Soundwave festival on our tour of Australia, so at the start of 2013, Ari and I flew over a few days early to dry out, get used to the time change, and generally take it easy before the band got there. That didn't work out, because our road crew showed up early as well and we just partied with them. By the time the tour kicked off, I was barely keeping it together. I have very little recollection of that tour. Duff McKagan of Guns N' Roses happened to be on the Soundwave tour with his band Loaded, and the guys asked him for advice on what they should do with me. Duff had had his own near-death experience from alcohol and had managed to turn his life completely around and was now thriving. The guys were hoping that he could offer some advice on how to handle this situation. He watched our show and me. He told them I was at a point where I would need to figure it out for myself, because there's not much you can do when someone is that far gone. I needed to crash and burn, and I was well on my way. I don't know why we didn't just shut it down and stop touring—and I think the whole band feels the same way now. We were dragging a dumpster fire aboard a train wreck racing around the world at top speed hoping it wouldn't crash or explode. I was so sick, but I didn't want to quit because we had tour dates on the books, and in my head I was saying, "I'm not a quitter." But I wasn't even capable of making coherent decisions at that point. It was like letting a toddler run your business and keep the household together.

Everything that was bad before, was now worse. My back pain, my anxiety, my resentment towards Stevo and Cone, their anger and attitude towards Ari and me—it was all worse. It came to a head on board a packed commercial flight traveling from Melbourne to Adelaide. Before the flight, we had all been drinking, and for a rare moment we were laughing and having a good time joking around in the bar with the Offspring guys. It was only an hour-long flight, but it was full and we couldn't all fit in business class. For some reason, the promoters had decided to put me and Ari and the Offspring in business while Stevo and Cone were in coach. On the plane, Stevo appeared in the aisle next to Ari and told her to get out of her seat and "get the fuck to the back of the plane." He kept ranting, saying that she didn't deserve to be here, that he was a founding member, and that this was all bullshit. I told him to calm down and that we would gladly go sit in *their* seats and he and Cone could sit up here. It meant nothing to us. We had just sat in the seats that were printed on the tickets. Stevo screamed back, "NO. You're going to sit here and SHE needs to go to the back of the plane." He was obviously hammered, and I told him to calm the fuck down and we'd just trade. He yelled some more expletives at Ari and then threw his ticket in our faces and stormed back to his seat. I was livid and ran back to where he was sitting. We got into a screaming match in the middle of the aisle while Cone watched silently. We never ended up swapping seats and we didn't talk for the rest of the day. The next morning, Ari and I got an email from Stevo apologizing sort of, basically saying, "Haha, you know me, when I have a few, I get a little nutty." It was short and felt disingenuous. This was the hypocrisy from the band that I had grown to resent. Those guys could drink, do drugs, get wild or crazy, act dangerously, yell and scream and get angry drunk, and the next day everyone laughed it off. If I did any of that, though, they would come down on me, because I would be jeopardizing their income.

We had one more tour to make it through before this three-year touring cycle would finally come to an end. We had started the *Screaming Bloody Murder* leg in the spring of 2010 believing we had the best record of our lives, and by the top of 2013, we were barely making it through a show and never wanted to see each other again—or at least that's how I felt. Ari and I kept to ourselves on this final tour as we made our way through Canada with our friends Billy Talent. I would sleep in my bunk on the tour bus until early evening when it was time to get ready for the show. I had started running, hoping it would help ease the neuropathy in my legs. It was getting to the point that I was having a hard time standing up on stage for a full show. After my run, I'd return to the bus, have a little bit of white wine, do my stretches, watch some Muhammad Ali fights on YouTube to get amped up, and knock back a bunch of Advil to kill the pain. My back had been so bad for so long that I was taking up to twelve Advil at once. I would then jump on stage and get through our set as quickly as possible. Then Ari and I would split and go find a place to play pool and drink Jack until it was time for bus call. I was happy when it was just Ari and me. We were great drinking buddies. While a lot has been made of my drinking problem, she wasn't far behind. In a lot of ways, we were very good for each other, but we definitely didn't discourage each other from drinking. We were both in the throes of our own alcoholism and didn't see much of a problem. We knew we drank too much, but it was always a problem for "later." We planned to take care of it all when we got home from the tour, which was ending soon.

I felt like I could coast through the rest of the tour just avoiding the band, along with my own problems. It was always a powder keg, though, and it was eventually going to blow. It finally did backstage in Edmonton. We'd had a surprisingly good set and it kind of felt like the old days on stage. It felt so good that I decided to go hang out in the dressing room with the guys after the show for once. I asked Ari to hang outside in the hall so the band could have a real moment together. It started out great, but then our security guard joked about us having so much fun on stage that we ran a few minutes over our normal set length. For some reason, this infuriated Stevo. He started screaming at me at the top of his lungs, a vein pulsing in his forehead: "We're fucking late because of you! You were fucking one minute late to stage today. I know, because I timed you." Even Cone got into it with me. I was so sick of Stevo's anger and them teaming up against me that instead of taking it like I always did, I yelled back, "Who the fuck cares, you fucking assholes! What the fuck does it matter if we're a few minutes over? We had a fucking great show, that's all that should matter." Stevo wasn't backing down. He was used to always being the loudest guy in the room and loved a good fight. He yelled back, "I fucking care! You're the one who doesn't give a shit about anything." Right then our tour manager, Bobo, walked in, unaware of the fight he was stepping into, and Stevo asked him, "How fucking late were we coming off stage? How many minutes?" Bobo was confused. "Late? You guys were a couple of minutes early tonight." Stevo was not having it, but Bobo had proof: "I record the show every night and you guys were about two minutes early tonight." I looked at Stevo and Cone and just shook my head. "Great, we just had this huge fucking fight about nothing," I said, and stormed out into the hall, slamming the door behind me. I sat there for a few minutes with tears welling up and thought to myself, *This is it, this is the last straw.* I turned to Ari and said, "I can't be in a band with these guys anymore." I didn't know what that meant logistically yet, but I knew that after this tour I never wanted to speak to them again.

I made it six more shows. We finally had a day off in Quebec, and I was having a really hard time walking. My back was in so much pain and how could it not be? I had more or less been ignoring it since 2010. Instead of properly dealing with it, I just kept putting on Band-Aids. Plus, all the running I had been doing to help my legs was actually making my back injury worse. I called my manager and asked for advice. He told me that if I couldn't make it through the last three shows I should just go home. He explained that the tickets were already sold, so the headliner, Billy Talent, wouldn't have to pay us. "Financially it's actually better for them," he said. "And physically it's better for you." I didn't want to cancel, figuring I could just get through it the same way I always did. I went to go find some food with Ari, but I couldn't make it to the end of the block without keeling over in pain. Every step I took made it worse, and I couldn't stand up straight. I had to have Ari help me back to the room.

I lay in bed and thought about my options. I wasn't sure if I could physically make it through the rest of the tour. Even if I did manage to perform, I knew what the worst case scenario looked like: I would go home in a wheelchair and the rest of the guys would go on vacation and I'd never hear from them. I didn't want to put myself through that again. Not for them. Not this time. I said fuck it, called my manager and alerted Bobo, telling them to get me a middle-of-the-night flight so I could sneak out without anyone knowing or making a scene. A car was scheduled to pick me up in the lobby at 4 a.m., and as Ari and I rode the elevator down to the lobby, I said to her, "I have a bad feeling we're going to run into the band guys right now. If we do, just say that we're going to sleep on the tour bus instead of in the hotel room." She looked at me and laughed, "It's 4 a.m., I highly doubt we're going to run into the band right now." The elevator doors opened, and the entire band and crew were standing there like they were intentionally waiting for us. Stevo was the only one who spoke. "So, where you guys heading with your bags?" he asked in a smarmy voice. I replied with my rehearsed response, "Oh, we're going to sleep on the bus so we don't have to wake up early in the morning." He smiled. "Oh really? Because there's a driver over there waiting to take you to the airport." I looked over at the waiting chauffeur and knew we were totally busted. I could only reply with the truth.

I explained that I was sneaking out, because my back was going out and I was afraid to go home in a wheelchair again. I couldn't finish my sentence, because Stevo cut me off. "Whatever, man," he said, and gave me a weak hug and walked away. He never hugged me and definitely never weakly hugged me, so I knew something was up. The rest of the band followed him, while some of the crew stuck around to say goodbye. Our drum tech Dan Moyse walked us to the car, and I asked him, "What the fuck was that? How did that happen?" He said the band and crew were all partying at the bar, and when they came back to the hotel, the driver came up to them and said, "Is one of you Deryck Whibley? I'm here to take you to the airport." It was just bad luck. I spent the drive to the airport freaking out to Ari. "I told you we would see them! I fucking knew it! I had the weirdest feeling! That's it, Stevo is quitting. That hug was him quitting." All I had been thinking about for months was moving on and, once this tour ended, never speaking to these guys again. But this wasn't the way I'd expected it to go down. I was caught off guard and having mixed emotions now that it was real. Ever the optimist, Ari couldn't believe that a hug could mean so much, but I knew. I kept repeating it over and over, "Trust me, I know him better than anyone, that was him quitting. I know it." The driver was apologizing profusely, thinking he had just broken up Sum 41. I kept telling him it wasn't his fault, but he felt terrible. About twenty minutes into our drive to the airport I started to feel strangely happy that it had all happened that way. It had ripped the Band-Aid right off. I didn't have to say anything anymore. It was all over.

Two weeks later I was sound asleep at home and my phone wouldn't stop ringing. I was in bed and just heard it ringing over and over. Finally

I decided to go answer it because it must be an emergency. When I saw Stevo's name, I knew what was happening. He got right to the point: "Hey, just letting you know I'm quitting the band. I can't do this anymore." I said, "Yeah I figured this call was coming. All good. Do what you gotta do." He said that, like when Dave left, he would write up a statement and let us approve. I said, "Great. I really appreciate that. I'll look out for it."

That wasn't what happened, though. Within an hour, Stevo had posted a statement on the band's official Facebook page. We didn't get a chance to see it before it went public. Even with all the shit that we'd gone through over the past few years, I expected that small bit of courtesy. But, just like that, Stevo was out.

CHAPTER 15

CAN IT GET MUCH WORSE?
YES

T his was going to be the best year of my life. No touring, no album to make, no Cone and Stevo. No one to answer to and no responsibility. Finally, for the first time since I was a kid, I would take a break and just be at home. It was a few weeks after the tour ended, and the first thing Ari and I wanted to do was dry out and take a real break from booze. We were shocked to realize how difficult it was. We made several real attempts to sober up, starting with a weekend at the Bacara Resort in Santa Barbara. It's so beautiful there that we were sure it would distract us enough to chill out and sober up. It was the total opposite. Being in that setting made us want to drink even more. We couldn't sit by the pool and *not* have a fun cocktail, after all. And it just felt wrong to dine at fancy restaurants and not have good wine with the meal (and maybe some Jack Daniel's to start). I was a little worried that for the first time I couldn't say no to a drink when I wanted to, but in true alcoholic fashion, I blamed it on the setting and not the actual addiction. I believed that all we needed to do was go somewhere where drinking wasn't as tempting. When we struck out at the Bacara, we decided to go stay with Ari's parents in San Jose, because there was no partying going on there. Well, there wasn't any partying until we got there. We ended up staying a whole month just hanging out, drinking, and having a good time. I still had some fear, because we weren't able to stop drinking even when we were with her parents, but once again we found our excuses, thinking, *We never see them and we're all having fun and bonding together. This is good for us as a family.*

The only thing that brought us back to L.A. was a call from my old friend Frank Zummo. He wanted me to jam on a song with his band, Street Drum Corps, in Las Vegas and I needed to practice and get ready for the show. I did rehearse and knew the songs, but I was a trashy drunken mess during the Vegas show, which shocked the SDC guys. I brought one of my signature guitars, specifically a Squire Deryck Whibley Telecaster model, to play during the show, but I was so drunk that I ended up giving it to a waiter as a tip. I've always been, and still am, a generous tipper, but this one probably takes the cake. He was ecstatic, even though I don't know if he had ever heard of the band. Even if he had, I was unrecognizable by this point. I know this, because around this time I was photographed going into a small Tom Petty and the Heartbreakers show at the Fonda Theatre in L.A., and I looked horribly bloated, sick, and totally hammered, and I was all of the above. I woke up the next evening to see that this photo had gone everywhere, and I was devastated. I told Ari, "This photo is going to haunt me for the rest of my life." She didn't believe it, but I know how this shit works. It will pop up over and over again, because assholes always love to remind you of the worst moments in your life, especially online. Even after all these years it still pops up if for some reason I have to Google the band. After that, Ari and I stopped going out of the house altogether. We just drank at home, watching movies, talking, and listening to music. We weren't always alone; we had friends who were always available to come over for some drinks and stay up all night with us, too.

By this point all my childhood "entourage" friends had disappeared. When Ari and I started to get more serious, I had asked them to move out. As soon as I wasn't funding their lifestyles anymore, they became critical of Ari and of us living together and, soon after, dropped me completely. I know that my drinking played a part, but when I was single and paying to keep the party going, it didn't seem to matter. My drinking only became an issue for them when I stopped footing the bill. This hurt, because these guys weren't random hangers-on, they were the ones that I grew up with, who were like brothers to me. I didn't want to think about it too much, so I just pushed it aside and Ari and I carried on.

The months rolled on in the same cycle of hanging out and drinking and drinking and drinking. One night I was deeply passed out in bed when I woke up because Mike was aggressively shaking me. He was rarely at the house since he moved out and was now living with his new girlfriend. I was startled to see him standing over me. I said, "What the fuck are you doing here? What's up?" He could barely make eye contact, but said sternly, "I need you to come with me." The way he said it made me instantly awake. I got out of bed and followed him, asking again what the hell was going on. He turned and said, "I found Ari in the garage. She was passed out in the driver's seat of the car parked in the garage with the engine running." I was so confused. It was a normal night and we had both gone to bed together, why was Ari driving somewhere? I asked Mike, "Where was she going? Did she just pass out or something?" He stared at me for a moment and said, "No, I think she was trying to kill herself." I was stunned. There was no way. Nothing bad had happened last night. It was a normal evening. We were drinking, watching movies, and then went to bed. "Are you sure?" I asked Mike, not believing it. "Did she say anything to you?" He explained that she didn't say much, but had told him that it was intentional. I had to go talk to her, because he had to be mistaken. Ari was always the optimist. She always found the good in situations. There was no way. Mike had put her on a couch, and when I found her she confirmed that she had tried to kill herself. She couldn't really say why, though. She had been lying in bed next to me and felt so hopeless, useless, and depressed and had been feeling that way for a long time. I was so confused. Why hadn't she talked to me? Why was this the first time I was hearing about it? How could she want to end her life? I brought Ari back to our room and tried to talk, but she was in no condition to have a real conversation. She was embarrassed and withdrawn and didn't want to talk at all. She just curled up in a ball in bed. I lay there holding her, terrified to fall asleep in case she tried to do it again.

As shitty as this whole situation was, in some ways we were very, very lucky. Mike had wanted to grab a few things from his old room in the house, but because he didn't want to see me, he came in the middle of the night. He happened to hear the car rumbling in the garage and thought it was odd and went to investigate. If he hadn't been avoiding us, Ari would have died. It's pretty fucked up to be grateful for alienating your family.

We tried talking about it more over the next few days, but neither of us was ever coherent enough (or sober enough) to get anywhere with it. I tried calling a suicide hotline to get advice, but it wasn't much help. Although it consumed my thoughts every day—and would continue to do so for years—we didn't really talk about it much. Ari said it was just a moment of weakness and that she felt better. Like all of our issues at this time, we just poured more alcohol on it. We simply moved on. I wished that I could help her, but I didn't know how to, and part of me also didn't understand it. I had never felt suicidal quite like that before. Sure I've been horribly sad and bummed out, but as I've said, my brain just automatically starts focusing on the positive relatively quickly. Even as a drunk I was happy and thought I was having a good time.

I knew deep down that this was a wake-up call. I knew we needed to stop drinking. I knew we needed to detox or see a professional. But we just kept putting it off, kept saying "not today, but definitely tomorrow." Of course, we had gone so far down the alcoholic rabbit hole by that point that the days all blended together and tomorrow never came.

Over the course of a year, time became a blur of constant drinking. It wasn't a bender, it was life. If you've never been drunk for months on end, here's what you should know: When you've been drinking that consistently, you're never actually sober. Ever. You never feel normal, because you never get a real night's sleep. You just pass out from drinking, wake up still drunk, drink more, and pass out again, never sleeping long enough to sober up, or get any actual rest at all. You're sleep deprived, hungover, and drunk simultaneously, and in a constant state of delirium. There are moments of clarity that never last long enough to act on them. Ari and I had blacked out the entire upstairs of the house, and since we were keeping ridiculous hours, we never knew what time it was—and didn't want to know, either. We were just avoiding reality as much as possible. At one point I fell trying to walk up the stairs and gave myself a huge black eye. I'd never even looked that bad from any of the fights I'd been in. I actually thought of getting rid of every mirror in the house and on more than one occasion almost smashed them completely because one glance at my face would sometimes force a moment of clarity. The sight of myself, bloated and puffy-eyed, was too painful to stare at for too long. I'd just look away and go back to pretending everything was great. We were hardly eating, and if we did eat, it was mostly pizza. All sorts of garbage, clothes, empty bottles, and pizza boxes piled up all over the house. If I was lucky, my body and mind would completely shut down and I could crash for a few hours. If I was really lucky, I'd wake up with some semblance of sobriety and I would tell myself, "Today is the day, we are stopping." I would make it a few hours, but then all the withdrawal and DTs would start and my hands and body would shake so much I could barely feed myself without it flying all over the place before it even got to my mouth. In rehab, I had learned how dangerous quitting alcohol could be. If it was done incorrectly, you could suffer severe brain damage or death from withdrawal seizures. The shaking started terrifying me, and I would go running for a drink out of fear of having a withdrawal-induced stroke. I'd usually puke up the first few attempts, but eventually after getting a certain amount of alcohol in my system, I'd finally feel normal. After a couple more drinks, because I'm a happy drunk, I'd be back having fun and saying the same old thing, "Tomorrow is the day I will stop." But again, tomorrow never comes.

There's a saying that *You can't rob somebody of their own rock bottom.* Which is basically what Duff McKagan had told the guys a year ago. I had to hit that bottom on my own for anything to actually change. That day came on April 15, 2014, three weeks after my thirty-fourth birthday. It was a pretty typical evening for Ari and me, hanging in the backyard, laughing, talking, maybe planning on watching a movie. I went inside and poured myself a drink of Grey Goose with the tiniest splash of Diet Dr Pepper and then collapsed on the kitchen floor. I was conscious, but barely lucid. I knew something was seriously wrong, but couldn't for the life of me figure out what was happening. I had both sharp and dull pain radiating all over my stomach and I felt incredibly sick. It was unlike any feeling I'd ever felt. Ari was in no shape to drive me to the hospital, and we were both unsure what was the best thing to do. *Maybe it will pass*, I thought, as I crawled on my hands and knees up the stairs to my bedroom. Ari called some friends for help, and by the time our friend arrived to take me to the hospital, I had passed out from the pain.

My next memory was waking up in a hospital and seeing my mother and Kevin hovering over me. When I opened my eyes, my mum jumped up with a big smile. "Deryck, hi!" I knew things must be bad, because they lived in Ajax. Based on her reaction, though, I thought maybe it was all just a scare and I was actually all right, but the memory ends there. The next thing I remember was waking up alone in the hospital, confused and groggy from the sedation. It was the middle of the night and no one was around. The room was very dark and gray, lit with dim blue lights, but through blurry vision I could see all the IVs and wires hooked up to me and I started angrily ripping them out. Then nurses rushed in and I heard people saying, "no, no, no," and then the memory fades.

I woke up in a different hospital. This one was much nicer and brighter and my primary care doctor was there, which led me to believe I was now at Cedars Sinai in Beverly Hills. I was still so confused, but felt safe that my doctor, Dr. David Ng, was taking care of me. Ari and my mum came in and broke the news: I had been in a coma for days. When I finally awoke, I had been completely sedated so I could sleep through the entire process of alcohol withdrawal, delirium tremens, and detox. My doctor explained the rest: My liver and kidneys had failed. The other hospital had given me drugs that made things worse, and if I had stayed there, I probably would have died. I was awake now and under proper care, but I wasn't out of the woods. In fact, Dr. Ng only gave me a fifty-fifty chance of making it. I was stunned. How did it get so bad?

Turns out that while my brain had a natural tolerance for alcohol and I rarely felt as drunk as I should've, my liver felt every single drink. I drank it into failure. The doctor had more to say. "We don't normally see this level of severity at your age," he explained. "You're having issues that a lifelong drinker in their late sixties comes in with. You're here now, though, and I have to tell you, if you make it through, I don't think you can ever drink again." I understood what he was saying, but I couldn't wrap my head around living my life completely sober. "What about just having a little wine with dinner?" I asked. He said something in response that instantly changed the way I thought about drinking forever. He said, "Deryck, is drinking a couple of glasses of wine at dinner really going to make your life *that* much better?" I looked at him, paused, then smiled and said, "No, it's not. What a great way to look at it." I figured if having two glasses of wine at dinner was going to make my life go from dull to exciting, then I had other, bigger problems to deal with.

I had slept (is that what you call it when you're in a medically induced coma?) through the worst of the detoxification process, so I actually felt unbelievably clear for the first time in years. I was so happy that I was finally free from the cycle I had trapped myself in for so long. I was still, however, in a hospital bed with three or four IVs in each arm, wires all over my body to connect me to machines, and getting up to twenty needles a day. My arms were covered in bruises, my stomach was riddled with ulcers from abusing Advil night after night on tour, and I had a two-month-old beard that I had no recollection of growing. I guess I really did hit my Jim Morrison period.

Even though I was feeling better, my doctor was right about it being touch and go. One time I was feeling fine and chatting with the nurse about when I could go home, when I started vomiting blood. The nurse yelled for help, and the whole team came rushing in and whisked me off to the ICU. This wasn't an isolated incident, either. I would feel fine and suddenly my organs would crash and I'd be rushed to the ICU again. I was in the hospital for an entire month.

Early on in my hospital stay, the doctors had put a little tube in my abdomen and hooked me up to a machine that would pump out all the bile I was holding in. All that bloating that was so thoughtfully documented by that now famous photo was never actually fat. It was all bile and liquid that my body was retaining. Day after day in the hospital my body would produce liters of this dark yellow bile and the staff would whisk it away. In just a few days, I went from my heaviest weight of 135 pounds down to 104 pounds. After all the bile was gone, I was emaciated. When I was first admitted, I was so jaundiced that my skin had a distinct yellow hue. I also had edema in my feet and ankles causing them to swell to the point it caused severe nerve damage in the bottoms of my feet. Ari and I had been so out of it for so long that we didn't notice the yellow skin or the swelling. I was going to have severe muscle atrophy from being in bed for so long, which was reversible, but some of the issues, like the nerve damage in my feet, could be permanent. My doctors told me to expect at least a year and a half of recovery to get back to any sense of normalcy mentally and physically. And that was if I could remain sober. I knew I wanted to get on my feet and back home as soon as possible. I asked if I could try and take a walk. I couldn't even stand two seconds on my feet. The pain was so intense from the nerve damage that it instantly brought me to tears—and that was while I was on a morphine drip. As I realized what I had done to my body, I broke down. I felt so low and pathetic. How could I have let myself get here? I was smarter than this. I felt so ashamed, so embarrassed, so angry, and so guilty. I'm my mother's only child and I almost killed myself with booze. My mum was a nurse herself and although I know she was terrified for my life, she never showed it and stayed strong and positive. Sleeping on the cot next to my bed the entire time taking care of me as if she worked at the hospital. I was also completely terrified of how my life would look moving forward. Me, sober? Could I even pull that off?

Ari was in terrible shape herself. Not as bad as me, but definitely not good. Everything had happened so fast. She had still been drunk when we got to the hospital that first night. Then my parents were in town and they called Mike, who came rushing over to the hospital. There was so much anger, blame, and fighting going on about what had happened, how it had happened, and what to do next. While my parents and Mike were fighting over my care and deciding if I should be transferred to Cedars Sinai or not, Ari was puking in the bathroom and crying. She had been drinking almost as much as me and couldn't stop to detox or check into rehab while I was in the hospital. She was chugging vodka to try and stop the withdrawal symptoms when she hit her rock bottom: crying on the bathroom floor in a hospital while the person she loved was dying in the next room. She knew this was the turning point for her, too. We were going to have to do this together if either one of us was going to survive. She poured the rest of the bottle into the toilet and came back out to my room. That was the last drink she ever had. She went cold turkey.

When I finally got cleared to go, it still wasn't over. I had been in the hospital for about four and a half weeks and would still need to come back daily for tests. I was glad to be home, but I was scared for my health, for Ari, and for my career. Would I ever get back on stage? Was my career over? Would I ever be able to walk normally again? My muscles were incredibly atrophied after my hospital stay, but the real problem was that my feet were in so much pain that when I tried to stand up, I would instantly collapse in agony. It felt like I was perpetually walking on broken glass. I was so thin and sick, my face was sunken and gaunt, and my hair was falling out in clumps. While my body was very slowly mending, my brain had its own work to do. I still couldn't form full sentences and got confused easily. I tried picking up a guitar and couldn't force my fingers to play a chord, which was actually the most heartbreaking part. I'd known this wasn't going to be easy, but it was way worse than I'd thought. I felt like I was starting from zero, having to teach myself how to do the most basic tasks from scratch. It took months of sitting and thinking, getting my brain working again, before I was ready to try any real physical therapy. I couldn't be on my feet for more than a few minutes without wanting to burst into tears from the pain, and I was humiliated by falling to my knees after only a couple of steps. It was during these long days that I realized that Stevo had quit the band on April 17, and a year later, almost to the day, I went into the hospital. The scariest part about that, and the reason it stuck out, was that it felt like he had only quit a week ago. An entire year had gone by in the blink of an eye. So much wasted time.

I reached out to the two people that I knew had seen and done it all a million times. I needed a boost, some encouragement, and some reassurance that I was going to be okay. One of those people was Tommy Lee. He had been sober for a number of years already, and when we spoke he instantly made me feel like I wasn't alone and shouldn't be embarrassed, because "there's a lot of us out there." The other person who got on the phone with me was Iggy Pop. He gave me the few encouraging words that completely changed the game for me. He said, "You need to forget who the fuck you *think* you are, and get back to who you *really* are." Those words resonated so much, because in an instant it all became so clear, how I'd gotten to this place. I had this image of myself as the guy with a huge tolerance, who could out-drink people twice my size, stay up later, sleep less, and still work harder than anyone. When I started self-medicating for my back pain and panic disorder, I had crossed an invisible line and fallen into a physical addiction where my body became dependent on alcohol to function. And once I continued further beyond that line, it just stopped functioning altogether. Sure, I had been able to pick it up and put it down for the first fifteen years of drinking, but in those last two years, I completely trained my body to *need* alcohol. No wonder I was spending $2,000 a week on booze.

I was motivated and determined to get my life back on track. All I could think about was music. I missed playing my songs. I missed being on stage. I missed writing new music. I missed the fans and the Sum 41 family around the world. I had learned a long time ago not to look at the comments online, but someone told me I should see what fans were saying. The messages they left were so positive and supportive, like "We need you back on stage," "Your music changed my life," and "The world wouldn't be the same without you." I was so used to being trashed online that I didn't think it was possible to see such positive things on the internet. The fans became a huge motivator for me. I needed to get back out there and see them, to do what I always did best—play fucking music for people.

By the fall of 2014 I had been out of the hospital for about four months, and was ready to get back to my life. I put myself on a grueling daily schedule of therapy, exercise, physical therapy, and working on music. I went around the house putting up photos of me on stage at huge festivals. I wrote encouraging messages on pieces of tape and stuck them to the walls. I started going to AA meetings, but they didn't really suit me. I preferred a one-on-one, back-and-forth conversation, so I started going to therapy again. I would do that in the mornings, then go to physical therapy sessions at my house with my friend and trainer Craig Hollander, and then do my own workouts. In the evenings, I would go into my studio and work on relearning guitar and trying to write music until about 2 or 3 a.m. and then repeat every day.

For months it felt like I was getting nowhere. I was doing great with not wanting to drink, but I wasn't seeing any progress with my walking, strength, pain relief, or even music. Every time I saw the neurologists about my feet, they never had any answers either; it was always the same: The pain will either be permanent or it will go away. *Oh great, why am I here once a week then?* Worse than all of the physical ailments, though, was that my creativity was gone. It was bad enough that I had to learn to play guitar again, but I couldn't write songs at all. I was struggling to get even some semblance of a guitar riff or a cool lyric. It felt worse than writer's block, because it was like I didn't know how to write any music whatsoever.

It didn't feel possible, but my life took another turn for the worse when I got a call from my accountant. It appeared that Mike, who I had known since I was five years old, had been stealing from me for the past few years. He was able to get away with it because when I first brought him on as my assistant, I gave him a credit card. I trusted him like my brother and had told my accountants never to question his transactions. He knew about this and, apparently as soon as I stopped paying attention, he took advantage of it. My accountants didn't question when he bought himself a car or jewelry for his girlfriend, because I had told them not to. While we had been estranged since I asked him to move out of the house, he had continued his scam, along with other childhood friends who had been charging groceries and their living expenses to me. Now it was all coming out into the open. This hurt a lot.

Even though he had moved out years ago, I still had Mike's room exactly the way he'd left it. I was so upset by his betrayal that I had to get rid of it all. While I was in there, I found more receipts for things that he'd purchased for himself on my credit cards. My spirit was shattered. I thought I'd done the thing that you're *supposed* to do when you have success—stick with the people who knew you before you were famous. I brought many of my childhood friends along for the ride, employed them, gave them jobs with salaries and on top of it paid for a lot of other things. I had taken care of them, and so many of them betrayed me in some other way. And when my life got tough, and I was the one who needed help, they bailed. It's like *Entourage*, except at the end of my series I find out that Eric, Drama, and Turtle were using me the entire time and then split when times got tough. It dawned on me that the only people who had ever really screwed me over or stolen from me were some of the people I was closest to. It was never strangers or people in the music industry. It was always the people I loved, cared for, and trusted the most who fucked me over.

I went into a very dark place after that realization. It was too hard to process this betrayal, especially after almost drinking myself to death and spending months and months trying to claw my way back and seeing little to no progress. I started having really dark thoughts. Like *What's the fucking point of all of this? Just say fuck it, who cares if booze is going to kill me? I might as well just drink and enjoy whatever life I have left because I don't want to live like this anyway.*

Dark thoughts like this were not normal for me and they scared me. I stopped and conducted a small thought experiment: *What are you actually fighting for?* I replied in my head: *Well, I want everything back, and more.* I couldn't help but notice that it rhymed. I thought, could that be a lyric? I wrote it down, and once I did that, a few more lines came out and suddenly I had the words to a song, and I actually liked them.

What I'm fighting for
Everything back and more
And I'm not gonna let this go
I'm ready to settle the score
Get ready 'cause this is war.

It completely summed up where I was at mentally, how I felt, what I wanted, and what I needed to do to get there. It was my new mission statement. Those lyrics meant, *I've got unfinished business. I won't count myself out. It's going to be the hardest thing I've ever done in my life, but if I fight harder than I ever have before, I can win.*

Those few words were like a gift from the universe. My outlook changed completely and I never looked back. I'm not religious or even that spiritual, usually just believing in the power of hard work, but I realized that I needed to have faith to get through this one. *Just believe. It may seem impossible, but if you believe you can do it, you will do it.* I threw myself into a harder and more challenging workout and found multiple physical therapists. I wouldn't allow myself to be discouraged by slow progress anymore. I reminded myself, "People have done much harder things in life, so stop fucking whining. You can do this."

There was still the issue of Sum 41. Sure, I was working on music for what I planned on being a new Sum 41 album, but I still never wanted to speak to Cone or Stevo again. As far as I was concerned, they were dead to me. At this point I was unsure of who else would be in this version of Sum 41, but I knew in order for me to get better I had to have the goal of writing and recording an album. Dave Brownsound and I had rekindled our old friendship even before I went into the hospital. When I got out of the hospital, he was on a plane to come see me a few weeks later. We talked about playing music again, but I told him that the band was so broken it might not exist. On top of that, the band didn't actually have a record deal anymore. At the end of 2012, long before I was in the hospital, our relationship with Island Def Jam had gone past the point of no return. We hated being on the label and they didn't know what to do with our music. We had signed such a huge record deal with them in the late nineties that we were still contractually obligated to give them one more album—and they would owe us a million dollars as an advance. We said, "Look, this clearly isn't working out for either of us. Why don't you keep the million dollars you owe us and just let us go clean." They agreed and we were free. As great as that was, it was also scary to be out there on our own, and frankly, there weren't many labels that wanted to sign us—and that was before Stevo left.

TIME WON'T WAIT

*A*ri and I had been through a lot together in a short period of time. Sometimes these things can destroy a couple, but it only made our relationship stronger as we both worked on our mental health and sobriety. One of the hardest things about recovering—and recovery in general—is figuring out how to be social again. Ari and I had gotten rid of most of the people in our lives that represented anything negative, but when we tried to hang out with anyone new, it was uncomfortable and awkward and made us feel anxious. It seemed like we were destined to be our only friends forever at this point. One day I received an out-of-the-blue text from Mikey Way from My Chemical Romance asking how I was doing. Sum 41 and My Chem had done shows together in the past. When I was at my worst with drinking, Mikey was at his worst in his own way, too, and we would hang out at my house all fucked up and not making much sense together. I hadn't heard from him in over a year, but he reached out to let me know that he was sober now, too, and we should get together. Turned out that he and his now wife, Kristen, lived down the street from us, and we all became good friends during a tough time. We went to concerts, dinners, and just hung out at each other's house. It helped Ari and me realize that being social was possible, it just needed to be with the right people. Mikey and I are still super tight. I think being able to lean on each other made it possible for him and me to get through this incredibly difficult period in our lives, and I'm forever grateful that he reached out that day.

I had also started playing music with friends again. Frank Zummo and I had been getting together often and jamming at my house. Way back when Stevo first announced he was quitting the band, Frank had suggested he could step in, and we enjoyed playing Sum 41 songs together. Since Dave was interested in rejoining the band, I thought trying to mend my differences with Cone could be a good idea. It was hard for me to call him, though. I would pick up the phone, start to dial, and then say, "not today," and hang up. Eventually, with the help of a lot of therapy, I was able to make that call. Cone and I started talking and began the long process of putting the pieces of our relationship back together. It was important to both of us to talk just as friends and not dredge up the bullshit of the past. We didn't talk about the last night on tour or all the fights we had or even Stevo quitting the band. Instead we talked about the birth of his first child and I told him what had happened in the hospital. It was a small first step, but it felt positive.

I started to have some momentum in my life. I was finally progressing physically. This idea of Sum 41 with Zummo on drums and Dave back in the band seemed incredibly promising. Plus, I had written some songs that were making me feel like I could write a full album. To help, I came up with a new writing trick where I set up a TV in my studio and played Quentin Tarantino and Tim Burton movies on silent with a guitar in my hand, letting the images inspire me. I started writing riffs and bits of music that I jokingly referred to as "Hard Score Punk," which would eventually become the album *13 Voices*.

Life was feeling good again, and in December of 2014, I proposed to Ariana at the Beverly Hills Hotel. I had rose petals laid out from the doorway all the way to the bed, where they were laid out in the shape of a big heart. Then I got down on my knee and presented her a ring and for some reason she was completely shocked—or at least pretended to be. We had been through so much together in the past four years, and all the ups and downs had only made us stronger. I couldn't wait to spend the rest of my life with her. Instead of getting drunk on champagne like in the old days, we jumped in a Rolls-Royce Phantom and had the driver take us to Mel's Diner for milkshakes. It was the perfect night—and one we'll actually remember!

At this point, I felt it was finally time to tell Ari about the whole experience with Greig Nori. It was the one secret I had still kept, partly because I was still embarrassed by it, but also because I didn't really think about him much. She reacted the same way as Avril, saying, "That's fucking abuse!" But I still didn't think it was. She was adamant, though: "He groomed you from a young teen and *mentally* forced you. You said no, you didn't want to do this anymore, and he told you it had to continue or you would lose everything. That's psychological, mental, and physical abuse." I hadn't heard the terms "grooming" or "mental abuse" yet and had always brushed off the Greig experience as just some shitty thing that happened. I wasn't any kind of victim. The only reason Greig was on my mind was because I was around the age he was when we met. I was sixteen back then and thirty-four now, and it was dawning on me how much power someone in that position could have over a kid from a broken home who idolized him. Grooming and molding him into what you wanted him to be. I saw how it could be tough for a kid in that position to stand a chance. When Ari pointed out all the things he had done that were potential grooming behavior, it made me question why Greig had started hanging out with me in the first place. All of a sudden, at this age, the picture started to become much more clear and obvious. Once again, Greig started to consume my thoughts.

It started to eat away at me that, throughout much of my life and career, some of the people closest to me had taken away so much. I was sick of it. I decided to file a lawsuit against Greig Nori to get my publishing back. I had never bothered looking into it before, because back when he was setting up all of those contracts, Greig had told me that it would be legally impossible to ever reverse them. Then one night I was having dinner with my old friend Michael McCarty, who had signed me to EMI publishing back in the day, and told him that I felt that Greig had unfairly taken more than his share of writing credits from my early songs. I was still upset that the splits were irreversible and there was nothing I could ever do about it. Michael was shocked, but he told me that I absolutely could change publishing splits after the fact. There are no rules as long as the parties agree. I was stunned. All those years I had been thinking there was nothing I could do about it.

After almost a year of sobriety, I just kept feeling better and better. I found that even laughing felt better. Ari and I had laughed all the time when we were drinking, but when I found something funny now, it was such a genuine feeling that I hadn't really felt since I was a kid. I was sleeping better and I was in less pain in my feet. My therapy was helping me cope with my anxiety and panic, and I believed that it could help me with Cone. We were speaking, but I didn't know if I could get into a room with him yet. I was still so angry over how he and Stevo had treated me. I knew they had every right to be upset with me about my drinking, but I felt that if the roles were reversed and either of them had been struggling, I would have handled it differently. I wouldn't have yelled at them or made them feel like such a piece-of-shit loser about it, because what does an alcoholic do when they feel bad? They fucking drink more. I would've said something like "This person, our fucking brother, is terribly sick and we need to do everything we can to help him." Don't get me wrong, I don't blame anyone but myself for the hell I went through, but I know I would have handled things differently if they were the ones with the problem. I knew if Cone was going to be in my life, I needed help to let those feelings go. I spent months working on changing my perception of him. Over time, I felt better and more receptive to the idea of building Sum 41 back up with Dave, Tom, Zummo, and even Cone.

We took it slow. Tom and Cone had never met Zummo before, so they came to L.A. and we jammed old Sum 41 songs in my living room. I had missed playing so much and Zummo is such a solid and unbelievable talent that we just threw him more songs and he learned them on the spot. Zummo had been in so many different bands and played as a studio drummer, so he easily understood the fast punk rock or metal stuff. When we played something a little more mid-tempo or hard rock, he brought a sort of Dave Grohl/Tommy Lee vibe that just felt solid, exciting, and fun. What sealed the deal was when we played the song "Pieces," which for me *had* to sound a certain way or it would fall flat, and he nailed it. Unfortunately, as much as the guys agreed Zummo was a great drummer, they were still gunning for Stevo to come back. I hadn't even proposed the idea of bringing Dave back into the fold yet, which I knew would probably make Tom feel pushed aside, and I wasn't ready to grapple with the idea of Stevo coming back, too.

The bigger issue was that I still couldn't stand or walk very much, because the pain in my feet and back was better but not gone. I had to play sitting down most of the time, which didn't feel very rock 'n' roll. I felt great about the music, but had no fucking clue if I was actually going to be able to go out on stage and perform. It wasn't just physical either; I had no idea if I could perform totally sober, either. I was really nervous that this could be a total embarrassment. I decided to face the issue straight on. I booked three solo shows in three-hundred- to five-hundred-capacity clubs, billed as Deryck Whibley Playing Songs of Sum 41. I had Zummo on drums and my two friends Devin Bronson and Mitchell Marlow on guitar and bass, and asked Mikey Way to play a few songs with us, too. I knew there would be all kinds of pressure and expectation for the first Sum 41 shows after my stint in the hospital and with a new drummer, so I wanted to take the heat personally. If I was going to fail, fall on my face, or have to cancel, it would be on me, not the band. Some of the guys disagreed and felt we should've done these shows as Sum 41, but I wanted to protect the band and make our eventual return something special.

The shows couldn't have gone better. From the very first moment I walked on stage, I was almost in tears. People seemed so happy that I was okay, holding up signs saying "Welcome back, Deryck!" Everyone sang along at the top of their lungs with so much heart and passion. Within minutes of being on stage, I knew that this was where I belonged. I also knew that even if it hurt me, I was going to go out on tour. I still had some balance and pain issues, but if I modified my movements, I could do what I needed to do on stage. I told my manager and agents to start booking Sum 41 tours. I was ready!

Alternative Press reached out to see if we were interested in participating in a six-page career retrospective of Sum 41 and if we would perform at the AP Awards that summer. It was the biggest thing we'd been offered in a decade and I said yes to both. It was exactly the type of show to reintroduce Sum 41 and to announce that, after nine years, Dave Brownsound was back in the band. For the article, the magazine wanted to interview the whole band, individually, along with people from our past, including Greig Nori and, of course, Stevo. I was surprised to hear Stevo declined to be interviewed. He had nothing to say about the band? It had been two years since he quit. Was he still so mad that he wouldn't even talk about the band he had spent his entire adult life in? A couple of days later, I got a message from Stevo that he'd like to talk. We had a lot to catch up on from the last two years, including my near-death experience and his new fatherhood, so I thought it would be a cordial chat. I was wrong. I was asking Stevo about his new son, when he interrupted me and started screaming at me like it was still three years ago and we were still knee-deep in the shit. He yelled, "Why would I be a part of some article when I have nothing good to say about being in the fucking band?" and "I knew you were going to end up in the hospital, it was so fucking obvious!" And then he hung up on me. I was stunned. Not because he yelled, but because was that the point of this call? Had he been holding in that anger since the last day of the tour two fucking years ago? I had spent the last two years worrying about being on a dialysis machine for the rest of my life, not about shit that happened at the end of the Billy Talent tour. Thank god I was in a strong and confident place with my sobriety, because otherwise that could have been a massive trigger.

Stevo called back and apologized for hanging up, but not for yell-ing. He wanted me to meet him tomorrow to have it all out in person. One thing I had learned over the last two years was the importance of boundaries. So I did something I had never really done with Stevo before: I said no. "I can't meet you tomorrow, I'm busy," I said. "And I have no interest in yelling about ancient history. I've lived so many lives in the past two years." He screamed at me, "Yes you can! And you will!" I laughed and said, "Stevo, you can't just *demand* that I meet you tomorrow. I have a life. I have things booked for tomorrow." He didn't like that and started yelling, "You fucking owe me, you OWE me!" I had spent enough time in therapy to know this conversation was going nowhere, and there was no place for this type of shit in my life anymore. So as he kept yelling, demanding we meet, I calmly just kept repeating, "Maybe in the future, but not right now." It went on and on with me repeating that same phrase about six more times until eventually he gave up and we got off the phone.

The phone call confirmed that not only did I *not* want that kind of energy in my life, but I *couldn't* have it around me. I immediately started feeling incredibly anxious. I started thinking about what my life would be like if he was back in the band: constantly feeling judged and walking on eggshells afraid of his disapproval and angry outbursts. I talked about the call with my therapist, and as we looked back at my relationship with Stevo, I realized that for years I had desperately sought his approval. And then I noticed that so did Cone, Dave, Tom, Greig Nori, and almost everyone we worked with back in the day. Everyone wanted Stevo's approval. It wasn't easy to get, either. He was intelligent and very disapproving and let you know how he felt all the time. He was always the loudest guy in the room and never held back his thoughts. Don't get me wrong, we were all close friends, and back in the day, we were merciless when we teased each other. No one was ever safe, but this was different. Stevo was mercurial with a "holier than thou" attitude, and what was acceptable to him one day was not the next. Like when we were in China and Ari got yelled at for smoking and then Stevo turned around and lit one up himself. Or he would scream about Tom and I trashing the bus but then be excited to show people the hilarious footage of the carnage. For years, I never knew if something would make him laugh or yell. Stevo's judgment of me and disapproval of whatever I did made me feel anxious whenever he was around. I just couldn't have that in my life anymore.

I guess the one good thing about that call was that it brought me closure. I hadn't really thought about Stevo or him quitting the band in a long time. I wasn't mad at him. I knew he wasn't a bad person. In fact, I know he is a really great human being who was an amazing friend for a long time. We just ran ourselves into the ground together and we found relief from the years of relentless pressure and stress in all the wrong ways. Mine was drinking, Stevo's seemed to be anger. Cone, who was the perpetual little brother and odd man out, wanted somewhere to belong so he sided with Stevo, which made me dislike them equally. Dave had quit, which in some ways broke our initial bond. Everyone played a part, and we had become unglued and the whole thing unraveled.

But all this was in the past now—and I didn't want to look back. I had been through fucking hell and only wanted to focus on the future and making Sum 41 bigger and better than ever. The first step was coming this summer. We had big plans for the AP Awards, to reintroduce Dave back in the band publicly. And to really make a splash we were going to perform the Run-D.M.C. song "King of Rock" with D.M.C. himself. We had performed the song back in the day and always loved how people's faces lit up when they heard the first few notes. Now we were going to perform that very song with one of our childhood heroes, from the band that inspired us to incorporate hip hop into our own music in the first place.

For some reason, the music industry loves to put on huge events and then give the bands no time to rehearse. I had put together a little demo of the medley we were going to perform and sent it out to everyone in the band and D.M.C. so they could learn it. The medley was basically a Sum 41 highlight reel, with sections of "Still Waiting," "In Too Deep," "Fat Lip," "King of Rock," and "What We're All About," all played as one long song. We showed up in Cleveland the day of the show, did a quick run-through in soundcheck, and then just had to hope it all worked out come showtime. We all shared a dressing room with D.M.C. and his crew and he held court. He had great old stories from back in the day with Russell Simmons, Rick Rubin, the Beastie Boys. He told us how Run-D.M.C. and early hip hop got started and gave us the actual breakdown of how "Walk This Way" with Aerosmith came to be. The most surprising story he told was how Sum 41 had actually inspired *him* when he was in a dark place in his own life and feeling irrelevant in the early 2000s. When "Fat Lip" came out, he could see that we had the old-school spirit and had been influenced by his band and his generation of hip hop. He realized that his legacy was living on in the new generation of music. We were really touched to hear that.

When it came time to get on stage together, I was nervous as hell. I didn't need to be. The show was incredible. The crowd was going wild, even starting a mosh pit. When Dave came out halfway through, there was a massive roar, and it got even louder when D.M.C. grabbed the mic. It felt just like the MTV twentieth anniversary performance all over again. It also reminded me that fuck, this was a great fucking band to be in.

After that night, once again, the tide began to change for Sum 41. Suddenly we had that all-important momentum on our side again. The press was calling for interviews and quotes. We were offered the headlining spot on the next year's Warped Tour, as well as the Kerrang! Tour in the UK. We were offered great slots on other huge festivals around the world. Our headlining tour sold out immediately. Our next year was already filling up and we hadn't even released new music yet.

When I got home from the AP Awards, Ari and I got married. It was a beautiful ceremony at the Hotel Bel-Air. Unlike the pressure and insecurity that surrounded my last wedding day, this one felt like an amazing, casual party with all of our friends and family. We'd come through the dark side together, more solid and more in love than we were before. It literally was the best day of my life. Nothing had ever felt so right in my personal life. I had never felt this deeply in love and knew that it would only continue to grow stronger. Which it has. The only downside was that I was so deep into trying to finish the next album, we didn't take a honeymoon. The day after the wedding, I was back in the studio. I had six months until we officially started the Sum 41 machine back up.

CHAPTER 17

THE GIFT OF INJURY

After everything that I had been through with my health and how public it became, I knew there would be interest in a new Sum 41 record and tour. However, I also knew that if we weren't good, we'd be written off, probably forever. Now that Dave was back and Zummo was joining, we were essentially a new band; a five-piece with three guitar players trying to find our groove. A band is like a marriage, and playing music is like the sex. Imagine being with one partner for seventeen years and suddenly trying it with somebody new. It's definitely going to be awkward at first and take a while to find the right rhythm, but it will eventually be great. In addition to getting to know each other, we had to start looking for a record deal, too. Not surprisingly, there wasn't a ton of interest to sign a somewhat dated-sounding band whose members were thirtysomething. Luckily, there was one label, Hopeless Records, who seemed to understand who we were, what we were capable of, and how hungry we were. They had the interest and the ability to help make us relevant again. It had been almost three years since we were last on stage and over a decade since we'd had a successful song on the radio. In show business years, we were washed up, dead in the water, nonexistent. Hopeless Records believed in us. We loved their passion, their team, and their history of breaking bands like Avenged Sevenfold and All Time Low. We signed a one-record deal with them and now had a partner to get our music career back on track.

With the record deal signed and a tour booked, I wanted—and needed!—to be a better version of myself in every possible way. Luckily I had no permanent damage to any internal organs and was essentially unscathed. I was committed to getting Sum 41 back on top again. The first step towards getting ready for the grind of touring was to finally fix my back problems once and for all. I started working with an amazing trainer named Dr. Craig Liebenson, at L.A. Sports and Spine, who usually spent his days working on professional athletes from teams like the L.A. Clippers, not newly sober punk rockers. He was the sort of doctor who was very excited when I came to him with multiple injuries. The first day we worked together he said, "Congratulations! You have the gift of injury." I thought he was making a weird joke about me being a total fucking mess. Turns out, he was serious. To his way of thinking, injuries were a gift because they gave us the opportunity to repair the damage and then build it back better than before. That really resonated with me and helped shift my focus to seeing the positive in my recovery process. At the same time, I also started getting my voice ready for the road by taking vocal training, which I had never done before. I saw two different coaches, named Ron Anderson and Valerie Morehouse, who taught me very different aspects of singing and warming up. I knew that I sang incorrectly and was always shouting from my throat, and I wanted to learn the right way to do things. I didn't want to scrape by making myself hoarse by screaming over a sore throat night after night anymore. With all the work I put into myself offstage, I started to feel stronger, with more energy and stamina than I had when I was twenty years old. I started eating a mostly plant-based, GERD-free, anti-inflammatory diet. I began meditating daily. I trained multiple times a day. As the tours went on, I gave up playing guitar onstage because I had too much energy to just stand in one spot and sing. I needed to move around. It was important to me to come back stronger than I'd ever been and to turn this band into a force that people took more seriously than ever.

We hit the Kerrang! Tour in February 2016 and shook off the rust.

By the end of the Warped Tour that summer, we were a machine. We were better than we'd ever been and the responses each night were massive. As far as we could tell, our audience looked to be the same age as always, still filled with kids in their late teens and early twenties, just like back on the *Does This Look Infected?* and *Chuck* tours. There were a lot of the older fans, as well, but they usually hung out near the back, avoiding the mosh pits and body surfers riding over the rowdy crowd. People kept telling us that crowds don't usually get this wild anymore and everyone just stares at their phones now, but for some reason Sum 41 shows are as insane as they were back in the nineties.

We released our first record in five years on October 7, 2016. The title, *13 Voices*, came from when I first started figuring out my way through sobriety. I had so many people in my ear telling me you need to go to rehab, you need to go to this meeting or that meeting, you need to talk to this person or that one, and if you don't, you'll never stay sober, you'll relapse and die! It was only once I shut them all out, and focused on getting my life on track in my own way, that I was able to forget about drinking altogether. Knock on wood, I've never relapsed. I did, however, accidentally drink a beer once. We were on the *13 Voices* tour and I was drinking non-alcoholic Heineken beers with some people in my hotel room. I drank three over the course of the night, and when I looked at my empties I noticed that while the labels were identical, one was a different color. I looked at it closer and realized it said "5% alcohol." Oops! I guess someone had handed me a real beer by accident. It didn't taste any different and I didn't feel it, but most importantly it didn't make me want to pick up drinking again whatsoever. I just laughed it off and made a note to be more careful next time.

Our schedule was now reminiscent of the early days of the band; we were constantly on the road doing long tours and rarely coming home for breaks. We were hitting countries and cities we'd never played before. We were starting small in larger clubs and small theaters, building up our audience, like we had done in the past. Our new single, "War," was doing well on radio in Europe, and we could feel things were growing. The best part was when people started singing along to the new songs as much as the old ones. Another aspect that was better than the old days was our press coverage. For the first time, it felt like people were actually interested in the music and what I had to say as an artist. The articles they wrote about us were flattering, and we were getting praise about our live shows. I couldn't say for certain why this shift happened. Maybe it was because we were older or because we weren't trying to make people laugh and instead focused on the music. Or maybe it was just because of the severity of my health issues. All I knew was that I wasn't going to question it. Instead, I just enjoyed talking to journalists and telling our story to people who were interested in covering us, and I was grateful to be talking to them. No one was making comparisons to other bands the way they did in the past. This was hard to wrap my head around and took a while to get used to. I still sometimes think people are being sarcastic if they come up to me and tell me our music was somehow meaningful in their lives or we've influenced them in one way or another.

At the end of 2017, I jumped into writing the next record, which would be called *Order in Decline*. Tour had just ended, and just like in the old days, I started writing immediately upon return. This time, though, I wasn't being forced by a manager or a label, I wanted to jump into song-writing because I was so inspired and excited. All the songs came very quickly. It took about three weeks to have an album's worth of them. Fifteen years ago, I had written *Does This Look Infected?* in about the same amount of time, but was riddled with stress, self-doubt, and anxiety. In just a few years, I had completely turned my life around and was in a much healthier and happier place. Still, I found myself writing about a lot of anger and frustration, which were apparently still buried somewhere deep inside. As great as my life was now, those thoughts could hide in the subconscious, and I exorcised them through my music.

While writing, I found myself thinking about my breakup with Avril, the fact that I'd never met my father, and even my disgust for the forty-fifth president of the United States. Don't get me wrong, I'm not actually *for* any politician. I think they're all fucking bad. This one just seemed particularly vile. I wrote about it all, because even when I wanted to change the topic, the more I tried to force myself to write about different themes, the worse my lyrics became. My words wouldn't make sense and I didn't feel any attachment to what I was singing. You have to let the music lead you or else it just doesn't work. I've learned those lessons now and I just let the creativity guide me.

Another thought I couldn't get out of my mind was Ariana's attempted suicide. From the moment it happened, it was in my thoughts every single day. I couldn't shake the image. It was on my mind more than usual, partly because I had recently performed the song "The Catalyst" with Linkin Park at the Hollywood Bowl, in a concert designed to honor the memory of Chester Bennington, who had taken his own life earlier that year. I was asked to perform the night before the show and didn't get to do any rehearsals with everyone, which was nerve-wracking to say the least, but I was honored to be on stage with those guys. Being part of that show also made me realize that Ari and I really hadn't discussed her suicide attempt since it happened.

A few weeks after that concert, Ari was away visiting her family, and her absence hit me so hard I broke down and cried. I realized that not only did we not deal with what happened that night, but we had never acknowledged what she had gone through trying to get sober. We had *only* dealt with my sobriety. When I got out of the hospital, no one had been there to help her. She was taking care of me while trying to figure out her sobriety all on her own. No one ever asked her how she was doing, or how she was coping whatsoever. The focus was all on getting *me* better. She had gone through so much, and I had never really acknowledged it before, and that gutted me. I thought about everything I wanted to say, everything I felt. I needed her to know I would be lost without her. That I was terrified she might try it again. That when the house was quiet and I didn't know where she was, I would search the house convinced that

I might find her dead somewhere. I needed her to know that she meant everything to me and I couldn't live without her and couldn't imagine the damage her death would leave behind.

Like most things in my life, those thoughts turned into music. I wrote a song called "Catching Fire" that said everything I wanted to say:

I never told you how I felt
Though I thought I'd said it all
And I never knew you needed help
Well, 'cause you always seemed so tough

But now I'm here alone
Without you by my side
If only I had known
That you kept it all inside
Now I'm trying to understand
Just trying to find a way
But forgive you I just can't
It's all just too much for me to take

And if I failed you, well, I swear I tried my best
But now you're gone, so all your tears can lay to rest
Just so you know
You meant the world to us, I know that it's too late
And all I want's another chance, I can't accept that you have left

Look at all this damage done
Are you happy with yourself?
And we thought the best was yet to come
And I thought I knew you, oh, so well
And the days just go by
While the moment seems to last

Like catching fire
All is gone, and it all went up so fast

When she got home, I played it for her. It was emotional for both of us, but it allowed us to finally open up and start talking about the scars we both had from that sad night. She had no idea that I was still thinking about it, and I explained that I *couldn't stop* thinking about it. It taught us that as close as we are and as much time as we spend together, we still need to check in with each other. It's easy to get caught up in daily life thinking everything is okay when sometimes something is lurking under the surface. The song made it onto the album, but when it was released, I wasn't ready to tell the world what it was about. I didn't want to put that kind of attention on Ari. About a year later, when suicide rates were skyrocketing during the pandemic, she decided that she wanted to use the song and her story as a way to help others. She bravely told her story to *People* magazine in the hopes of making other people feel less alone. She blew me away with how open and free she was. It was her very first interview, and she nailed it, and I was so proud and honestly also felt a little inadequate. I had been struggling with interviews for years, and she was a natural!

Order in Decline came out in July 2019 and we hit the road. Right away I saw that our dedication and hard work was paying off. The shows just kept getting bigger; we were selling more tickets, and playing in more countries. The new music was doing well, and it seemed to resonate with our fans and the music industry. All it took was nonstop touring and putting out the best music possible. As great as it all was, the grueling schedule was starting to take its toll on me. Again. We had booked a full tour through 2019 that was scheduled to roll through 2020. Then we wanted to mark the twentieth anniversary of *All Killer No Filler* in 2021 with another world tour. There was already talk of another record after that. I was excited, but part of me was also dreading it. That little hint of dread made me start questioning whether I was losing my passion for this life or if I was burning out. I hadn't stopped pushing hard since I got out of the hospital in 2014, so maybe five years on, I just needed a break, but with our schedule of shows, I couldn't really just take time off. While we were finishing up the European leg of the tour, there was a lot of talk in the news about a new deadly virus that was starting to spread. A few weeks after we got home in late February, the world went into full Covid-19 lockdowns.

There is no denying that 2020 was a heartbreaking year in so many ways, between the Covid-related deaths, George Floyd's death, the 2020 election cycle, and global unrest. But, though it's hard to admit since the world was falling apart in 2020, that forced break was exactly what I needed at the right time in my life. Plus, there was one really bright spot for me in 2020: Lydon Igby Whibley was born February 23, 2020, one week before the Covid lockdowns started. Ari and I had picked that name a few years earlier while on tour in Prague. Ever the movie buffs, we both loved the name Igby from the movie *Igby Goes Down*. We thought it would be too cruel to make that his first name, though, so we named him Lydon after the singer of the Sex Pistols, John Lydon, aka Johnny Rotten. It was a tribute to the reason I started playing punk rock in the first place. I was a dad, and that was better than any award or selling out any tours or having any hit song. When the rest of the year's tours were canceled, I wasn't upset, I felt relieved and thankful to be able to stay home with my first child. His arrival felt even more special because Ari and I had been down such a long and difficult road together to get to this point. Not only did we have years of struggle getting our lives back on track, but getting pregnant had been its own difficult journey. Like so many other people, we had an extremely hard time conceiving, and after years of trying, and seeing every doctor, taking every test, doing everything we could, nothing was working. It just didn't seem like it was in the cards for us. We processed the loss of that dream during a long walk through New York City right before we left for a European tour. Ari and I sat on a bench in Madison Square Park and I told her, "I married you because I want to be with *you*.

It doesn't matter if we can't have kids. If that's how it's going to be then, we'll just travel the world together, spend every minute with each other and have the greatest time imaginable for the rest of our lives." We both agreed that we just needed each other to be happy. We headed off to Europe for a quick summer festival run, and a few weeks later, and to our complete surprise, we came home pregnant.

We spent most of 2020 taking turns watching little Igby, giving each other both a decent night's sleep. I would take the late shift, Ari would do the mornings, and we'd be up together through the day as a team. I used those late nights with my son sleeping next to me to begin reworking Sum 41 songs into acoustic and piano versions. It was something I had been thinking about for a while, and those quiet nights gave me the time to flesh the music out. I couldn't just transpose the songs "as is" into acoustic versions, they had to be fully rewritten in most circumstances. I made a few quick demos, and when they started sounding really good, I added a string quartet using keyboard synths. It was exciting and creatively different than anything I'd ever done before. I'd never written a score before, but with the help of a composer named Nico Stadi I created a whole new landscape for these songs. I reached out to a Sum 41 fan called ThePunkCellist that I had seen on Instagram, who did punk rock covers with his cello. To replace the synths strings, we got him to play cello and asked a musician named Avery Bright to play violin. Soon, there were almost twenty songs and a whole album was being made entirely remotely.

During the pandemic, I also got a few phone calls from managers and record labels asking me if I would write music for their artists. The strange thing was, they all wanted pop punk songs. I thought, *I haven't written a pop punk song in about seventeen years, I don't even know if I could do it if I tried.* I decided to see if I could come up with anything, just because it would be a fun challenge, if nothing else. I sat down and quickly wrote one song, "Landmines," and then another called "Waiting on a Twist of Fate." I was surprised how effortless it was and, even more surprising, that I actually liked them both. I realized that I didn't want to give these away.

As the year went by, I would write some stuff here and there, but I wasn't taking it very seriously and never thinking of it as work for Sum 41. Some of the songs were heavy, some pop punk, and some ideas were completely different than anything I'd ever written before. I had no idea what I would do with any of it. I just kept collecting music. It was around this time I got a phone call from my old pal and the former president of EMI Michael McCarty. He informed me that all sorts of deals were being offered to purchase artist's music publishing catalogues and would I be interested in selling mine? My first response was "No, I'm not interested. Why would I get rid of my songs? I don't need the money and I want to control where my songs are placed in movies and commercials." He said fair enough and hung up. I went to bed that night imagining I had sold all my songs and had nothing to my name anymore. I woke up the next day and felt incredibly inspired and creatively charged. I started writing new music immediately. I called my manager and told him, "I think I'm interested in selling. Let's see what kind of deal we can make." The idea of having nothing wasn't scaring me, it was actually inspiring me. Just the mere idea of selling my songs made me want to write new ones. Soon we had made a deal with a company called Harbor View that I felt comfortable with. Because of the way my original EMI deal was structured, a certain portion of royalties would revert back to me, allowing me to still own a percentage of all my old songs. Most importantly, it would give me veto power on where the songs were used in the future. To me it was a win-win.

One trick that Ari and I learned as new parents was that one of the best ways to get Igby to chill was to strap him in his car seat and hit the road. During lockdown, there was no traffic in L.A., and you could get all the way from Hollywood to Malibu in twenty minutes, so we went on a lot of drives. I realized that there was one soundtrack that always got Igby to stop crying: nineties punk rock music. I made a playlist of all my old favorites, like NOFX, Strung Out, Lagwagon, Pennywise, Rocket from the Crypt, No Use for a Name, and so on. After listening to that every day, I started to notice that I was writing pop punk songs again with ease. They started to pour out of me, and they were all in the same vein as the early Sum 41 records. I loved that the music that inspired my early songs was inspiring me again. I hadn't lost it. In fact, in some ways, I could articulate myself better now—and I could certainly sing better. I made demos like always, finishing as much of the songs as I could before I was ready to show anybody. I still didn't think these songs would be the next Sum 41 album, but I was having fun with this old sound.

Eventually I had collected a lot of songs, but I needed to listen to them all to try and figure out what to do with them. I put the eight pop punk ones I had written along with six or seven heavier ones I had also been writing on a disc, jumped in the car, and hit play. As I drove around listening, it started to dawn on me that maybe these all could be a Sum 41 record. If I kept writing, I could probably fill out a double album.

I sat down and wrote more songs and then sent everything to the rest of the band, but didn't tell them what I was thinking. One by one, each guy came to me and said, "What do you think about making this a double album?" Ever since *Underclass Hero*, I'd always been a believer in letting the music tell *you* what to do, not to let your mind get too involved. Something I heard Bono say once (and it's true) is that songs aren't your babies, they are your parents, they tell *you* what to do. *Heaven :x: Hell* came together completely by accident in the middle of the pandemic, and it was like a gift.

I decided to coproduce the album with my friend Mike Green. We had been writing and working together for a few years and had found a good rhythm that made great songs. When it came time to record the album, the guys put down their bass and guitar parts at home and sent them to me and Mike. Most of my vocal performances and a lot of the rhythm guitars that I had used in the demos ended up staying as the final takes. They just had a feel and vibe that worked best with the songs. They're carefree and unpolished.

Near the end of the recording process I was lucky enough to acquire Jerry Finn's white modded Marshall 100-watt Plexi amp, the actual amp

I used on *All Killer*. It had been twenty-two years since I had plugged into that amp, and when I did, it sounded exactly the same as I remembered it. I couldn't resist and had to rerecord the rhythm guitars for "Landmines" with it. I just wanted that full-circle moment.

I was taught by the great analog producers and engineers, such as Jerry Finn, Rob Cavallo, Doug McKean, Joe McGrath, and Jack Joseph Puig, and I still use the techniques they taught me. When it comes to mixing the records, I've learned so many techniques, tricks, and tips from working with Tom and Chris Lord-Alge, as well as Andy Wallace. I lean heavier into using analog equipment, but also take advantage of digital. I'm not a purist, I just want what sounds great, and I'll take it any way I can get it. Having all of these great teachers has been an in-person master class, but at the end of the day, you need to rely on your own ears and instincts to get you where you want to go.

As the lockdowns came to a close and touring started back up, our schedule was booked to make up for all the shows we'd missed due to the pandemic. It had been two years off, and as excited as I was to have new music, I still wasn't looking forward to touring. I figured I just needed to get back into it and I would feel better. To an extent that was true. When I got back on the road, it was great to see the guys and even better to get back up on stage and play the old songs again. It was everything that happened off stage that was exhausting me. It was the grind of the nonstop travel, the logistics, and the close quarters, on top of handling all the business of the band, the band politics, and dealing with so many decisions that affected people's lives in our organization. I didn't want to deal with it anymore. It felt too big and too much for me to want to deal with it anymore. It was consuming my life. It just wasn't fulfilling. I didn't want to be juggling all of that while being away from home ten months out of the year.

While everything felt important and exciting when we were playing for fans, when I left the stage, I found myself asking, *Do I really want to do this anymore? How long can I keep this up for?* Then, I would get on stage again and those thoughts would go out the window as I rode that amazing high feeling like I could never give this up. Quitting or breaking up the band was not an option for me, ever. I've worked too fucking hard to get to this place. Besides, while the grind of touring and administration and decision-making was taking its toll on me, there was still so much I loved about being in the band. By the *Screaming Bloody Murder* album, we decided we weren't going to live and die by radio or MTV anymore. Instead we wanted to focus on the fans and build and maintain a fan base by touring and performing live, night after night. It turned out to be the best decision we ever made. We watched our fan base grow and grow as the shows got bigger and bigger, playing in more countries than we ever had in our career. Eventually we surpassed the number of fans we'd had in the early days when our music was constantly on the radio. We created a cultlike audience of *only* super fans and it was incredible. So was performing for people who knew every single word to every song and sang along with so much passion. Hearing from fans that *our* songs were the ones that got them through hard times and breakups, helped them cope with depression, and were the ones they chose to dance to at their weddings made it all worthwhile.

It wasn't just the fans, either. The five of us were the best version of Sum 41 we'd ever been, both on stage and in the studio. Everything the band and I had been through, and everything we'd accomplished, was more than I'd ever dreamed of. Sure, it had been hard and we'd had some major lows, but the highs had been even more incredible. I wouldn't have changed any of it, not even the lowest moments of my life, because without all those tough times, I never would have learned anything. I wouldn't know how to recognize the great moments if everything just worked all the time. I wouldn't be as happy as I am today. How could I walk away from this? Everything was the best it had ever been for Sum 41. And then it dawned on me. That's *why* I needed to walk away now. I didn't want to bring this band down. If my passion and enthusiasm started to wane, then I would pull Sum 41 down. I can't fake anything I do. I didn't want to drag around a burnt-out, lesser-than version of Sum 41. We'd done that. I didn't want to just go through the motions, putting on boring shows and making mediocre music, just for a paycheck. I'd made a decision a long time ago to never do anything for money, and I'd stuck to it. I refused to be the miserable rock star sitting backstage in a sold-out arena dreading to go out on stage.

It took a long time and a lot of soul-searching to finally allow myself to say, "I think it's time I let Sum 41 go." I wasn't sure if the band knew something had been off about me lately. I knew I had been distant from them, the same way Dave was before he left. Even if the band had noticed I wasn't quite myself, I knew this was going to hit them hard. I wasn't sure how to tell them, though. I had been thinking about this for a while and I didn't think it would be fair for me to drop a bomb on them and then say, "So . . . what do you think?" I also wanted to be able to articulate my thoughts in the clearest and most honest way possible without feeling nervous, forgetting to say something important, or fumbling my words. So I wrote a heartfelt email laying out how I felt, why I felt the way I did, and why it was important for me to make this change in my life. At the end of my email I said, "Don't respond. Just sit and think about it, discuss with your families, and when you're ready, let's talk." A few days later I spoke to each member separately. We spoke on the phone for a few hours and the mood was sad, but completely loving and understanding. We were able to talk calmly and maturely about it all. I apologized for not doing it in person but felt this was the best way, and every single one of them agreed and thanked me for giving them the time to process it. Even though there was incredible sadness, the guys couldn't have taken it better. We're brothers and this is a family, and at the end of the day, we're all fortunate to have each other. Even Stevo reached out for the first time since he'd yelled and hung up on me back in 2015. He sent me heartfelt email apologizing for how bad things had gotten between us and not being there for me when I needed him most. He admitted that his own drinking and anger had gotten the better of him in those days, too. Sending that note was big of him, and I was blown away. I could finally let go of a lot of the guilt and confusion that had plagued me for many years after the way things ended between such good friends and bandmates.

I'm forty-four and have two amazing children, an unbelievable wife, a great relationship with my mum and Kevin, Nan and Papa are still doing amazing, and I have managed to get rid of all the negative and unwanted people in my life. I am surrounded in joy. I have no idea what I'm going to do in my next forty years, but I think you can probably tell by now that I'm not going to be sitting around doing nothing. I can't not work. I will find something else that I'm passionate about and throw myself headfirst into it. One thing for sure is, I will finally take Ari on that honeymoon I owe her.

On February 28, 2023, our beautiful daughter Quentin Arlo Whibley was born, one of the happiest days of my life. Parenting is new and I find it surprisingly natural so far, even though I never had a stable father figure as a role model. I feel confident that I can rely on instincts, rather than example. My instincts have always served me right. I only fail when I choose not to listen to them. I know that I'm in for the ride of my life raising two kids in this world that only seems to get crazier by the year. After everything I've been through, I hope that I can understand and relate to and guide them through all the heaven and hell they will one day experience. I do know that it won't be boring. At three years old, Lydon Igby decided to pull the fire alarm in the middle of class, evacuating the whole school, and having the fire department show up for a false alarm, and I got called to his principal's office to discuss. I guess it's payback time.

I didn't want to call it quits without saying goodbye to our fans. I wanted them to have one more album and tour to remember us by. I truly believe *Heaven :x: Hell* is our best record, the one that best exemplifies Sum 41's style. The title not only represents the light and dark side of the band musically, but it encapsulates the story of our career. It's all uniquely us. For years we straddled the line between pop punk and metal. We played both types of festivals with people looking at us strange as the only punk band at the metal show. Then it became normal and no one questioned it anymore. It took us over twenty years to get to the point of being accepted, but we finally got there.

I was excited for this record to come out and this tour to begin. Not because I wanted to get it over with, but because I felt so strongly about who we were as a band and the final record we made. It's a record we never intended to make, full of songs I never intended to write, but it all came together naturally and organically, and I love the end result. When our first single "Landmines" was released on September 27, 2023, I was conditioned to not expect radio to play it or for anyone other than our core fan base to notice it. But the exact opposite happened. The video and song spread online, and streaming numbers quickly surpassed all expectations. We had momentum again. For the first time in over a decade, radio embraced us and we were back on the *Billboard* charts. The song kept creeping up the alternative airplay charts, like the little song that could. Eventually it hit the number one spot. We were back on top, twenty-two years after "Fat Lip" topped the chart—and "Landmines" was in the number one spot for longer! The full album, *Heaven :x: Hell*, was released soon afterwards and debuted higher in multiple countries than any record in our entire history. I was forty-three years old, and Sum 41 had the number one song in the U.S. and in our home country of Canada, too! The first song that was released after I had sold my entire catalogue of music became a hit. It was proof to me that you don't have to lose your gift once you get into your forties. You can still thrive. I had an immense feeling of accomplishment, and this time I wasn't going to let it pass by like I did when I was twenty-one. I wanted to savor the moment and look back at everything it had taken to get there. When I got home from tour, I took Ari for dinner and a helicopter ride over Las Vegas to cement the fact that we were on top of the world again. She had been by my side through all of it, encouraging me, and always being my biggest champion. She never got upset with me or made me feel guilty for spending so much time on the road or locked in the studio working. She always knew that the only thing harder than being the Mac is staying the Mac.

I've had to work hard for everything I have, and I still needed a ton of help and a lot of luck to make all my dreams come true. I've had to pick myself up a few more times than most, but all the hell has made me appreciate the heaven even more. Without it, I'd never learn or evolve. And that's what I love about life. I'm fascinated to find out what's next. I'm proud of the journey. I had to be weak to learn how to be strong. I had to lose it all to know how to win. I had to crash and burn to find the strength to rise. It's been exciting, it's been dangerous, it's been heaven and hell, but above all it's been honest. I've never taken what wasn't mine, I've never screwed anyone over in business, I've never chased musical trends, and I've never sold anything but music. I get a kick when I look around and realize that every dollar I've ever made, every opportunity I've ever had, has come from just picking up a guitar and writing some songs. I wrote them through the good times and the bad. Some were easy, some were tough, but all of them are near and dear to my heart. It still amazes me that the dream came true. We were the high school band that made it.

Being in this band had become fun again, after a lot of years of it being a daily struggle. Long gone were the days of drinking every drop of booze in sight, taking every drug we were offered, smashing every backstage or dressing room, and partying with strippers, models, and Playmates till the sun came up. No more trashing vans and tour buses or being banned from hotels or kicked off airplanes. Now, we took pride in being at our best and proving that we were still relevant. We had been written off so many fucking times in the past and always came back better than before. Every time someone called us a "flash in the pan" or said "this band will be gone next year," I would always think, *You don't get to decide when we're done. We'll tell you when it's over.*

And now it's over. I always knew we would write our own story.

Melissa Locker, thank you for coming in and saving the day and making me sound like the best version of myself.

ACKNOWLEDGMENTS

First off, I'd like to thank my family. My incredible mother, Michelle Gordon, who is one of the strongest and toughest people I know. I've learned so much about resilience and fighting against the odds from you. My wife, Ariana Whibley, who is always in my corner giving me strength, courage, and logic when I need it most (which is a lot). My two beautiful children, Lydon and Quentin. I can't wait to see what you grow up to become. And of course, Kevin Gordon, who just might be the biggest Sum 41 fan on the planet and is funny, witty, caring, and one amazing grandad to two lucky kids. Nan and Papa, I am so lucky to have you in my life. Brent and Jolie Cooper and family, thank you for taking me in and treating me like your own, even though when you met me, I was a mess! Thanks, of course, to the only brothers I've truly had in my life, my bandmates. In order of appearance in my life: Dave Brownsound, Cone McCaslin, Stevo32, Tom Thacker, Frank Zummo. Through the good times and bad times, we will always be bonded for life.

The amazing team of people in my life: Ron Laffitte, Chris Nary, Larry Tull, Jordan Keller, Meredith McGinnis, Dustin Kovacic, Ray Macdonald, Chris "Snake Man" Taylor. Thanks to Dayna Ghiraldi and Dave Shapiro for the early feedback. This wouldn't have happened without you. Geoff Funk, Geoff Meall, and Tom Kemp. Lisa Gallagher, for always making my life easier, thinking ten steps ahead, and keeping everything moving in the best direction possible! Thanks to Shawn Dailey and Anthony Bozza. To everyone at Gallery Books, including Jen Bergstrom, Aimée Bell, Emma

Van Deun, Sally Marvin, Jen Long, Sydney Morris, Kell Wilson, Rebecca Strobel, and Sierra Fang-Horvath! You made this process very easy and enjoyable. I always felt fully supported, so thank you! To Mona Houck.

Thanks to all my friends who mean the world to me: Melanie Harris, Matt Brann, Ian Bulloch, Todd Morse and family, Craig Hollander (I wouldn't be standing without you), Devin and Jessica Bronson, Lee and Erin Levin and family, Asher, Mike Green and family, Chantel Kendall, Marc Costanzo, Tina Kennedy, Avril Lavigne, Mikey Way and family. Thanks as well to Fat Mike, NOFX, and Pennywise for inspiring us to start Sum 41. Thanks to Chris and Tom Lord-Alge, Tommy Lee, Matt Sorum, Duff McKagan, John Feldman, Kevin Lyman, Iggy Pop, Tomás Mier, Rob Stevenson, Lyor Cohen, Livia Tortella, Sheila Richmond, Howie Mura, Stu Bergen, Jim Caparro, John Reid, Kimi Kato, Matthew Tilley, Julie Greenwald, and the late Lewis Largent for taking the chance on four bratty punk rock kids from Canada and making their dreams come true. I know there are more people, and I'm sorry if you're not listed. I love you and I thank you, too. I know I'll never hear the end of this.

ABOUT THE AUTHOR

DERYCK WHIBLEY is a Canadian singer-songwriter and record producer who plays rhythm guitar and keyboards. He is the founder and primary songwriter of the band Sum 41.